Corrections:
Dilemmas and Directions

Peter J. Benekos
Mercyhurst College

Alida V. Merlo
Westfield State College

ACJS Series Editor, Ralph A. Weisheit

Academy of Criminal Justice Sciences
Northern Kentucky University
402 Nunn Hall
Highland Heights, KY 41076

Anderson Publishing Co.
Criminal Justice Division
P.O. Box 1576
Cincinnati, OH 45202-1576

Corrections: Dilemmas and Directions

ISBN 0-87084-235-8

Library of Congress Catalog Number 92-81967

Kelly Humble *Managing Editor*   *Project Editor* Gail Eccleston

Cover Design by John H. Walker

Preface

The subject of corrections has long fascinated researchers in criminal justice. Peter Benekos and Alido Merlo have assembled an important collection of articles that illustrate the specific concerns facing corrections in the 1990s. At the same time, these articles show how institutions that are supposedly closed and isolated from the rest of society directly reflect changes in the outside world. They make this explicit in their introductory chapter, but each subsequent chapter makes the point anew. America's disillusionment with inadequate governmental management of prisons makes prison privatization an appealing alternative. Political corruption and bank scandals remind us of the importance of ethical decision-making. AIDS and prison gangs are among the prison issues that mirror problems in society. As in the rest of society, women's issues and concerns about professionalism are also raised in the study of prisons. Thus, the articles assembled here represent several of the many ways in which prisons are microcosms of American society.

Americans have a love-hate relationship with prisons. There is general public support for long prison sentences for convicted felons, but there is little enthusiasm for funding prison maintenance or construction. Consequently, prison overcrowding and skyrocketing costs in times of restricted state and federal budgets make it essential to explore corrections alternatives. The last four chapters of the book do just that, considering shock incarceration, probation, the use of technology in community supervision, and the renewed interest in community correctional centers.

The problems and issues facing corrections in the 1990s are many and no single book can adequately address them all. However, this book provides a thoughtful discussion of some of the most important problems. Like previous books in the ACJS/Anderson Monograph Series, this monograph is written for two audiences. First, it is presented in a style accessible to those with little prior knowledge of each specific topic. Second, it is comprehensive enough to be a useful resource for those who already have a general familiarity with the issues. Most importantly, this monograph will stimulate all readers to think more about this issue which in one way or another effects everyone in our society.

Dr. Ralph A. Weisheit
Illinois State University

Acknowledgments

A number of people have facilitated the completion of this volume. The Academy of Criminal Justice Sciences Series Editor, Ralph Weisheit, and the Project Editor at Anderson Publishing Co., Gail Eccleston, were very helpful.

Special thanks go to my mother, Clara Merlo, for her wisdom, encouragement and love, and to my husband, Kevin Ashley, for everything he does each day.

—*Alida V. Merlo*

Special thanks to my parents, John and Lil Benekos, for their support, and to my wife, Pat, for her understanding and encouragement.

—*Peter J. Benekos*

Contents

Introduction:
The Politics of Corrections

Alida V. Merlo
Westfield State College

Peter J. Benekos
Mercyhurst College

The public's perceptions of crime are that it is increasing dramatically, that it affects all people uniformly, that the fear of crime is justifiable, and that there is a quick and easy solution. That solution is to build more prisons and to revise the criminal codes to mandate long-term incarceration. Unfortunately, the solution is not without its problems, not the least of which is cost; prisons are very expensive to build, staff, and maintain. The belief that punishment, as opposed to treatment, is likely to deter future crime has widespread support. Policies reflecting this conservative ideology are partially responsible for the crisis that corrections is now experiencing. The incarceration rate in the United States is higher than that of any other country in the world, prisons and jails are overcrowded, funding for new prison construction is scarce, and the recidivism rate for offenders is high.

There are no quick fixes to the dilemmas that corrections is experiencing. Offenders who have been convicted of crimes and who are the "clients" of corrections often have drug and alcohol problems, have been exposed to the AIDS virus, lack meaningful vocational and life skills, and are illiterate. Correctional administrators are not only required to deal with this population, but their policies must also reflect the prevailing political exigencies and ideology. The creation, expansion, elimination, or maintenance of institutions and programs is contingent on public perceptions and public funding.

In the way that crime was made a national issue in the 1960s and placed on the political and social agenda in the United States (Cronin, Cronin & Milakovich, 1981), corrections has become its own issue in the 1980s and

1990s. While drugs, gangs, and violence continue to heighten the fear of crime, efforts to deal with crime as a public policy issue have intensified the "trend toward punitiveness among policymakers, a punitiveness founded on feelings of frustration, anxiety and loss of control" (Fairchild & Webb, 1985:9). As a consequence, corrections as a liberal, rehabilitative strategy of the 1950s and 1960s has been co-opted into conservative, retributive systems in which formal social control has expanded to unimagined proportions. The irony of the get-tough legislative crime control policies, however, is not only an emerging view that these policies have been futile (Walker, 1989) but that they have also created a crisis in corrections that has generated its own political agenda and policy issues.

PRESIDENTIAL ELECTIONS AND POLITICS

In the 1964 presidential election, and under the banner of "law and order," Barry Goldwater raised the issue of crime and challenged Lyndon Johnson's "war on poverty" with his agenda for a "war on crime" (Cronin et al., 1981). On one hand, the voters were presented with a get-tough response to crime that included expanding police powers and legislating tougher laws; on the other hand, they were offered social reform, civil rights, and increased education and employment opportunities. In their assessment of this "nationalization" of the crime issue, Cronin, Cronin, and Milakovich concluded that even though Johnson won the election, the "law and order issue just wouldn't go away" and became fixed in the public's mind and on the national agenda (1981:22).

Six elections later, in 1988, Vice-President George Bush invoked the get-tough issue when he challenged Massachusetts Governor Michael Dukakis on his state's correctional policies that permitted a convicted murderer serving a life sentence to participate in the furlough program. The case involved Willie Horton, an inmate who escaped while on furlough (his eleventh), traveled to Maryland, broke into a couple's home, raped a woman and assaulted her fiancé with a knife (Fidrich cited in Byrne, 1989).

During the campaign, the Bush political "sound bite" portrayed the Willie Horton incident with the image of a revolving prison door. This cast Dukakis as soft on crime and "effectively crystalized a complex problem by presenting it as a dramatic case history of one individual" (The Sentencing Project, 1989:3). This issue plagued Dukakis throughout the campaign and, while it was not solely responsible for his defeat, it was a salient theme that captured the public's imagination, suggested racial undertones, played on the public's fear of crime, and reinforced the political advantage of the get-tough agenda. In the aftermath of the incident, Governor Dukakis signed legislation that excluded first-degree lifers from participating in the furlough program.

As effective as the Bush campaign staff was in exploiting the Horton incident by making furloughs an emotional issue and a symbol of liberal policy, the Dukakis staff was equally ineffective in countering the campaign or using the opportunity to inform the public that furloughs were a regular program of the Federal Bureau of Prisons as well as state prison systems. In fact, in 1987, while George Bush was Vice-President and Willie Horton escaped while on furlough, almost 15,000 federal furloughs and 185,000 state furloughs were granted (Malcolm, 1989).

In analyzing this campaign issue, The Sentencing Project attributed success to Bush's position because "the educational process (of informing the public about the issue) never took place and no alternative proposals were presented" (1989:3). In other words:

> the failure of the Dukakis campaign to discuss positive experiences of furlough programs around the country or otherwise respond only reinforced the perception of these programs as endangering public safety.

Correctional Lessons

In spite of the general success of furlough programs, the Horton case and the politics of the 1988 election offer three lessons for corrections. First, as the crime issue has been used effectively to evoke a series of images, corrections and correctional policies are equally attractive political platforms that can be simplified and symbolized to capitalize on public sentiments. Because "electoral campaigns are difficult forums for rational discussion" (The Sentencing Project, 1989:4) candidates can polarize policies and appeal to the "law and order" theme already established in American politics. For example, in the 1988 campaign, images were evoked that Dukakis was for "criminals" while Bush was for "victims." The success of this strategy predicts an increase in the politicalization of corrections.

As a consequence of this "imaging" of corrections in the context of "symbolic politics," correctional administrators are also presented with a lesson: the "decision-making stakes for each of the key decisionmakers in the correctional system" will be raised (Byrne, 1989:481). As Byrne observed,

> policymakers and administrators are likely to be monitored more closely in the future as they attempt to develop sentencing policy, to deal with crowded institutions, to control institutionalized offenders, and to supervise offenders in the community (1989:481).

This lesson was not missed by Virginia Governor L. Douglas Wilder in his consideration of whether to commute the death sentence of Joseph M. Giarratano. In describing the Giarratano case, Kaplan and Cohn noted that Governor Wilder is "a man with national political ambitions who can't afford to be Willie Hortonized" (1991:56). Because of the "emotion and rhetoric" that have been generated, The Sentencing Project anticipates an unreceptive environment in which "any criminal justice reform proposals may be doomed in the near future" (1989:1).

As legislators and administrators confront these implications of the Willie Horton effects, a third lesson has become increasingly apparent. With concern for greater accountability and with the influence of politics, policy-makers will seek short-term, reactive solutions to the problems of crime and criminal justice that will require more control and will result in increased numbers of offenders under correctional supervision and in institutional confinement. As Byrne concluded, "the simple truth is that while getting 'tough' with offenders is certainly good politics, it is not necessarily good policy" (1989:481). The consequences are evident as crowding has become a major correctional dilemma.

Prison Crowding

The Sentencing Project released a study at the end of 1990 that reported that the United States has achieved the highest known rate of incarceration (1990). With 426 jail and prison inmates per 100,000 residents, the United States had surpassed the incarceration rates of both South Africa (333 per 100,000) and the now-defunct Soviet Union (268 per 100,000). With a 1990 federal and state prison population in excess of 704,000 inmates, the decade of the 1980s experienced a 113 percent increase (from 329,821 in 1980) in the number of offenders confined (Bureau of Justice Statistics, 1990a). The percentage increase in 1989 alone was 12 percent and added over 76,000 prisoners to the nation's prison population. Based on Bureau of Justice Statistics figures, this required an additional 1,500 new prison beds per week (1990a).

While these figures represent record-high levels for incarcerated offenders, the increase in the number of offenders supervised in the community has also been phenomenal. The Bureau of Justice Statistics reported that more than three million offenders were on probation and parole at the end of 1990—2,670,234 on probation and 531,407 on parole (1991). Since 1980, this represents a 126 percent increase in the probation population and a 107 percent increase in the parole population.

These population figures indicate that since the end of 1980, when approximately 1.8 million persons were under some form of correctional control and supervision, to the end of 1989 when the number had increased to 4.1 million—1 out of every 46 adults—corrections has grown beyond its capacity as public policies have expanded the scope of social control. Reflecting both the public's fear of crime—*get tough*—and the politician's fear of reform—*don't be soft*—crime policy has been consistent with a conservative agenda that has focused on deterrence, incapacitation, and punishment. And while some contend that there is "no relationship between the incarceration rate and violent crime" (O'Brien cited in Malcolm, 1991:B16), the growing number of prisoners and prisons is becoming its own issue and a major corrections dilemma.

As the annual cost of incarceration policies reaches $16 billion (The Sentencing Project, 1990), economic pressures begin to create their own realities. Commenting on these overwhelming costs, Kenneth McGinnis, Director of the Department of Corrections in Illinois, observed that "prisons will simply bankrupt the states unless we find cheaper ways to punish and figure out how to keep all these people from returning" (cited in Malcolm, 1991:B16).

Economics and Correctional Policy

The economic realities of the overutilization of incarceration are forcing a number of states to consider alternatives. In 1990, 62 new institutions were opened in the United States at a cost of more than $1.7 billion (Camp & Camp, 1991:40). Additionally, more than $441 million were spent to renovate or expand existing facilities (Camp & Camp, 1991:43). Most states cannot continue to support correctional philosophies that mandate these funding levels for construction and renovation.

At the same time that prison construction costs are soaring, state and federal budgets are shrinking. Although Americans want criminals to be incarcerated, they are not necessarily prepared to allocate a disproportionately large share of the state's budget to fund these institutions. As a result, there is increasing pressure for correctional administrators and legislators to develop new initiatives. It is no coincidence that short-term incarceration programs, private prisons, intermediate sanctions like electronic surveillance, house arrest, and intensive probation, are frequently touted as alternatives. The greater reliance on traditional probation services is also a manifestation of the frustration associated with prison and jail overcrowding.

From the political perspective, both conservative and liberal policymakers share some consensus that prevailing correctional policies need to be "reformed." Conservatives are increasingly reluctant to continue funding long-term incarceration even though they espouse punitive justice. They are seeking to reduce costs and still deter criminals. Liberals have long contended that alternatives to traditional incarceration are not only cheaper but also more humane and more effective. The indication that both groups are now willing to consider similar sanctions—albeit for different reasons—suggests that the policies of the 1990s may be more moderate than previously envisioned.

Although legislatures and the judiciary are not likely to abandon the conservative agenda, they are likely to question the utility of policies that not only are economically impossible to continue to fund, but also have resulted in 24,878 lawsuits, 95 class action suits, and 15 court-appointed masters or other overseers in 1990 (Camp & Camp, 1991:6). It is in just such a milieu that changes are most likely to occur.

OVERVIEW

Each of the authors in this volume examines a specific area, issue, population or dilemma in adult corrections, and provides some observations and recommendations regarding future directions in corrections. The authors argue that there are no quick and easy solutions to the prison problem. Rather than relying on the use of incarceration as the preferred punishment, a variety of intermediate sanctions seems to be more appropriate. However, as the offender population continues to grow, there are several problems and challenges that administrators, policymakers, legislators, and the public will need to address.

Because prisons and prison populations present more salient dilemmas for corrections, six of the chapters focus on specific prison and jail issues. The four remaining chapters address the less restrictive or short-term correctional alternatives including shock incarceration, probation, intermediate sanctions, and halfway houses.

In Chapter 1, Ford and Moore provide an overview of jail management for the 1990s by focusing on the problems that administrators must deal with in an era of reduced funding. Although the jail population tends to be more youthful, heterogeneous, and transient than the prison population with which it is often confused, there are some initiatives that can be undertaken to address overcrowding, inmate control, staff training and deployment, liability, and the external environment. The fact that jails and prisons are frequently perceived by the public as identical institutions makes efforts to secure public support especially important.

One of the responses to prison overcrowding and the costs of incarceration is to contract with the private sector (1) to build prisons and jails for the government and, in some instances, (2) to authorize private corporations to operate and manage correctional facilities. Although the private sector has been involved in the delivery of services for juveniles and adults in a supportive role for a long time, the movement to privatize corrections involves private agencies administering prisons, jails, and juvenile facilities in a more comprehensive and independent manner than previously utilized. In the second chapter, Merlo discusses some of the ethical implications of contracting with the private sector to provide these services. Although privatization is perceived as a quick, easy, and cost-efficient solution to America's prison problems, there are a number of issues that merit more careful consideration.

Later chapters in the book focus on problems unique to prisons. There are four special issues that have been addressed: AIDS, gangs, female offenders, and correctional officers.

One of the more significant problems to be addressed is the increasing prevalence of the HIV virus in prison populations. A recent survey by Camp and Camp revealed that there were 2,164 inmates in state and federal institutions in the United States who were documented AIDS cases (Camp & Camp, 1991:30). In Chapter 4, Olivero examines the AIDS epidemic and its implications for correctional administrators. He illustrates the extent of the problem, and analyzes the various AIDS policies that currently exist in correctional institutions in the United States, the case law regarding testing and segregation of offenders, and the education and prevention programs that are offered for correctional staff and inmates.

In addition to AIDS, prison administrators must also confront inmate gangs and the prevalence of gang violence. In their chapter, Fong, Vogel, and Buentello consider the Texas prison system and that state's experience with gangs. They provide some historical background on the gang problem and give a detailed analysis of the demographic and social characteristics of two prominent gangs in the Texas system.

In Chapter 5, Pollock-Byrne examines data on women offenders and their sentences. The female offender of the 1990s faces an increasing likelihood of being sentenced to prison for her crime. Recent litigation suggests that the courts tend to support the equal treatment of male and female inmates. Men and women in prison are to have equal numbers of, and access to, programs, treatment, and services. However, there is some concern that the equal treatment approach may replace the differential needs approach that historically has characterized women's prisons and will result in women and men having access to fewer programs and services.

Chapter 6 focuses on correctional officers. Blair and Kratcoski analyzed longitudinal data on correctional officers. In the context of prison crowding, policy changes, and perceived increases in occupational stress, the authors' research examined individual and structural correlates of the professional attitudes and views of prison officers. Their data suggest that professionalism remained relatively unchanged over an eight-year period.

The subsequent chapters of the anthology shift focus to issues and initiatives in institutional and community corrections. In an effort to deal with overcrowding and to satisfy the demands that prison programs become more innovative, shock incarceration programs have been developed in a number of states. In Chapter 7, Benekos reviews the concept and evolution of shock incarceration programs and summarizes findings from the boot camp program in New York State. Despite their apparent popularity with the public, shock incarceration programs target a very specific population: youthful, first-time, nonviolent offenders. Their programs service a very small percentage of a state's incarcerated population.

In view of the fact that the number of adults serving under probation supervision increased 126 percent in the last decade (Bureau of Justice Statistics, 1990b), Chapter 8 explores the impact of large probation caseloads on probation officers. With over 2.5 million offenders on probation status, probation systems have experienced increased demands but have received relatively fewer resources. According to Sieh, the consequence has been a "decrementalism" of probation. Under these conditions, Sieh describes the stress and frustration of probation work and offers the observations, reactions, and recommendations of a sample of probation officers.

In response to the overcrowding in prison and probation systems, several "intermediate punishments" are being developed. Three initiatives—intensive supervision, house arrest, and electronic monitoring—are described and evaluated in Chapter 9. Whitehead reviews several controversial issues including the effectiveness and cost-savings of these developments and concludes that legislators and policymakers need to reconsider some of the basic assumptions and issues regarding punishment.

The final chapter also considers an intermediate sanction. McCarthy reviews recent developments in the use of residential centers as alternatives to incarceration. This chapter describes various innovative approaches for using centers to meet sentencing needs and correctional initiatives. McCarthy concludes that the use of centers will continue to increase and will become more multidimensional in purpose.

These chapters examine some of the challenges and constraints confronting corrections administrators and policymakers at the end of the twentieth century. The authors' reviews suggest that economic rather than ideological concerns are determining correctional initiatives. The dilemma of developing these cost-limited policies and programs in a get-tough political environment will continue to be an issue for corrections. This volume contributes to the understanding of these new directions.

REFERENCES

Bureau of Justice Statistics (1991). "Probation and Parole 1990." Washington, DC: U.S. Department of Justice.

———— (1990a). "Prisoners in 1989." Washington, DC: U.S. Department of Justice, May.

———— (1990b). "Probation and Parole 1989." Washington, DC: U.S. Department of Justice, November.

Byrne, J. (1989). "Reintegrating the Concept of Community into Community-Based Corrections." *Crime & Delinquency,* 35(3):471-499.

Camp, G.M. & C.G. Camp (1991). *The Corrections Yearbook—1991, Adult Corrections.* South Salem, NY: Criminal Justice Institute Inc.

Cronin, T.E., T.Z. Cronin & M.E. Milakovich (1981). *United States v. Crime in the Streets.* Bloomington, IN: Indiana University Press.

Fairchild, E.S. & V.J. Webb (eds.) (1985). *The Politics of Crime and Criminal Justice.* Newbury Park, CA: Sage Publications.

Kaplin, D.A. & B. Cohn (1991). "Pardon Me, Governor Wilder." *Newsweek,* (March 4):56.

Malcolm, A. (1989). "Administration Moves to Curb Prison Furloughs." *New York Times,* (August 27):A18.

_____ (1991). "More Cells for More Prisoners, but to What End?" *New York Times,* (January 18):B16.

The Sentencing Project (1989). *The Lessons of Willie Horton.* Washington, DC.

_____ (1990). *Americans Behind Bars: A Comparison of International Rates of Incarceration.* Washington, DC.

Walker, S. (1989). *Sense and Nonsense About Crime: A Policy Guide,* Second Edition. Pacific Grove, CA: Brooks/Cole.

1

Fiscal Challenges Facing Local Correctional Facilities

Marilyn Chandler Ford
Volusia County, Florida Department of Corrections

Francis T. Moore
Volusia County, Florida Department of Corrections

INTRODUCTION

Corrections achieved high public visibility during the 1980s. This attention can be attributed to a burgeoning inmate population, enhanced by increases in violent crime. In response, there has been an infusion of money into corrections. Such high levels of funding will not continue. This chapter discusses how corrections can meet the fiscal challenges of the 1990s. A financial framework is used to discuss some of the most pertinent issues in correctional management. As we illustrate, sound correctional management and fiscal responsibility are often interdependent.

Inmate populations increased during the 1980s beyond available bed space and beyond expectation. Daily prisoner counts doubled at all levels—local, state, and federal (Bureau of Justice Statistics, 1990a, 1990b). The problem has continued unabated. For example, the 1989 growth rate at state and federal correctional institutions was greater than the percentage increase recorded during 1988 (13.1 percent and 7.3 percent, respectively). The local experience is no different. In 1986, 55 percent of the jail managers responding to the National Assessment Survey reported their facilities held more than 100 percent capacity. Just four years later, the proportion over capacity had risen to 68 percent (Guynes, 1990).

Corrections has traditionally been saddled with a reactive mission to pro-vide a variety of services for offenders, and to do so with comparatively lim-ited funding, facilities, and equipment. Concerns about crime and punishment coupled with inmate overcrowding provided a ripe opportunity for correctional administrators. Seeing the potential to gain resources for a segment of the jus-tice system that usually is at the end of the receiving line, correctional admin-istrators capitalized on the climate of concern. Correctional budgets rose precipitously to contend with the problems of crowding and crime. National figures reveal that between 1960 and 1985, state and local governments increased their per capita spending on law enforcement by 73 percent, while corrections budgets jumped 218 percent (Strasser, 1989). Further, between 1986 and 1990, the annual median operating budget for jails across the nation rose by more than $1 million, from more than $2.2 million to $3.4 million (Guynes, 1990). In many jurisdictions jails became the major cost leaders in local budgets.

The effect was not unlike that which occurred when the courts began rec-ognizing inmate rights as constitutional guarantees. Correctional administra-tors initially challenged inmate petitions. Soon, however, many correctional managers embraced the petitions when they realized that local governments were responsible for funding and implementing the courts' orders. Improving the environment for inmates also improved the environment for staff.

However, continued increases in funding cannot be sustained. Corrections competes with services within the criminal justice sector, as well as in the broader public arena, for limited tax dollars (Kemp, 1983). In addition, critics assert that the lopsided expenditures for criminal justice (cities spent 20 per-cent more for law enforcement than for education in 1988-1989) come at the expense of programs that more appropriately reduce proclivities to crime (Chambliss cited in *Criminal Justice Newsletter,* 1991a:7). The reality is that government will not continue to fund corrections without limit in the 1990s. Correctional managers have begun to realize that the never ending flow of funds is an illusion. Further, correctional administrators are learning that unlimited financial resources are no silver bullet; they still will not substitute for sound correctional management. In the 1990s correctional administrators will have to look at options other than budget growth to accommodate rising inmate populations.

This chapter examines the issue of fiscal responsibility: how correctional managers can deal with soaring jail costs without the discretion and flexibility of the 1980s. Although many of the observations apply to prisons, we focus specifically on the unique problems and solutions for jails. And although the suggestions may have value for the smaller correctional facility, the orientation is predominantly toward the larger, urban jail.

JAILS vs. PRISONS

Smith (1984:76) aptly notes the paucity of research at the local correctional level. Two explanations for this limited inquiry are offered. First, Smith attributes it to the "obvious inadequacy" of jails in terms of structure, staff, programs, and tenor when compared to state institutions. Second, he cites the fascination of the prison. Regardless of the adequacy of either explanation (and there are certainly other reasons he did not consider, such as access for study or limited research dollars), the prison does occupy a more prominent place in the public consciousness. Not surprisingly, the public also fails to distinguish between the two types of correctional institutions.

Jails and prisons share common ground, although the functions they serve and the challenges they pose differ more in degree and kind than is normally thought. The difference in function gives rise to concomitant differences in inmate population. For example, one of the jail's functions is to confine, before trial or sentencing, individuals who are determined to be risks for release. For most jails, particularly urban jails, the majority of the population consists of nonsentenced individuals. In Florida, for example, the proportion of pretrial and presentence detainees typically averages about 60 percent of the daily inmate population (Florida Department of Corrections, 1991), while nationally it is over 52 percent (Bureau of Justice Statistics, 1990a).

There is a certain heterogeneity to the jail population that is not as evident in prison populations. Jails are way stations for those with problems not readily addressed elsewhere: the mentally disturbed, the inebriate, and the public nuisance. Research on career criminals suggests that jails contain a more diverse group of law violators. There is a certain amount of selectivity, and hence homogeneity, in prison populations because most states sentence persons to prison only as a last resort (Petersilia, 1981). The heterogeneity of jail populations has become even more exaggerated due to the large number of offenders at state institutions. Where crowding in prisons has substantially reduced the actual term of incarceration served by inmates, judges may select local jail sentences as more fitting dispositional options (Finn, 1984; Guynes, 1990). Additionally, it is common for state and federal prisoners to be housed in local facilities due to prison overcrowding (Bureau of Justice Statistics, 1990a; Guynes, 1990; Vanagunas & England, 1988).

Jails are further distinguished by the transitory nature of their inmate populations. Rates of admissions and releases are high. During the year ending June 30, 1989, there were over 19 million jail admissions and releases (Bureau of Justice Statistics, 1990a). Movement into and out of custody also occurs rapidly. Jail managers reported that typically 40 percent of releases occur within 48 hours of admission (Guynes, 1990). Our own experience in Volusia County (Daytona Beach), Florida, is consistent with the national trend. Over 45 percent of jail admissions are released from custody within 48 hours of entry and 60 percent are released within one week (Volusia County, Florida Department of Corrections, 1991).

Finally, there is the perspective of the inmate during this initial period of confinement. In prisons there is a general acceptance by inmates of their legal fate long since determined. This is not true for most persons confined in jails. As Gibbs (cited in Smith 1988:78) relates, the jail inmate encounters a sudden street-jail transition, separation from significant others, and uncertainty about his/her legal status. These concerns shape the inmate's experience and coincidentally shape issues that jail personnel must address.

How can an agency that is less well funded (as all local government agencies tend to be), with a more diverse inmate population, and often less qualified staff, be more efficient? The remainder of the chapter considers this issue. Five areas that we believe need to be addressed to effectively manage jails are discussed:

1. Institutional crowding

2. Inmate control

3. Staff selection, training, and utilization

4. Liability

5. The external environment of the jail

These concerns intersect; points of convergence are noted where appropriate. Throughout this chapter we emphasize a proactive stance, the need for a systematic approach, and the use of data as key ingredients to accomplish more for less in the jail environment.

MANAGING OVERCROWDING

The nation's jail population more than doubled in the 10 years between 1978 and 1988 (Bureau of Justice Statistics, 1990a). Data from the national Jail Census for 1988 show that 343,569 persons were confined in local correctional institutions compared to 158,394 persons confined at the time of the 1978 census. At midyear 1989, local jails held an estimated 395,553 persons, 15 percent more than the previous year, and overall jail occupancy was 108 percent of the rated capacity of the nation's jails (Bureau of Justice Statistics, 1990a:1). Not surprisingly, overcrowding was ranked as the number one issue facing the criminal justice system by jail managers responding to the 1990 National Assessment Survey (Guynes, 1990). Essentially the same results were found in the surveys of judges and trial court administrators (Nugent & McEwen, 1988).

Overcrowding is often a major contributor to lawsuits related to jail conditions. Findings of the 1989 Annual Survey of Jails, a sample of one-third of the jails nationwide, revealed that one-quarter of the 508 jurisdictions with large jail populations (i.e., holding over 100 inmates daily) had at least one facility under court order to limit population, and 23 percent were under court order to improve one or more conditions of confinement, predominantly overcrowded living units (Bureau of Justice Statistics, 1990a). In the 1990 National Assessment Survey, 36 percent of the 280 responding jail managers reported facilities under court order to improve conditions of confinement (Guynes, 1990).

Aside from the unpleasantness of court intervention, the jail manager experiences more immediate negative consequences due to overcrowding. Operating at or near capacity impairs meaningful classification systems and separation of inmates. Seventy-three percent of the jail managers responding to the 1990 National Assessment survey reported inadequate space to permit the housing separation needed for classification (Guynes, 1990:3; see also Clements, 1982). Overcrowding also places greater demands on jail managers because of the diverse inmate population. For example, the pretrial detainee is legally entitled to more freedoms than the convicted or sentenced inmate. Such requirements impose additional limits on housing decisions. In turn, this complicates the administration's ability to manage the jail effectively and ensure the safety of inmates and staff. Finally, jail overcrowding requires immediate additional costs and aggravates future costs.

Legislative and Judicial Approaches

What have been the responses to overcrowding? Correctional administrators have used one of three strategies: front-end options, back-end options, or capacity-expansion options (Austin & Krisberg, 1985). Briefly, these options reduce admissions, accelerate releases, and increase the number of correctional beds available.

A frequent means to relieve overcrowding has been back-end options. For sentenced inmates this has included enlarged grants of gain time for good behavior and increased use of transitional community correctional programs. A related mechanism is legislative caps on inmate populations, which are tied to emergency release powers. The caps require release of inmates when the facility's population reaches a certain proportion of capacity, typically 95 percent or higher. Population caps and emergency release powers have been used in a variety of jurisdictions: Florida, Illinois, Michigan, and Tennessee.

Both Florida and Texas are prime examples of jurisdictions with population caps at both the local and state levels. In Florida, state prisons routinely release inmates due to court-imposed population caps, as do 39 of the state's 67 county jails (Strasser, 1989). The tension that exists when both types of institutions labor under such caps is illustrated by the trouble that occurred in Houston, Texas in late 1990. Local officials blamed the state when more than 250 inmates were released because the backlog of state prisoners in the jail exceeded the court-ordered cap on inmates awaiting transfer to state prisons.

However, state officials maintained that the county should have released its own inmates before resorting to the release of convicted felons (*Criminal Justice Newsletter,* 1990).

Unhappily, back-end options function better for alleviating overcrowding in state prisons than in jails. This is due to several factors, not the least of which are the limited resources of local governments. There are fewer locally operated transitional correctional programs available (e.g., halfway houses). Additionally, local authorities may not have a legal basis for expanding gain time awards. Where such authority exists, there is a reluctance to extend such awards for fear the offender will recidivate and unfavorable public opinion will result (*Criminal Justice Newsletter,* 1991b). Emergency release powers are viewed as a last resort for similar reasons. Austin's (1986b) analysis of the Illinois early release program revealed mixed results: recidivism was not necessarily greater among the early releases, but the public viewed the program as unsuccessful due to the obvious (administrative) mitigation of punishment. Finally, by virtue of the shorter maximum sentences available locally, less relief is possible because increased gain time awards are levied in days and not the monthly increments typical at the state level.

Capacity-expansion options are the other most often used adaptation strategy. The least costly and most timely manner of accommodating more inmates has been to redefine facility capacity to permit double bunking. However, this is not an alternative for every jurisdiction. In many of the older jails it is impossible to double bunk and to stay within space requirements set by legal mandates. Thus, many jails have had to build. Whether construction has included new buildings, renovation of existing facilities, or the refitting of other, vacant facilities for correctional purposes, it is the most costly response to inmate crowding.

These back-end and capacity-expansion options are essentially reactive in nature. Furthermore, these measures too often prove inadequate. For example, the time involved in construction means that this measure does not provide immediate relief. Sustained growth also makes it difficult to build out of an overcrowding problem (Zimmerman, 1986). Additionally, authorizing emergency release powers and allowing additional construction permit public officials to avoid the more difficult options of pretrial release programs, speedier prosecutions, developing meaningful drug and alcohol treatment services, and mental health facilities. Many believe these latter options are likely to produce more beneficial long-term consequences (e.g., Finn, 1984; Harris, 1985).

Proactive Approaches

Jails have traditionally exercised little control over the number and nature of offenders committed to their custody. However, jails need not be passive receptacles. There is wide disparity in jail use (Ford, 1990; Klofas, 1988, 1991). This suggests that there are other front-end and back-end options available. Because jails are an important element within a dynamic system, there is a need to address their problems on a systemwide level. Moore and Ford (1989) discuss how jail administrators must think and act proactively. They illustrate how the jail manager can assist in developing policies that reduce admissions and shorten lengths of stay for nonsentenced inmates. There are two advantages to the proactive strategy. It can significantly reduce correctional costs, and the time for implementation is usually short.

The flow of persons through the correctional funnel into jails can be diminished. For example, admissions can be decreased by revising penalty structures and decriminalizing selected offenses. Admissions also can be reduced by altering bail procedures. By working with police and pretrial services, significant savings can be achieved in reducing the number of minor offenders entering the jail. Law enforcement officers can issue notices to appear or divert some people to more appropriate alternate systems (such as detoxification centers) instead of more costly jail detention.

Efforts to shorten lengths of stay for nonsentenced inmates will prove particularly cost-effective for large jails because the bulk of their populations are nonsentenced. Lengths of stay can be shortened by reducing case processing time. Court delay may be the single most important factor in reducing the need for jail construction. For example, the average time to arraignment may be decreased by instituting better case management procedures within the prosecutor's office, or by hiring additional prosecutors. Alternately, various types of court management programs may speed up the process by minimizing judge shopping and continuances—thus lessening overall delay. This demands that system participants be proactive too, and well-versed in system operations. It also means that certain elements of the system—the prosecutor's office and court dockets, for example—may be open to unwelcome attention and analysis.

There are situations, of course, in which construction will be necessary to accommodate a rising inmate population or to satisfy requirements that the jail administration provide a safe and humane environment. Yet jail managers should not be seduced into a building frenzy because of a sympathetic climate. Few administrators will find the easy solution of the 1980s. Decisionmakers are increasingly shying away from expensive public projects as a threat to local government's overall fiscal health. To conserve fiscal resources, construction programs must be based upon inmate growth trends, and they need to be paced for both the size and longevity of predicted growth. Unless construction efforts incorporate these criteria, an excess of beds will result (Blumstein, Cohen & Miller, 1980), with the possible consequence of the beds being filled solely because they are there (Mullen, 1985b; but see Klofas, 1991).

MANAGING INMATES

As noted previously, the jail serves multiple functions. Its inmate population consists of a diverse group of people, with assorted needs. Many of the jail inhabitants are simply individuals for whom we have no alternative resources. They are social deviates rather than criminals. This heterogeneity in population and in jail function complicates the delivery of services and the maintenance of a safe and humane environment. The jail manager must find a way to produce coherence despite this diversity.

Classification of Inmates

One approach to managing jails more effectively is through classification of inmates. As Austin (1986a:303-304) notes, "A properly functioning classification system is the 'brain' of prison management as it governs inmate movement, housing, and program participation, which in turn heavily influence fiscal decisions on staffing levels and future budget needs." While the desired outcomes of classification systems are easily specified, the components of a proper classification system are varied and not as easily enumerated.

Most jails classify on at least gender and a crude estimate of aggressive behavior.[1] Males are separated from females, and the violent are separated from the nonviolent. Jails, particularly the larger ones, benefit from making finer discriminations. Distinctions used more frequently in state facilities are appropriate for jail populations, especially as pressures of overcrowding mount.

Buchanan, Whitlow, and Austin (1986), in their national survey of objective classification systems, describe the predominant classification model used by state and federal authorities. The model, based on a prototype by the National Institute of Corrections, emphasizes dual custody concerns: security (architectural constraints) and handling (supervision) needs. Typically, security needs are a function of instant offense severity and prior criminal record, while supervision needs reflect prior institutional behavior, and current interpersonal and behavioral components. While architectural constraints and supervision needs are dichotomous, there is also obvious overlap. Offense severity and institutional behavior can relate both to the level of security needed for housing as well as to the amount of control needed when the inmate is inside or outside of his unit. For example, someone charged with a capital crime is likely to require maximum-security housing as well as maximum (or heavy) handling procedures.

Advantages of Classification

Classification can be used to achieve four primary fiscally responsible outcomes. First, some individuals may be classified out of the jail system to more appropriate, alternate systems. Second, certain individuals may be classified to less expensive correctional options within the institution. Third, inmates of particular classifications may benefit by efforts to release them from custody as soon as possible. Finally, classification can reduce lawsuits—a very real cost for jails.

Traditional taxonomies rely heavily on security (order) considerations while other concerns, such as mental health problems, are viewed as peripheral. Yet some of these seemingly marginal issues may well indicate a need to send the person elsewhere. It is necessary to consider whether the jail is the most appropriate place for an individual. By incorporating this inquiry into the classification process the jail administrator may be able to divert persons to alternate systems. Special needs populations (with limited public menace) may be removed from the jail system and placed in other, more rehabilitative milieus. Obvious referrals are those presenting mental health issues or drug and alcohol dependencies.

Classification efforts may also be used to ferret out those who should remain within the justice system, but who do not necessarily require the constraints of the custodial environment. Increasingly complex forms of nonsecure detention—for example, house arrest and electronic monitoring—have been developed, and are advocated as effective restraint alternatives to the jail (McCarthy, 1987). These programs may be used to control the size of inmate populations, hence reducing jail costs.

Another class of potential referrals includes persons with acute medical conditions. For example, someone suffering from a degenerative disease that impairs free movement could be placed on community supervision instead of remaining in jail. An amputee or someone in the advanced stages of AIDS are examples. The related savings can be significant, because medical care is one of the costliest items in the jail's budget. The diversion also presents less risk to the community because of the individual's impairment, and at least in the 1990s, the diversion is likely to be viewed as a proper *quid pro quo* for its financial benefit.

A second advantage of classification is its utility for managing individuals within the institution. Housing assignment can be tied to the number of high-security offenders, while security levels may be reduced by proper classification schemes. Inmates who pose lower security concerns may be housed at lower custody levels. This translates into savings because staffing levels are usually lighter for monitoring and handling lower-security inmates.

Grouping like individuals together also means that the jail can profit from the effects of homogeneity. Allocating persons who are similar in predetermined ways to the same housing locations is likely to reduce tensions within most units. Ideally, potentially lethal mixtures of inmates are avoided. Both staff and inmates may better predict and prepare for problems that are likely to occur. Cost avoidance is key; the jail administrator hopes to hold costs down by avoiding disturbances that lead to the destruction of property and injury to inmates and staff.

A third advantage of classification is that some inmate subgroups can be targeted so they are released as soon as practical. Savings are realized as bed space is freed. For example, time limits for completion of the presentence investigation (PSI) may be set according to custody status. For persons in jail the time limit can be abbreviated to shorten delay between adjudication and sentencing. In contrast, persons out on pretrial release can be assigned the longer periods for PSI completion. These time limits clearly focus scarce correctional resources by prioritizing cases for handling. Additionally, inmates who receive state prison terms can be identified and monitored so they are moved as rapidly as possible.

A final benefit of managing inmates occurs when the number of lawsuits is reduced. This is the other cost-avoidance goal of classification. As previously discussed, competent classification can increase intra-institutional control, and this increase in control can minimize the exposure of the institution and staff to legal challenges. The associated savings—from attorneys' fees, and potential compensatory and punitive damage awards—are not trivial. Aside from the monetary benefits, a valuable by-product of managing inmates successfully is a more stable atmosphere for staff and an enhanced public image. This issue is more fully explored later in the chapter.

MANAGING STAFF

The costs incurred in staff selection and training, which are amplified as a result of turnover, are not often quantified. However, jail managers acknowledge that the costs are real and may be substantial. In this section, staffing concerns and their implication for fiscal responsibility are discussed. The issues include staff selection, development, and retention; staff deployment; and the civilianization of the jail work force.

Selection and Retention

Correctional institutions historically have been deficient in attracting and retaining qualified individuals. The problem is tied to the public's notion of penal institutions, as well as to the comparatively less favorable aspects of the job. The slang used to refer to correctional officers—"hack," "screw," "turnkey," "bull"—conveys a generally poor image. Popular media portrayals, whether purely fictional or docudrama, are hardly more favorable (e.g., fictional—*Cool Hand Luke, The Glass House,* the James Cagney "Big House" prison movies; docudramas—*Attica, The Executioner's Song*). In fact, it is difficult to find a positive or honorable media characterization of a correctional officer or administrator (*Brubaker* is perhaps one of the few examples).

Staffing problems also relate to the organization of local correctional facilities. In a majority of jurisdictions jails are run by the sheriff's department. And, typically, jail duty is the norm for officers before assignment to road patrol. That the jail is seen as the gulag is not surprising. As Poole and Pogrebin (1988) observe, correctional officers report conflict between the assignment and career expectations, little commitment to task, a decrease in prestige and responsibility, and limited time in the position. In this context jail duty is like a hazing ritual—a rite of passage to be endured before the benefits of the police fraternity may be fully enjoyed.

This organizational structure also frustrates the development of professionalism among COs in local facilities. Viewed as less qualified and less skilled, both within the hierarchy of the law enforcement community and within the correctional subculture, jailers receive little recognition for their uniqueness and little support for developing a professional demeanor.

In addition to the poor image of jailers and a perceived lack of professionalism, the literature describes a number of stressors associated with the CO's job (see Philliber, 1987 for a review). The varying types of role conflict—treatment-custody conflict, person-role fit, role overload, and role ambiguity—constitute what Shamir and Drory (1982) have generically labeled "occupational tedium."

The problem is exacerbated by the overall employment picture. There is emerging concern about the dwindling number of educated, skilled workers. A job recruiter for McDonnell-Douglas noted in 1990 that of the four million resumés they had received in the previous five years, skill levels were so poor that 1 out of 20 applicants could not pass an eighth-grade-level reading and writing test.[2] The competition between the private sector and the public domain for qualified employees is already critical. These realities, taken in conjunction with projections that the labor pool will shrink as the current work force retires and is replaced by a smaller group of workers, suggest that competition for the qualified worker will grow even keener (Volcker Commission Report, 1989). The pressures in the broader labor market signal potentially greater difficulties for corrections recruitment efforts of the 1990s.

The issues of personnel selection, training, and retention are intertwined. If jail managers could identify at the outset individuals with characteristics compatible with the correctional task, turnover (and hence expenditures) might be reduced. Similarly, if job training could compensate for selection shortcomings, turnover could be minimized. Yet, despite increased emphasis on job redesign (known also as "job enrichment" or "job enhancement"),[3] too little information exists to assist in restructuring recruitment efforts and to ensure retention of qualified staff. In a review of the literature on correctional officers, Philliber (1987) concluded that current research is still not definitive about how to best select COs, how to predict turnover, and how to train and evaluate officers. Unfortunately, there has not been substantial work in the intervening years to alter that conclusion, and information about jailers in particular remains sparse. More and higher quality information is needed if jail managers hope to reduce costs in this area.

Deployment

Because a jail's operating budget is comprised primarily of personnel costs, jail managers can save through wise staff deployment. A continuing problem in all correctional settings is overtime. The jail administrator can address this problem through sophisticated scheduling, properly timed hiring efforts, and positive inducements to reduce staff sick time. In the latter instance, one mechanism is to periodically buy back unused sick time. The savings of this single innovation are impressive because overtime is typically paid out at twice the hourly rate but unused sick time can be purchased at the normal pay rate.

There are several ways in which staff schedules can be manipulated to ensure post coverage and yet minimize costs. They are variations on the same theme: staffing patterns should be adjustable as the jail's activities and inmate population fluctuate. This is analogous to what Tucker and Hyder (1976) termed "fluid patrol" in policing. By introducing flexibility into staff scheduling and allowing post boundaries to vary according to the needs of the jail, cost containment can be achieved. In order for these deployment strategies to be productive, critical posts and demand (peak and non-peak) times must be identified.

One means of balancing coverage with staffing costs is to define mandatory, as opposed to optimum, posts and staffing levels at each post. The mandatory level is the minimum necessary to operate the institution without undue incident. Optimum levels are the desirable but expendable standards. Mandatory posts and post staffing levels are always filled while optimum ones remain unfilled as staff shortages (sickness, annual leave) occur.

A second means of balancing institutional needs and costs is to view some posts as fixed and some posts as functional. Fixed posts carry set responsibilities and typically occur within a set location, for example, the Housing Unit Officer (HUO). In contrast, a functional post would consist of several interim duty assignments, limited in duration, and with changing responsibilities and locations. In our Department a Relief Officer is assigned to work from 5:00 a.m.-1:00 p.m., an atypical shift. The officer first helps to serve breakfast on the housing units. He/she spends from 8:30-11:30 a.m. on visitation duty, and concludes the shift by relieving the HUOs for lunch.

A different cost-effective approach is to prioritize housing so that nearly-empty housing units can be combined. Alternately, jailers should sometimes opt to double-cell inmates rather than to add beds to existing units or to create temporary housing units consisting of a few single-person cells. In our experience, the random use of beds in corridors and dayrooms contributes to an unstable environment, creating the need for additional staff—and sometimes more staff than if more traditional housing had been used (i.e., double-bunking).

Ideally, staff deployment should also rely upon information about inmate subgroups, the officer, and post requirements. Minimizing cost is more likely when the skill level of COs is matched to post assignment. Officers who are adept at managing difficult inmates should be assigned to the high-security units while less proficient officers can be assigned to less demanding posts.

Civilianization

Many tasks now performed by sworn staff can be transferred to civilian staff. Civilian staff generally cost less because there are fewer training requirements. In turn, this means the cost of civilian turnover is lower. If one assumes a constant rate of turnover in particular positions, converting them to civilian operations can produce substantial savings for the jail administrator. This allows more sworn corrections officers to become available for their primary job—the care and custody of inmates and order maintenance of the institution.

Interestingly, civilianization efforts do not always reduce costs (Heininger & Urbanek, 1983). Increased costs are more likely in positions requiring higher degrees of education, training, or specialization (Hennessy, 1976). For example, computer specialists and other technicians often require greater compensation.

Civilians have been most frequently used in clerical and administrative positions in corrections, like the booking office, which processes all jail admissions and releases. For larger jails, the work is primarily clerical in nature and it can easily be performed by trained civilians.

Acceptance of civilians in the more traditional criminal justice roles is not common. The civilianization of law enforcement is the primary example in the American justice system, although there have been isolated private or quasi-public efforts in probation (Lindquist, 1980). In the past 15 years the number and use of private police has grown significantly. Yet their workloads continue to be comprised of minor and non-crime-related calls for service (Cunningham & Taylor, 1985). In one of the few assessments of a private police force with traditional law enforcement duties, Walsh and Donovan (1989) found the private security force to be effective in crime prevention.

Full conversion to civilian correctional forces has also been slow. Privatization is not an idea that has wholesale acceptance, and for a variety of reasons (Mullen, 1985a; see Merlo this text). Jail managers have overwhelmingly expressed little need for contracting out total facility operations (87.4 percent reported "no need in the next three years" (Guynes, 1990:9)). Ultimately, the acceptance of civilians will be based on their successful performance rather than on strictly financial considerations (Heininger & Urbanek, 1983).

There are other non-custodial functions that may be converted to civilian operations to produce savings. Some jails already use private vendors, typically in the medical, mental health, basic education, and food services arenas. Jail managers appear ready to accept a greater role for private vendors in jails, particularly in the program areas (Guynes, 1990). Breeden and Brien (1984) note that cost containment is only one reason correctional administrators opt for contracted services. They cite six other problems that lead correctional managers to contract arrangements: staff turnover, lack of support services, standards compliance, inadequate record-keeping, burdensome administration, and inconsistent delivery of professional services. Additionally, in the purchase of service agreements, costs of one kind may be merely exchanged for costs of another kind. Interagency conflict between the contract holder and the service provider can be a hidden expense in these arrangements (Morrissey, Steadman, Kilburn & Lindsey, 1984).

MANAGING LIABILITY

The largest single potential cost factor in jail management lies in legal liability. Similar to medical malpractice claims, lawsuits challenging jail operations have proliferated in the past 15 years. This proliferation is a result of the growing tendency in the courts to recognize steadily increasing areas of government responsibility.

Because law is an evolutionary concept, today's dissent in a court decision is frequently a guideline for a future decision. With that in mind, correctional administrators can anticipate areas of change that will affect their operations. A prominent example of this is in the area of jail suicides. As recently as the 1970s, suicides in jail were considered unavoidable and the courts often dismissed claims against public officials. That approach changed during the late 1970s, however, and today jail officials are frequently held liable for suicides deemed to be predictable or preventable.

Given the costs involved in litigation and the payment of benefits awarded to families of jail suicide victims, special handling procedures are commonly instituted. These special precautions are based on what is known about the meaning and likelihood of suicidal gestures within the jail setting (Burks & DeHeer, 1986; Haynes, 1983; Hopes & Shaull, 1986). Because it is known that suicide attempts are most likely to occur within the first 3-72 hours of incarceration (Haynes, 1983), as well as shortly after conviction or sentencing (Hopes & Shaull, 1986), typical jail procedures emphasize identifying and monitoring individuals who exhibit suicidal behaviors at these times. Persons judged to be potentially suicidal are likely to be segregated from other inmates, although some recommend two-person cells (Hopes & Shaull, 1986). Periodic watch, physical restraint, and restrictions on materials that might be used to inflict injury or death (no metal or plastic eating utensils and use of paper clothing) are customary handling precautions (Burks & DeHeer, 1986; Hopes & Shaull, 1986).

This illustrates how established departmental policies and procedures are one mechanism to limit liability. Departmental procedures define acceptable on-the-job behaviors and prescribe the sequence of behaviors that staff are expected to follow. At the most basic level departmental policies structure staff discretion; they result in staff operating from a shared perspective.

However, because liability attaches in a wide variety of areas, correctional policies and procedures must be developed for a broad spectrum of conduct and be comprehensive in nature. The common understanding of correctional litigation is that it consists mainly of lawsuits based on violations of inmates' constitutional and civil rights (42 U.S.C. §1983 actions). However, as the manager of a public institution, the jail administrator faces a wider variety of legal issues. The jail manager has legal duties to all parties entering the premises: the public, staff, other officials, private contractors, and inmates. The types of liability range from state tort claims through constitutional issues to labor relations and contract administration.

Obviously, no jail administrator in a large facility can assure the level of compliance required without effective management structure and practice. Comprehensive and proactively developed policies and procedures are the most reliable means of addressing liability. Yet realistically, the existence of policies and procedures is not enough protection. Rather, it is the daily adherence to established procedures that minimizes exposure. The wise administrator ensures that, insofar as possible, a mechanism exists to facilitate staff compliance with departmental policies. Only as the staff follow departmental procedures is a barrier to liability erected.

The savings from reduced liability are both direct and indirect. Savings occur because of cost-avoidance as well as cost-reduction efforts. As wise management practices can lead to savings, they also reduce the administrator's exposure to liability.

MANAGING THE EXTERNAL ENVIRONMENT

The area of management with the greatest potential for both positive and negative impact on jail operations is the seldom-utilized external environment. Corrections professionals at all levels continuously voice frustration with the lack of public understanding of the difficulties they face. Similarly, other professionals express dismay when corrections attracts publicity and money while problem-free operations experience budget cutbacks and neglect.

These phenomena are to be expected in a profession that is little understood and often disdained. The responsibility for altering that image and creating a broad-based constituency is vested in the jail administrator. Implementation of this approach is not easy because there is no common denominator among the various roles in the criminal justice system. Arresting agencies naturally seek high percentages of case resolution and therefore are not concerned with jail crowding. Prosecutorial agencies share the same perspective. The judiciary is primarily concerned with the size of their dockets and the soundness of their decisions, regardless of whether defendants are incarcerated or not. Public defenders and defense attorneys focus their efforts on the individual clients, not the collective body of defendants, and certainly not on the limited portion of that group which is incarcerated.

As a result of the diverse focuses of these justice system agencies, the agency concerned with incarceration is the jail. Given this solitary responsibility, the jail manager needs to perform a variety of functions that are not readily apparent to the uninitiated. The jail administrator must coordinate his/her agency's position and image within the justice system, while simultaneously exercising control of agency expenditures. An effective way to do this is to develop a constituency of public support.

In Volusia County, Florida, this public support was achieved by publicizing the real costs of incarceration, the nature of the inmate population, and potential future jail costs. Data that showed the total costs of unnecessary or protracted incarceration were developed and disseminated in the media. At the same time, efforts were made to enhance the image and public exposure of Department of Corrections's staff. The result was public recognition of the costs associated with large jail populations and a growth in public confidence in the Department of Corrections, which enhanced the Department's credibility within the local criminal justice system and in the community.

To improve the Department's public image, many small but public activities were undertaken. This brought uniformed correctional personnel into direct contact with the public outside the institution's walls. Activities included participation in: civic events, such as the dedication of new buildings; neighborhood watch groups as trainers and speakers; charitable fundraising events; community disaster response activities; job fairs; university and secondary school career day programs; and similar non-institutional projects. These efforts, coupled with an effort to cooperate with area media to obtain positive exposure for corrections, not only led to an improved public image but also had a favorable effect on staff morale.

Along with the enhancement of public image and recognition of professional competence came public confidence in the local corrections agency. This helped to establish the credibility of the message that the Department of Corrections had been articulating in the media: that for fiscal reasons, control of the size of the incarcerated group was a desirable community goal. This goal has been accomplished so effectively that the largest law enforcement agency in the county took credit for its contribution in reducing the size of the jail population during a public meeting.

Accomplishments such as these are not easily attained and more difficult to sustain. The Department of Corrections's efforts took four years to reach fruition and required the maintenance of momentum in all areas of the external environment. Politicians, bureaucrats, law enforcement personnel, attorneys, oversight agencies, the media, and the public—all have an interest and varying degrees of influence in jail operations. All of these individuals and groups, as well as the staff and inmates of a particular institution, must receive a consistent image of the jail, and its operations and goals. Obviously, to attain this the jail administrator must blend the qualities of diplomacy, politics, leadership, and foresight.

CONCLUSION

This chapter has focused on five areas that can be managed to reduce jail expenditures. We began our analysis with a review of correctional problem-solving and the legacy of the 1980s. During the 1980s, when initially facing what appeared to be insurmountable overcrowding, some jurisdictions appropriated more money to solve the problem. They believed overcrowding and the jail's internal problems could be ameliorated if sufficient financial resources were allocated. As we have entered the 1990s, financial resources have eroded and it has become clear that money alone will never replace competent correctional management.

Our discussion has emphasized proactive management, a systematic approach, and the need for data to inform the venture. Several years ago Alvin Cohn (1987) discussed the future of correctional management and the need for proactive managers. In his discussion Cohn used the term *stewardship*. It is a term that fits our vision of the effective jail manager.

The proactive correctional administrator practices aggressive management. Several images resonate from this style: leadership, support groups, calculated risks. Sound (proactive) correctional management and fiscal responsibility are often interdependent. Although not an absolute, the proactive jail manager acts in such a manner that while achieving financial health, other agency objectives—such as improved institutional control or decreased staff turnover—are also satisfied.

The proactive jail manager moves forward in a planned fashion to achieve organizational goals. He/she recognizes lean financial times, but is not paralyzed by them. Instead, the aggressive jail manager reviews how the job might be done better or with fewer resources (e.g., Burt, 1980).

Our second major theme has been that the jail administrator must employ a systemwide view. This reiterates a common observation: the criminal justice enterprise, although often times disjointed, is a system. What occurs at one stage affects the others, particularly when influencing the size of the jail's population. The jail manager needs to employ the broader view.

Without this perspective it is more difficult to impact on jail crowding, and consequently contain correctional expenditures. Additionally, the systemwide view is also critical if the jailer is to manage the external environment to his/her benefit.

A third theme has been the need for data. Each of the strategies detailed here rely on data. Data are necessary to inform the process, both at the outset for establishing the current state of affairs and at various later points to evaluate performance. Many jails do not currently have well constructed or easily retrievable data sets. These will be required for effective management in the future (Flood, 1989).

In addition, quantitative study is needed. Research findings on correctional officers, while growing, remain largely impressionistic (Philliber, 1987). Clear conclusions are few and are attenuated by small samples and research sites of questionable comparability. Moreover, research specifically on jails and jailers is notably lacking. More and higher quality data are needed.

Finally, the basis for these recommendations is our belief in the integrity of local correctional facilities, jail managers, and their staffs. Many problems confront the jail today. We are not convinced that the obstacles to producing a safe and humane environment for all—inmates and staff alike—are any more difficult than in previous times. It may simply be that the obstacles are different today.

We contend that this decade will be a time when local correctional agencies make unprecedented gains toward professionalism. We are optimistic that continued research on correctional officers, and jailers in particular, will expand and enhance public understanding. Our belief is that positive public recognition will follow.

NOTES

[1]   Given the Juvenile Justice and Delinquency Prevention Act of 1974, which mandated removal of all juveniles from adult jails and detention centers, most juveniles are no longer confined in adult facilities. Thus, age was not included as one of the primary attributes for classification. However, many of the larger jails still use age to classify inmates.

[2]   Session presented at the annual conference of the American Jail Association, Reno, Nevada, May, 1990.

[3]   These concepts gained prominence in the past 10 years, primarily as part of the new generation jail ideology (e.g., Zupan, 1991; Zupan & Menke, 1991). The definition emphasizes greater participation of correctional officers in decision-making and participatory management. While job enrichment/enhancement gained greater currency from the new generation jail designs, the concept may be separated from architectural style *per se*, and such efforts have been advocated within more traditional settings (e.g., Toch & Klofas, 1982).

REFERENCES

Austin, J. (1986a). "Evaluating How Well Your Classification System Is Operating: A Practical Approach." *Crime and Delinquency,* 32(July):302-322.

_____ (1986b). "Using Early Release to Relieve Prison Crowding: A Dilemma in Public Policy." *Crime and Delinquency,* 32(October):404-502.

Austin, J. & B. Krisberg (1985). "Incarceration in the United States: The Extent and Future of the Problem." *The Annals of the American Academy of Political and Social Science,* 478(March):15-30.

Blumstein, A., J. Cohen & H.A. Miller (1980). "Demographically Dissaggregated Projections of Prison Populations." *Journal of Criminal Justice,* 8:1-26.

Bolduc, A. (1985). "Jail Crowding." *The Annals of the American Academy of Political and Social Science,* 478(March):47-57.

Breeden, H.E. & P.L. Brien (1984). "Contracting Food and Medical Services: Megatrend or Fad?" *Corrections Today,* 46(August):52, 54.

Buchanan, R.A., K.L. Whitlow & J. Austin (1986). "National Evaluation of Objective Prison Classification Systems: The Current State of the Art." *Crime and Delinquency,* 32(July):272-290.

Bureau of Justice Statistics (1990a). *Jail Inmates,* 1989. Washington, DC: U.S. Government Printing Office.

_____ (1990b). *Prisoners in 1989.* Washington, DC: U.S. Government Printing Office.

Burks, D.N. & N.D. DeHeer (1986). "Jail Suicide Prevention." *Corrections Today,* 48(February):52, 73, 88.

Burt, M.R. (1980). "Creativity and Feedback Can Stretch the Budget." *Corrections Today,* 42(July/August):64-65.

Clements, C.B. (1982). "The Relationship of Offender Classification to the Problems of Prison Overcrowding." *Crime and Delinquency,* 28 (January):72-81.

Cohn, A.W. (1987). "The Failure of Correctional Management—The Potential for Reversal." *Federal Probation,* (December):3-7.

Criminal Justice Newsletter (1990). "Jail Overcrowding in Houston Results in Release of Inmates." 21(20)(Oct. 15):5.

_____ (1991a). "Group Cites Shift in Priority from Education to Justice." 22(12)(June 17):7.

————— (1991b). "Texas Parole Board Under Fire: Prison Crowding Raises Pressure," 22(9)(May 1):6.

Cunningham, W.C. & T.H. Taylor (1985). "Doing More With Less: Private Security Options for Decreasing Police Workload." *The Police Chief,* 52(May):62-63.

Finn, P. (1984). "Judicial Responses to Prison Crowding." *Judicature,* 67(February):318-325.

Flood, J.P. (1989). "Jail Records." *American Jails,* 3(Fall):39-40, 43.

Florida Department of Corrections (1991). *County Detention Facilities: Daily Inmate Population Data, Monthly Report.* Tallahassee, FL: Office of the Inspector General.

Ford, M.C. (1990). "Comparative Rankings for ADPs, Incarceration Rates, and Pretrial Detainees," Unpublished research report (Mimeographed).

Guynes, R. (1990). *National Assessment Program: Survey Results for Jail Administrators.* Washington, DC: National Institute of Justice.

Harris, M.K. (1985). "Reducing Prison Crowding and Nonprison Penalties." *The Annals of the American Academy of Political and Social Science,* 478(March):150-160.

Hayes, L. (1983). "And Darkness Closes In...A National Study of Jail Suicides." *Criminal Justice and Behavior,* 10(December):461-484.

Heininger, B.L. & J. Urbanek (1983). "Civilianization of the American Police: 1970-1980." *Journal of Police Science and Administration,* 11(June):200-205.

Hennessy, J.J. (1976). "The Use of Civilians in Police Work." *The Police Chief,* 43(April):36-37.

Hopes, B. & R. Shaull (1986). "Jail Suicide Prevention: Effective Programs Can Save Lives." *Corrections Today,* 48(December):64, 66, 70.

Kemp, R.L. (1983). "Retrenchment Management: Coping With Fewer Tax Dollars." *The Police Chief,* 50(November):39-41.

Klofas, J. (1988). "Measuring Jail Use: A Comparative Analysis of Local Corrections." Paper presented at the annual meeting of the American Society of Criminology, Chicago, March.

————— (1991). "Disaggregating Jail Use: Variety and Change in Local Corrections over a Ten-Year Period." In J.A. Thompson & G.L. Mays (eds.) *American Jails: Public Policy Issues,* pp. 40-58. Chicago, IL: Nelson-Hall.

Lindquist, C.A. (1980). "The Private Sector in Corrections: Contracting Probation Services from Community Organizations." *Federal Probation,* 44,1:58-67.

McCarthy, B.R. (ed.) (1987). *Intermediate Punishments: Intensive Supervision, Home Confinement, and Electronic Surveillance*. Monsey, NY: Willow Tree Press.

Moore, F.T. & M.C. Ford (1989). "A Model to Reduce Overcrowding." *American Jails*, 3(Fall):16-19, 21, 22.

Morrissey, J., H.J. Steadman, H. Kilburn, Jr. & M.L. Lindsey (1984). "The Effectiveness of Jail Mental Health Programs: An Interorganizational Assessment." *Criminal Justice and Behavior*, 11(June):235-256.

Mullen, J. (1985a). *Corrections and the Private Sector*. Washington, DC: National Institute of Justice.

_____ (1985b). "Prison Crowding and the Evolution of Public Policy." *The Annals of the American Academy of Political and Social Science*, 478(March):31-46.

Nugent, H. & J.T. McEwen (1988). *Judges and Trial Court Administrators Assess Nation's Criminal Justice Needs*. Washington, DC: National Institute of Justice.

Petersilia, J. (1981). "The Career Criminal Concept: Its Applicability to Prison Management." *Corrections Today*, 43(May/June):42, 43, 46, 48, 50, 51.

Philliber, S. (1987). "Thy Brother's Keeper: A Review of The Literature on Correctional Officers." *Justice Quarterly*, 4(March):9-37.

Poole, E.D. & M.R. Pogrebin (1988). "Deputy Sheriffs as Jail Guards: A Study of Correctional Policy Orientations and Career Phases." *Criminal Justice and Behavior*, 15(June):190-209.

Shamir, B. & A. Drory (1982). "Occupational Tedium Among Prison Officers." *Criminal Justice and Behavior*, 9(March):79-99.

Smith, D.E. (1984). "Local Corrections: A Profile of Inmate Concerns." *Criminal Justice and Behavior*, 11(March):75-99.

Strasser, F. (1989). "Making the Punishment Fit the Crime...And the Prison Budget." *Governing*, (January):36-41.

Toch, H. & J. Klofas (1982). "Alienation and Desire for Job Enrichment Among Correction Officers." *Federal Probation*, 46:35-44.

Tucker, M.L. & A.K. Hyder (1976). "Economic Realities Force Effective Manpower Utilization." *The Police Chief*, 43(April):32-33.

Vanagunas, S. & D. England (1988). "The Domino Effect: State and Federal Crowding Put Local Jails on the Receiving End." *Corrections Today*, 50(August):196-199.

Volcker Commission Report (1989). *Leadership for America: Rebuilding the Public Sector*. Lexington, MA: Lexington Books.

Volusia County, Florida Department of Corrections (1991). "Inmates' Lengths of Stay." Unpublished raw data.

Walsh, W.F. & E.J. Donovan (1989). "Private Security and Community Policing: Evaluation and Comment." *Journal of Criminal Justice*, 17:187-197.

Zimmerman, S.E. (1986). "Planning for Growth." *Corrections Today*, 48(February):60, 62, 64, 66.

Zupan, L.L. (1991). *Jails: Reform and the New Generation Philosophy.* Cincinnati, OH: Anderson Publishing Co.

Zupan, L.L. & B.A. Menke (1991). "The New Generation Jail: An Overview." In J.A. Thompson & G.L. Mays (eds.) *American Jails: Public Policy Issues,* pp. 180-194. Chicago, IL: Nelson-Hall.

2

Ethical Issues and the Private Sector*

Alida V. Merlo
Westfield State College

INTRODUCTION

All of us are familiar with the crisis in corrections. Overcrowded facilities, court-ordered limits on the population, the staggering costs of incarceration, and the recidivism rate remind us daily of the problems that the United States is confronting in both the juvenile and adult correctional systems in the 1990s. Local, state, and federal governments are reviewing their alternatives and, in some instances, are looking to the private sector for help in confronting the crisis. This chapter will examine some important ethical issues that must be recognized when considering the use of the private sector.

Several factors make the identification of ethical problems in corrections intriguing. First and foremost, the United States is currently experiencing a rapid expansion in the number of prisons throughout the country. Camp and Camp (1991:40) report that 23 states and the federal government have added 62 new institutions designed to accommodate 36,373 inmates at a total cost of more than $1.7 billion in 1990. By all indications, there does not seem to be any end to this trend. Second, corrections is big business and involves big money. In 30 jurisdictions, additions or renovations to 102 existing facilities were under construction in 1990. Additionally, 36 states, the District of Columbia, and the Federal Bureau of Prisons plan to increase their bed space

---

* This chapter is a revision of a paper that was presented at the Academy of Criminal Justice Sciences Annual Meeting on March 16, 1990 in Denver, Colorado.

by 87,664. The construction costs for additional beds reported by 34 agencies exceed $3.2 billion (Camp & Camp, 1991:43-44). Third, historically, corrections is the only subsystem of the adult criminal justice system that has embraced privatization and has relied on it. Fourth, correctional clients and their institutions are without advocates. The public is not interested in knowing what happens with respect to prison administration or inmate problems as long as the offenders do not intrude on its personal space. Additionally, prisons are not included among the public's priorities (education, roads, improved law enforcement, and hospitals) for allocation of tax revenues (Ellison, 1986-1987:718).

Although exploring ethical issues in the privatization of corrections is especially interesting now because of the tremendous growth of prisons and the large amount of capital being spent, the private sector was involved in corrections long before this recent trend. For example, during the Eisenhower administration, the federal government began the process of converting publicly administered functions to the private sector (United States Department of Justice, Office of Juvenile Justice and Delinquency Prevention, 1988:3-2). However, it was not until the Reagan administration that the real impetus for privatization occurred. In addition to corrections, the private sector has established itself in air traffic control, transit systems, hospitals, and solid waste collection (United States Department of Justice, Office of Juvenile Justice and Delinquency Prevention, 1988:3-2).

Privatization in corrections is used to describe a variety of arrangements. The obvious and most common usage involves private agencies contracting with the public sector to provide specific services. Privatization also refers to private companies owning and operating institutions. These arrangements are referred to as "COCOs"—contractor-owned and contractor-operated (McDonald, 1990:15). Privatization in corrections also characterizes facilities and institutions administered by the public sector but owned by the private sector. Last, privatization denotes a publicly owned facility or institution that the private sector operates. These are known as "GOCOs"—government-owned and contractor-operated (McDonald, 1990:15). Private corporations providing services or administering programs and facilities may be categorized as "for profit" or "not for profit."

Federal, state, and local governments frequently contract with private providers for educational/vocational training, halfway houses, and medical services for both adult and juvenile offenders. However, the transition from providing assistance and support to the public sector to the role of actually owning, managing, and administering correctional facilities in recent years has been controversial (U.S. Department of Justice, Office of Juvenile Justice and Delinquency Prevention, 1988:3-4). It was not until the private agencies decided to aggressively pursue a more active role in the delivery of services and the management of institutions that the public sector began to question and analyze the extent of private sector involvement. This chapter focuses on this more recent trend.

Although the literature on privatization is fairly extensive, the actual number of privately administered adult correctional facilities is surprisingly small. Logan (1990:20) contends that there were approximately 24 adult confinement institutions operated by about 12 companies with 9,000 beds in mid-1989. These facilities were found in 12 states (Logan, 1990).

ARGUMENTS AND CONSIDERATIONS FOR CORRECTIONAL PRIVATIZATION

Competition as an Incentive

One of the reasons often cited for relying on the private sector is the expectation that competition will improve the correctional system. Proponents argue that the involvement of the private sector will make the services offered to the offender better because the state will no longer have a monopoly on prisons and jails (Logan & Rausch, 1985). Theoretically, this present lack of competition can be eliminated when the state establishes a bidding process for private agencies to deliver services.

The existence of a competitive bidding process that encourages two or more private agencies to submit proposals does not, on its surface, preclude ethical dilemmas. It is quite possible that deception can occur. For example, advocates of a private system of corrections can stress its competitive nature and its potential to be far superior to the public system while being aware of the fact that only one or two private companies will have the necessary resources to bid on a prison or jail (Bowditch & Everett, 1987; Gentry, 1986). The bidding process can also be tainted by collusion when one or more companies make an informal arrangement not to compete with each other.

Additionally, those individuals who are responsible for selecting the contractors may deceive the public about the process. The qualifications and interests of the contract reviewers may be suspect. In some instances, the public sector might employ a private management team to advertise for the requests for proposals, to screen the proposals, and to recommend the finalists. The objectivity of these intermediaries may be influenced by their personal beliefs, friendships, and possible conflicting interests in the outcome of the process.

Even if the bids are reviewed by public sector employees, there is no guarantee that conflict of interest dilemmas can be prevented. For example, two kinds of actions were noted in a 700-page audit of Housing and Urban Development's Moderate Rehabilitation Program that led to an investigation of HUD. The first involved distribution of grants by top HUD officials to well-connected Republicans; and the second involved consulting fees paid to intermediaries. Former Interior Secretary James G. Watt, for example, received lucrative consulting fees for assisting clients to secure federal housing subsidies (Johnston, 1989:B5).

The potential for such activity has already been demonstrated in private corrections. News reports indicated that two Hamilton County, Tennessee commissioners who voted to renew the Corrections Corporation of America contract to administer the county workhouse in the 1980s had private business contracts with the company (Morgan cited in Press, 1990:30).

Individuals have been able to profit from influencing government decisions in corrections without privatization. For example, real estate developers, with some insider knowledge, purchased land in remote areas of one state, cognizant of the need for prison space and the state's search for suitable locations. They then offered to sell the land to the state for a sizable profit.

Some observers question the extent to which the bidding process will coerce the government to accept services that may be inferior or inadequate. They envision a scenario in which all the bids that have been submitted are either too similar or not really appropriate for the state's needs. The state may then be in the unenviable position of having to select one because it has no other alternatives.

The low likelihood of an open bidding process with equal opportunity for all is another cause for concern. The assumption that a bidding process alone will facilitate the involvement of a number of providers and generate competition has not been documented in the literature. In fact, from November of 1985 through September of 1986 when the staffs of the Council of State Governments and the Urban Institute studied privatization in the United States, they found that not all governments utilized "...fully competitive procedures when contracting for the operation of correctional facilities" (Hackett, Hatry, Levinson, Allen, Chi & Feigenbaum, 1987:4). The large amount of capital required for involvement may also discourage the smaller providers from submitting proposals. Thus, the diversity envisioned through privatization may be illusory.

Opponents contend that as governments delegate more and more authority to the private sector to deal with offenders, it will become more difficult to monitor their activities (Field, 1987). They suggest that the private sector will become more autonomous and that the public sector will be even less inclined to keep track of what is happening. The "out of sight/out of mind" attitude that has characterized corrections will become more prevalent once the private sector has a stronghold in the delivery of services.

Economic Considerations

Advocates of privatization argue that there are tremendous economic benefits to utilizing the private sector. Not only do they contend that the private corporations can construct prisons more cheaply and more quickly because there are no statutory bidding requirements to hinder their project's progress, but they also suggest that the private prison will produce revenue for the state and local government because the corporations will pay business and property taxes. No state or federal prison is subject to such taxes (Evans, 1987:258).

The time lag associated with public construction projects is not an entirely negative phenomenon. Some critics of privatization contend that it forces the public to address the real costs of get-tough policies. Private construction may mask the true costs because the funding decisions are made by government officials rather than the voters (Porter, 1990; Press, 1990). As long as the private contractors can finance, build, and administer prisons with relative ease, opponents argue that there will be no impetus for the public to evaluate correctional policies, assess overcrowding, and explore alternatives to traditional incarceration and large institutions (see DiIulio, 1990; Sevick & Cikins, 1987).

Unfortunately, the private construction of facilities is not a panacea. The collapse of the skywalk in Kansas City and reports of the shoddy construction of nuclear power plants suggest that the private sector is not immune to problems. Additionally, some opponents of privatization fear that the government will be coerced to enact favorable tax exemptions or make special arrangements to reduce taxes if the state is totally dependent upon the private sector. Too much reliance on the private sector may place the state or local government in the position of employee versus employer.

Private prisons are frequently advocated because of their lower construction and administration costs. Very little research has been conducted on privately administered institutions. In one study comparing three private and three public correctional facilities, Sellers (1989) found support for the private sector argument that their costs are lower than those of public facilities. Additionally, private institutions offered more programs than the public institutions (See also Brakel, 1988). However, no large prisons were included in Sellers' study and Brakel's research utilized a case study approach of one institution.

Flexibility in Negotiations

Another advantage of contracting with the private sector is its flexibility. Without bureaucratic red tape, proponents suggest that services can be delegated to private agencies, implemented, and then revised as necessary without delays (Hutto, 1990). Critics are not so optimistic about the prospects of the government quickly terminating a contract and successfully soliciting bids from other private agencies to step in and do better. What happens if a contractor defaults? A large amount of capital would have been invested and the results could affect offenders and the public for years.

Opponents also question the government's willingness to terminate the contract when it is committed to privatization and its options are limited.

Private contractors may effectively preclude flexibility when they develop strong liaisons with influential legislators. Even if the government contracting agency is interested in terminating a contract or selecting a new vendor, the private contractor may be able to thwart such attempts through its independent influence in the legislature (see Arnaud & Mack, 1982:353).

There is also the dilemma of negotiating the contract. In some instances, there have been complaints that experienced contract attorneys have represented the private contractors while the government is represented by the agency's contract specialists who do not have the equivalent legal expertise and experience (Arnaud & Mack, 1982). One may ask whose interests are being served in such a situation. The procedures for making certain that the public is fully informed about the bidding and contracting process and the safeguards to ensure its fairness are issues that have not been fully addressed.

Although model legislation designed to preclude unethical conduct has been proposed, its author asserts that no legislation can completely prevent illegal or unethical behavior in the contracting process (Robbins, 1988:453). There is an expectation that government officials will monitor these activities closely while providing notice to those individuals who may contemplate violating the law (Robbins, 1988:453).

Any discussion of the bidding process must also take into account the evaluation and monitoring of the contract. Ideally, the government would stipulate in the final contract all of the procedures for monitoring the private agency's performance. However, any bid that is submitted, typically, would include only preliminary evaluation and monitoring techniques that the private agency has designed for its own protection and convenience (Merlo, 1986).

ETHICAL ARGUMENTS IN THE UTILIZATION OF THE PRIVATE SECTOR

Delegation of Responsibility

The foremost ethical issue in the privatization of corrections involves the state's ability to assign to a private agency or organization the power and authority to deprive citizens of their liberty. Simply stated, the private agency will be exercising the state's constitutional police power (Holley, 1988:339). The possibility that, as a non-governmental agency, it would use deadly force on an inmate attempting to escape, eliminate an inmate's good time credits, or conduct disciplinary hearings that may result in an inmate's being placed in solitary confinement is problematic (DiIulio, 1988a, 1988b, 1990; Robbins, 1986). Corrections professionals have tremendous discretion that should not simply be delegated to a private agency.

Proponents argue that the private sector is already heavily involved in the exercise of discretion in juvenile corrections and that the transfer of that authority to adult corrections can occur smoothly. To facilitate or preclude that transition, some states have enacted new legislation or revised earlier legislation (Hutto, 1990; Keating, 1985).

Opponents contend that it is morally wrong for the state to abdicate its responsibility to punish offenders to a private nongovernment agency. Decisions on length of confinement, place of confinement, and discipline cannot be reassigned to private agencies in the same way as garbage collection services (Keating, 1985). The analogy is made to other areas: Is society prepared to substitute private policing for public policing and private courts for public courts? If not, how does it see no moral difference between private and public corrections (DiIulio, 1988b:82)?

Profit Motive

Another ethical issue concerns the profit motive of the private provider (Lekachman, 1987). If fees are to be paid to private contractors on a per diem basis, there may be an incentive to maintain a steady stream of clients entering the system. In such an instance, control over decisions affecting incarceration and parole policies becomes critical to the private provider's profit making (Bowditch & Everett, 1987; *Privatization of Corrections,* 1986:14). How might private employees who recommend inmates to the parole board or who have some input into release decisions respond when, for example, they are aware of the corporation's fiscal problems?

Some observers suggest that the possibility of a government providing opportunities to private citizens to make a profit in the punishment of others merits closer scrutiny (Keating, 1985:50). Such an argument does not account for the fact that a number of private providers are non-profit corporations and therefore do not realize a profit in their willingness to detain offenders.

Conflict of Interest

One of the most frequently cited ethical issues deals with conflict of interest. The revelations made during the investigation of HUD in the summer of 1989 provided an opportunity to observe how some government officials left public office, met the requisite waiting period limitations, and then returned "...to lobby former colleagues for projects" (Johnston, 1989: A1, B5).

When public sector officeholders leave government, they take with them two kinds of information: "A general understanding and knowledge of the way government operates and specific confidential information about government policy or about private sector entities regulated by the government" (Starr & Sharp, 1984:40).

The private corporations are cognizant of the wealth of information available to them from former governmental corrections personnel. Not surpris-

ingly, the corporations have been quite successful in appointing them to
boards of directors or offices (Keating, 1985:16-17).

In 1985, in hearings before a subcommittee of the Committee on
Governmental Affairs of the 99th Congress, Ann McBride of Common Cause
testified that "...the problem is not what people do after they leave government, but what they do while in government in expectation of future employment" (cited in Roberts, 1988:183). The number of people who left the
Department of Defense and took positions with defense contractors or moved
from contractor jobs to the Defense Department in 1983 totaled 2,100
(Roberts, 1988).

Although the defense and corrections budgets are in no way comparable, it
is likely that individuals will trade on their experience, background, and association with their former colleagues. There are special problems presented in
the transition of employment from the public to the private sector. Beard
(1978) suggests that it may take years to detect any perceived impropriety; for
example, this could occur when an official accepts a position in a company
that had received favorable treatment from his/her earlier judgment and rul-
ings. Beard contends that the problem is particularly difficult to prove when
the previous favor was to neglect a possible area of inquiry or to take no
action (1978:236).

Individuals who are legally empowered to make decisions and who
receive special treatment or services from the corporations also may have a
conflict of interest. In the early 1980s, a Speaker of the Tennessee House of
Representatives was a stockholder (along with Governor Lamar Alexander's
wife) in Corrections Corporation of America. Later, the corporation was
awarded contracts to deliver services to Tennessee offenders (Keating, 1985).
What safeguards are in place to prevent a government official in charge of
contracts from repeatedly selecting the same company or being entertained by
the favored corporation for the weekend?

The possibility that a private prison lobby will develop and endeavor to
convince the public and legislators to demand more prison space and longer
sentences is a major source of concern (Elvin, 1985). Self-interested individuals could testify before legislative committees about the increase in crime
and the need for more get-tough policies, and then offer to assist the government in the construction and operation of these facilities. The pervasive punitive ideology coupled with the fiscal constraints would enhance the public's
acceptance of and dependence on private corporations.

Contract Monitoring and Regulation

Monitoring the contract, a critical link in the process, is frequently
neglected or minimized. First and foremost, the government has an obligation
to review all of its contracted services and to take an active role in the super-

vision and evaluation of private agencies that provide such services. The delivery of services to a population that is without power or advocates is especially problematic (Silvester, 1990). The facts that prisons are closed societies and offenders have no real representatives mean that the government must be vigilant in its monitoring activities.

Some proponents of privatization suggest that one advantage of the contract process is that it requires the government to stipulate what its goals really are and then to formulate the criteria to be utilized in evaluating the successful attainment of those goals (Logan, 1987:37). Historically, public correctional agencies have not been required to review their goals and prioritize them. The introduction of private sector contracting makes it possible for the state to chart its course more openly and then work toward a solution to its problems (Logan, 1987:37).

Although one would agree that the government should clearly stipulate its correctional goals, opponents of privatization suggest that the public sector can become more accountable and more effective without private sector competition. They contend that the ability of the government to monitor contracts successfully is replete with problems. One problem involves the flexibility of the contractor. In an attempt to establish and maintain accountability, some contracts may specify what can and cannot be changed. DiIulio (1990:162) suggests that although monitors could be authorized to grant variances or exemptions when necessary, there could be problems with such discretionary authority.

Bowditch and Everett (1987) list three potential problems when government regulates private agencies. First, the public regulatory mechanism could manifest a conflict of interest if the government endorses the goal of the industry. For example, consider the nuclear power industry. Second, industry lobbyists could exert considerable control over government policy and regulation by suggesting that the industry concerns are national concerns or exercising their political power and influence to prevent consideration of alternative ideas. Last, the government regulatory body would have the same view on goals, organization, and priorities as the industry if the agency's staff were trained with the industry (Bowditch & Everett, 1987:449).

Critics also question the ability of the government to successfully establish a regulatory agency and to allocate the resources and money that would be necessary to staff and monitor it. In their research of state and local governments that contracted with the private sector, Hackett et al. (1987:7) found a lack of careful monitoring of the agency's performance. There is also the issue of outsider involvement in the evaluation process. This raises two important questions: What safeguards will be employed to make certain that kickbacks and bribes are not being paid to officials? Will the public have to rely on the agency to police itself?

If private sector agencies "promise" that they can do it better, they have to be held fully accountable. Unfortunately, the evaluation of private providers is sometimes limited to a cost-effective, "bottom-line" assessment. As a result, the issue often becomes, "Can private companies do it more cheaply?" From this perspective, observers might ask if society is ready to delegate its responsibilities to inmates to the lowest bidder?

In one recent report on three private institutions, troublesome problems in the areas of staff salaries, lack of privacy for inmates, understaffing, inadequate facilities, and turnover rates were documented (Schuman, 1989:32). If the goal is to provide care as cheaply as possible to inmates, one wonders if inhumane treatment of inmates may result. It is not obvious which criteria of evaluation will be utilized by the government.

CONCLUSION

One of the more subtle ways that the private sector providers can protect their interests in corrections and assure their continued involvement is in the area of research. Bowditch and Everett (1987) suggest that private agencies could affect policy by becoming involved in and funding research organizations that are responsible for developing policy options. It would be in the company's best interests to have research data that examine the benefits of a large prison system. In such an instance, financial considerations would determine society's utilization of prisons and evidence would support prisons as the most appropriate method for dealing with offenders (Bowditch & Everett, 1987:451).

Other critics contend that private agencies and organizations will be more selective than public institutions in accepting clientele. The private sector's ability to choose individuals for its programs and to contractually limit the size of the population are two luxuries the public sector does not have. Inmates in crowded public institutions must rely on courts to remedy crowding.

Another possibility is that a two-tier system for separate classes of offenders might evolve. Under current prison regulations, administrators can transfer inmates to other institutions. It has been suggested that the private sector might ultimately refuse to deal with the more serious offenders (a process called "creaming") and force the government to establish special institutions for troublesome inmates. Virtually any recalcitrant offender or any outspoken inmate might be administratively transferred to public or more restrictive settings.

Perhaps the most troubling aspect of the privatization of corrections can best be illustrated by recent judicial intervention. Wecht (1987) contends that privatization will mandate "...greater judicial willingness to review prison practices to guarantee the rights of prisoners" (1987:815). In the case of *Wilson v. Seiter,* 111 S. Ct. 2321 (1991), however, the United States Supreme Court ruled that prison conditions such as poor sanitation in the dining halls and in food preparation and improper ventilation do not violate an inmate's

Eighth Amendment rights unless the inmate can prove that prison officials acted with "deliberate indifference" (111 S. Ct. 2323). The Court's decision suggests that it is less likely to monitor prison conditions and act as an advocate for inmate rights.

Apparently, some public agencies, elected officials, and the public have determined that there is a difference between private and public policing and private and public courts but not between private and public corrections. The fact that correctional institutions are filled with powerless offenders who are perceived as a burden to society may help facilitate the transfer of state responsibility to private corporations. As DiIulio contends, it is not entirely obvious how these distinctions are made (1990:176).

The government's reliance on the private sector in recent years has been due, in part, to the public's disenchantment and frustration with corrections systems, the rising costs of incarceration, the demand for more prison space, and the perception and fear of crime. Although private prisons appear to be a relatively easy way to solve the prison problem, they are not without problems. This chapter has identified some of the ethical issues that merit closer consideration as government agencies attempt to respond to increasing problems and costs of incarceration by deferring to the private sector.

TABLE OF CASES

Wilson v. Seiter, 111 S. Ct. 2321 (1991).

REFERENCES

Arnaud, J.A. & T.C. Mack (1982). "The Deinstitutionalization of Status Offenders in Massachusetts: The Role of the Private Sector." In J.L. Handler & J. Katz (eds.) *Neither Angels Nor Thieves: Studies in the Deinstitutionalization of Status Offenders,* pp. 335-372. Washington, DC: National Academy Press.

Beard, E. (1978). "Conflict of Interest and Public Service." In R.T. DeGeorge & J.A. Pichler (eds.) *Ethics, Free Enterprise & Public Policy,* pp. 232-247. New York, NY: Oxford University Press.

Bowditch, C. & R.S. Everett (1987). "Private Prisons: Problems Within the Solution." *Justice Quarterly,* 4(September):441-453.

Brakel, S.J. (1988). "Prison Management, Private Enterprise Style: The Inmates' Evaluation." *New England Journal on Criminal and Civil Confinement,* 14(2):175-244.

Camp, C.G. & G.M. Camp (1984). *Private Sector Involvement in Prison Services and Operations.* Washington, DC: U.S. Department of Justice, National Institute of Corrections.

Camp, G.M. & C.G. Camp (1991). *The Corrections Yearbook—1991, Adult Corrections.* South Salem, NY: Criminal Justice Institute Inc.

Cullen, F.T. (1986). "The Privatization of Treatment: Prison Reform in the 1980s." *Federal Probation,* 50(1):8-17.

Denhardt, K.G. (1988). *The Ethics of Public Service.* Westport, CT: Greenwood Press.

DiIulio, J.J. (1986). "Prisons, Profits, and the Public Good: The Privatization of Corrections." *Research Bulletin,* (1) Huntsville, TX: Sam Houston State University.

_____ (1988a). *Private Prisons.* Washington, DC: U.S. Department of Justice, National Institute of Justice.

_____ (1988b). "What's Wrong with Private Prisons." *The Public Interest,* 92(Summer):66-84.

_____ (1990). "The Duty to Govern: A Critical Perspective on the Private Management of Prisons and Jails." In D.C. McDonald (ed.) *Private Prisons and Public Interest,* pp. 155-178. New Brunswick, NJ: Rutgers University Press.

Durham, A.M. (1989). "Rehabilitation and Correctional Privatization: Observations of the 19th Century Experience and Implications for Modern Corrections." *Federal Probation,* 52(March):43-53.

Ellison, W.J. (1986-1987). "Privatization of Corrections: A Critique and Analysis of Contemporary Views." *Cumberland Law Review,* 17:683-729.

Elvin, J. (1985). "A Civil Liberties View of Private Prisons." *The Prison Journal,* 65(2):48-53.

Ericson, R.V., M.W. McMahon & D.G. Evans (1987). "Punishing for Profit: Reflections on the Revival of Privatization in Corrections." *Canadian Journal of Criminology,* 29(October):355-387.

Evans, B.B. (1987). "Private Prisons." *Emory Law Journal,* 36(Winter):253-283.

Field, J.E. (1987). "Making Prisons Private: An Improper Delegation of a Governmental Power." *Hofstra Law Review,* 15:649-675.

Gentry, J.T. (1986). "The Panopticon Revisited: The Problem of Monitoring Private Prisons." *The Yale Law Journal,* 96:353-375.

Hackett, J.C., H.P. Hatry, R.B. Levinson, J. Allen, K. Chi & E.D. Feigenbaum (1987). *Contracting for the Operation of Prisons and Jails,* 1-8. Washington, DC: U.S. Department of Justice, National Institute of Justice.

Holley, C.E. (1988). "Privatization of Corrections: Is the State Out on a Limb When the Company Goes Bankrupt?" *Vanderbilt Law Review,* 41:317-341.

Hutto, T.D. (1990). "The Privatization of Prisons." In J.W. Murphy & J.E. Dison (eds.) *Are Prisons Any Better? Twenty Years of Correctional Reform,* pp. 111-127. London: Sage Publications.

Johnston, D. (1989). "Former H.U.D. Officials Built Profitable Housing Business." *New York Times,* 14 July 1989. A1, B5.

Keating, J.M. (1985). *Seeking Profit in Punishment: The Private Management of Correctional Institutions.* Washington, DC: American Federation of State, County and Municipal Employees.

Lekachman, R. (1987). "The Craze for 'Privatization': Dubious Social Results of a Reaganite Dogma." *Dissent,* 34(Summer):302-307.

Logan, C.H. (1987). "The Propriety of Proprietary Prisons." *Federal Probation,* 51(September):35-40.

_____ (1990). *Private Prisons: Cons and Pros.* New York: Oxford University Press.

Logan, C.H. & S.P. Rausch (1985). "Punish and Profit: The Emergence of Private Enterprise Prisons." *Justice Quarterly,* 2(3):303-318.

McDonald, D.C. (1990). "Introduction." In D.C. McDonald (ed.) *Private Prisons and the Public Interest,* pp. 1-18. New Brunswick, NJ: Rutgers University Press.

McKinney, J.B. (1988). "Fraud, Waste, and Abuse in Government." In J.S. Bowman & F.A. Elliston (eds.) *Ethics, Government and Public Policy,* pp. 267-286. Westport, CT: Greenwood Press.

Merlo, A.V. (1986). "The Private Sector in Juvenile Corrections." Paper presented at the American Society of Criminology annual meeting, October, Atlanta, Georgia.

Mullen, J., K.J. Chabotar & D.M. Carrow (1985). *The Privatization of Corrections.* Washington, DC: U.S. Department of Justice, National Institute of Justice.

Pollock-Byrne, J. (1989). *Ethics in Crime & Justice: Dilemmas and Decisions.* Belmont, CA: Brooks/Cole.

Porter, R.G. (1990). "The Privatisation of Prisons in the United States: A Policy that Britain Should Not Emulate." *The Howard Journal,* 29(May):65-81.

Press, A. (1990). "The Good, the Bad, and the Ugly: Private Prisons in the 1980's." In D.C. McDonald (ed.) *Private Prisons and the Public Interest,* pp. 19-41. New Brunswick, NJ: Rutgers University Press.

Privatization of Corrections (1986). Hearings before the Subcommittee on Courts, Civil Liberties, and the Administration of Justice of the Committee on the Judiciary, House of Representatives, Ninety-Ninth Congress, First and Second Sessions, November 13, 1985 and March 18, 1986 Washington, DC: U.S. Government Printing Office.

Roberts, R.N. (1988). *White House Ethics: The History of the Politics of Conflict of Interest Regulation*. Westport, CT: Greenwood Press.

Robbins, I.P. (1986). "Privatization of Corrections: Defining the Issues." *Judicature*, 69(6):324-331.

———— (1988). *The Legal Dimensions of Private Incarceration*. Washington, DC: American Bar Association.

Schuman, A.M. (1989). "The Cost of Correctional Services: Exploring a Poorly Charted Terrain." *Research in Corrections*, 2(February):27-34.

Sellers, M.P. (1989). "Private and Public Prisons: A Comparison of Costs, Programs and Facilities." *International Journal of Offender Therapy and Comparative Criminology*, 33(3):241-256.

Sevick, J.R. & W.I. Cikins (1987). "Introduction." In J. Sevick & W.I. Cikins (eds.) *Constructing Correctional Facilities: Is There a Role for the Private Sector?*, pp. 1-12. Washington, DC: The Brookings Institute.

Silvester, D.B. (1990). "Ethics and Privatization in Criminal Justice: Does Education Have a Role to Play?." *Journal of Criminal Justice*, 18(1):65-70.

Starr, M. & M. Sharp (1984). *Ethical Conduct in the Public Sector: Report of the Task Force on Conflict of Interest*. Ottawa, Canada: Canadian Government Publishing Center.

United States Department of Justice: Office of Juvenile Justice and Delinquency Prevention (1988). *Involving the Private Sector in Public Policy and Program Development*. Washington, DC: U.S. Government Printing Office.

Wecht, D.N. (1987) "Breaking the Code of Deference: Judicial Review of Private Prisons." *The Yale Law Journal*, 96:815-837.

3

AIDS in Prisons:
Judicial and Administrative
Dilemmas and Strategies

J. Michael Olivero
Central Washington University

INTRODUCTION

The presence of AIDS in prisons and jails in the United States illustrates many diverse and complex dilemmas. One level of analysis can be focused upon correctional administrators as they attempt to mediate among various interests: infected inmates, noninfected inmates, fearful inmates, correctional staff, legislative mandates, judicial mandates, and the public. Their dilemma is the focus of this chapter.

Acquired Immune Deficiency Syndrome (AIDS) is a disease that impairs the body's immune system. The disease ranges from asymptomatic infection, which defies detection, to nonterminal diseases, to the terminal stages of AIDS and death from diseases that ordinarily do not present a problem for people with properly functioning immune systems. AIDS is transmitted from person to person, through an exchange of body fluids, associated with sexual activity or sharing intravenous (IV) hypodermic needles. People infected with AIDS may not know they are infected, may show no indication of being ill, or may test negative for infection, and yet they can transmit the disease to other people (Olivero, 1989).

Correctional administrators faced major problems before the advent of AIDS. Conditions within many jails and prisons were deplorable. Most jail and prison conditions did not meet Constitutional standards, especially in regard to medical care (Vaid, 1987). The presence of large numbers of inmates with a communicable disease that is incurable is an administrative nightmare when compounded by already existing problems.

THE SCOPE AND NATURE OF AIDS
IN JAILS AND PRISONS

The National Institute of Justice and the American Correctional Association conducted a national survey of all federal and state prisons and 38 county and city correctional systems to assess the incidence of AIDS infection among inmates since 1985 and to attempt to identify policies and changes in policies to address the AIDS issue. The results of the survey indicate that between 1981 and October 1986, there were 784 confirmed AIDS cases in participating state and federal correctional systems (Hammet, 1987). Between October of 1987, and October of 1988, the numbers increased from 1,964 to 3,136 confirmed AIDS cases (Hammet, 1988; 1989).

These early findings may have been just the tip of the iceberg. By 1989, there were 3,661 confirmed AIDS cases in state and federal correctional systems. Additionally, there were 1,750 cases in 38 large county and city jails. This amounted to roughly a 600 percent increase since 1985 and a 72 percent leap since 1988 (Hammet, Moini & Abt Associates, 1990). In 1989, it was estimated that out of every 1,000 prisoners entering California's prison system, 20 inmates were infected with the AIDS virus (McNeil-Lehrer, 1989).

In the next few years, the number of AIDS-infected inmates is certain to increase. The relationship between AIDS and correctional populations is mostly attributed to the presence of illegal intravenous drug users (Hammet, 1989; Greenspan, 1988). When first identified, the rate of infection within correctional facilities did not keep pace with increases in the general population. For example, in 1987, there was a 59 percent increase in those dying from full-blown AIDS in correctional facilities and a 61 percent increase in deaths in the general population of the United States (Hammet, 1988).[1] By contrast, in 1988 and 1989 there was a 72 percent increase in the total number of AIDS cases in correctional populations, and an estimated 50 percent increase in society at large. These findings suggest that new cases of those dying from AIDS are increasing more in correctional facilities than the population at large. The overwhelming majority of these were illegal intravenous drug users (Hammet et al., 1990). On the other hand, the findings may be misleading due to the large size of the population in the United States, in comparison with the size of the population within prisons.

Intravenous Drug Use

There are many reasons why dramatic increases in the numbers of AIDS-infected prisoners can be expected. As long as drugs remain illegal or people using illegal intravenous drugs commit crimes, there will be persons with histories of intravenous drug use in correctional facilities. Additionally, the method of injection that many illegal intravenous drug users employ places them at greater risk for contracting AIDS.

Many users inject the drug at "shooting galleries" where unsterilized hypodermic needles are shared by multiple users. Each user draws his/her own blood in the syringe so that it mixes with the drug. In doing so, each user injects whatever diseases the previous users carry into his own blood system, including the AIDS virus (Inciardi, 1990).

The highest increases in AIDS cases in the past two years have been among illegal intravenous drug users (Hammet, 1988). The prevalence of AIDS among homosexual males, the previous highest at-risk group for AIDS, has declined. The decrease is attributed to safe sex practices and an attentiveness to educational messages by the male homosexual community (Olivero, 1990). Illegal intravenous drug users may not benefit from AIDS educational messages.

This failure may be related to the fact that both intravenous drug users and criminals are accustomed to taking risks (Miah & Olivero, 1989; Inciardi, 1990). Limited research on inmate knowledge of AIDS and its relationship to their behavior to avoid infection indicates that many inmates know the avenues of AIDS transmission, yet they involve themselves in high-risk behaviors (Miah & Olivero, 1990).[2] Lainer and McCarthy (1989) found that incarcerated juvenile male offenders were not concerned about contracting AIDS, likening it to other matters, such as pregnancy, and shared the belief that "it can't happen to me."

This cavalier attitude may be cross-cultural. Morgado and Olivero (1991), while researching knowledge of AIDS and AIDS-related behaviors among Mexican inmates, found that Mexican and American prison inmates held similar levels of knowledge. However, they continued to engage in behaviors that would place them at risk of contracting AIDS.

No one knows the prevalence of illegal intravenous drug use inside jails and prisons. One possibility is that the scarcity of hypodermic needles within correctional facilities leads to greater sharing. Further, tattooing involving needles is also common in prisons. This is another means of transmitting AIDS (Hammet, 1988).

Sexual Transmission

There are also increases in the number of those infected with AIDS in prison as the result of homosexual activity among male inmates. Anal intercourse is one of the primary means of AIDS infection (Friedland & Klein, 1987). Sexual activity among incarcerated offenders is widespread (Olivero, 1990). Self-report data from inmates in Tennessee reveal that 18 percent had engaged in homosexual behavior while incarcerated. The Federal Bureau of Prisons reports that 28 percent of its prisoners have engaged in homosexual behavior while in prison (Hammet, 1988).

In addition to consensual sexual relationships within correctional populations, there is also homosexual rape. The possibility of infection through homosexual rape provides little deterrence to rapists because it is the victim and not the perpetrator who faces the greatest risk of contracting AIDS. Research indicates it is less likely for an AIDS-infected rape victim to transmit the disease through sexual activity than it is for the perpetrator (Vaid, 1987).

The incidence of sexual assault in correctional facilities may be quite high. In an early study of sexual assault in a Philadelphia jail, 2,000 inmates out of 60,000 indicated that they were the victims of sexual assault (Davis, 1968). Lockwood (1980) found that 28 percent of his sample were the target of sexual aggression at some time in their institutional custody. More recently, the Federal Bureau of Prisons estimated that between 9 percent and 20 percent of its prisoners were the target of sexual aggression (Hammet, 1989).

There have been instances in which inmates have sued prison officials alleging that they contracted AIDS through rape. A prisoner in Florida recently filed suit against prison officials alleging infection through gang rape (*Smith v. Department of Corrections,* 1987). The success of such cases will probably depend on the plaintiff's ability to prove that he was infected as the result of the rape and not infected at some other time. This would probably be difficult to substantiate because it is recognized that the test for AIDS will not always show infection until weeks or months after the time of infection. The plaintiff would have trouble proving he was not already infected, or not infected through some other manner.

There is some published evidence that sexually transmitted diseases and even AIDS may be spread in prison. Alcabes and Braslow (1988) traced the spread of gonorrhea among inmates who contracted the disease while incarcerated in a detention center in New York. The Federal Bureau of Prisons reported that there were 218 cases of syphilis and 115 cases of gonorrhea diagnosed after health screening upon prison admission in 1986 (Moran & Peterman, 1989).[3] Unfortunately, although outbreaks of sexually transmitted diseases within prisons are well known by experts, most of the data on transmission have gone unpublished (Moran & Peterman, 1989).

Results concerning the transmission of AIDS while in prison are somewhat conflicting. Inmates in a military prison were followed an average of 15 months after screening for the AIDS virus and none had antibodies to the AIDS virus upon retesting (Kelly, 1986). AIDS infection among state prison inmates was also examined in Maryland. Out of 422 inmates, two eventually became infected. Based on these findings, the researchers concluded that .4 percent of the prison population would become infected each year (Brewer, 1988). In both samples the number of inmates already in prison who were infected with the AIDS virus was unknown. However, 1 percent of the military sample and 6.6 percent of the Maryland sample were found infected upon admission into the systems.[4]

At any rate, studies that seek to ascertain transmission while in prison are problematic. The upper limit of the incubation period for AIDS has not been established and the AIDS test will sometimes not detect the presence of the virus for extended periods. Therefore, it is uncertain whether inmates were already infected upon entrance and received a false negative during testing (Blumberg, 1990).

AIDS POLICIES

The concentration of illegal intravenous drug users in correctional facilities and the possibility of spread through sexual contact while in prison is a major concern for correctional administrators. At issue is whether it is necessary to test for AIDS and, if so, what to do with those inmates who are identified as HIV positive. For example, is it necessary to segregate AIDS-infected inmates or can the spread of the disease be controlled through education about its transmission? What conditions will be present in AIDS-isolation wings or facilities, or what constitutes adequate medical treatment for infected inmates? In an attempt to address these questions, the issue of testing and segregation (including judicial interpretation), and AIDS education, will be examined.

Testing

The most controversial issue facing prisons is forced or mandatory AIDS testing (Greenspan, 1988). Proponents of mass screening argue that it is the most effective way to prevent the spread of the infection while in prison. Furthermore, it is seen as a means of achieving a variety of positive objectives, including:

> (1) to provide counseling to the infected; (2) to improve
> medical monitoring and care for the infected; and, (3) to
> provide specific counseling and supervision to infected
> inmates prior to release in an effort to reduce infection of
> others outside of prison (Clements, 1989).

The Federal Bureau of Prisons and the states of Alabama, Colorado, Georgia, Idaho, Iowa, Missouri, Nebraska, Nevada, New Hampshire, New Mexico, Oklahoma, South Dakota, and West Virginia, and Wyoming have mass, mandatory screening upon entry into their systems (Hammet, 1989). Between 1986 and 1987, the number of prisons using mass testing upon entrance increased from three to 13 (Hammet, 1989). As of October 1989, 16 (33%) state correctional systems and the Federal Bureau of Prisons screened all inmates upon entrance. This procedure represents the dominant policy (Hammet, 1990).[5]

Advances in methods to treat the AIDS infection and associated disorders have resulted in an increasing emphasis on early detection (Hammet, 1990). Sutton (1990), working in Alabama's correctional system, found that early treatment with AZT (azidothymidine)—a drug that retards the progress of the disease—lowers the costs of care for infected prisoners and increases their tolerance for the drug. Prior to the spring of 1989, Alabama's policy was to provide AZT to those who were AIDS infected, had a T-Helper cell (the cell that directs the white blood cells to attack foreign organisms) count below 250, and suffered from pneumocystic carinii (a form of pneumonia). Currently, the policy is a mandatory mass screening program and the provision of AZT upon request, regardless of the status or progress of the disease.

The AIDS test does not determine whether the individual has contracted AIDS. It is a test for antibodies to the AIDS infection, which may take a month or longer to develop. Hence, one could infect others, be asymptomatic, but test negative for the presence of antibodies. Problems with testing raise serious consequences for AIDS transmission within prison. Once inmates have been tested and found negative for the AIDS virus, they may believe themselves and others to be free from infection. Hence, they may practice unsafe sex while believing the risk is minimal (Vaid, 1987).

If testing does occur, the concern becomes the purpose of the testing, and how the results will be used. It is well known that inmates suffer negative treatment as the result of being found to be AIDS infected (Olivero, 1989). Correctional officers have refused to work with infected prisoners in 20 percent of the state and federal correctional systems (Hammet, 1988). There are other reports of correctional officers pushing food trays under cell doors, refusing requests for assistance, and wearing masks or gloves while escorting prisoners with AIDS (Olivero, 1990; Vaid, 1987).

Despite information that AIDS cannot be transmitted through casual contact, correctional officer labor unions continue to lobby for the disclosure of test results. In some instances, correctional officers have filed union grievances requesting the names of all prisoners suspected of having communicable diseases (Vaid, 1987). The Association of Federal, State, County and Municipal Employees (Correctional Officer's Union) has advocated mandatory testing of all prisoners for AIDS exposure, and the segregation of those found to have been exposed (Hammet, 1987).

Negative and harsh treatment of AIDS-infected inmates by noninfected inmates may exceed that of correctional officers. Prison administrators have found it necessary to segregate infected inmates for their own safety. For example, prisoners inadvertently filmed in an AIDS training film were beaten by other inmates because they were thought to have AIDS (*Noisy v. Bowles*, 1987). In another instance, noninfected inmates threatened to burn down the cells housing infected inmates to convince prison administrators to remove them from the prison's general population (Vaid, 1987).

The courts have held that the segregation of infected inmates for their safety is justified. The courts have also supported segregation policies despite the request of infected inmates to remain in the general population. For example, in *Cordero v. Coughlin* (1984), segregation was deemed appropriate to "protect both the AIDS victims and other prisoners from tensions and harm that could result from the fears of other inmates"(*Cordero v. Coughlin,* 1984:10) (see also *Lewis v. Prison Health Services, Inc.,* 1988).

The courts are reluctant to interfere in institutional policies concerning AIDS. Part of their hesitancy is based upon the rationale that it is undesirable to attempt to micro-manage prisons through the courts. In *Jarret v. Faulkner* (1987:929), the court refused to take a position concerning appropriate AIDS policies stating, "the problems of the prisons are not readily susceptible to resolution by decree." Furthermore, "The problem of protecting prisoners from AIDS is best left to the legislature and prison administrators"(*Jarret v. Faulkner,* 1987:929).

Not only have the courts been reluctant to micro-manage prison policies concerning AIDS, but they also have resisted pressure to mandate medical standards. In *Glick v. Henderson* (1988), inmates argued that all inmates and prison personnel should be tested for AIDS infection. Experts provided conflicting testimony as to whether testing was necessary. The court refused to make what it described as a medical standard decision, stating:

> [plaintiff] asks this Court to involve itself in a medical controversy and to dictate medical guidelines in an area where the medical profession has not yet spoken, a task this Court is hardly suited to do (*Glick v. Henderson,* 1988:539).

The courts have also used the same perspective, i.e., not micro-managing prisons or dictating AIDS medical guidelines, regarding the necessity of testing. In *Judd v. Packard* (1987:744), the court stated:

> Much is still unknown about AIDS, but any serious-minded individual can readily appreciate its potential for causing a plague of (or beyond) Biblical proportions. Furthermore, the danger of AIDS is heightened in the closed community of a penal institution where carriers of the HTLV-III virus may readily transmit it, whether willingly or unwittingly, to other inmates, through homosexual encounters or otherwise. Thus, the diagnosis, identification, and treatment of potential AIDS carriers, as a part of a program of AIDS prevention, certainly has a legitimate purpose, especially in the prison setting...[Furthermore,] It may be that prison

officials might face a 1983 suit for failing to isolate a known AIDS patient or carrier, if...[lack of action constitutes] grossly negligent or reckless conduct on the part of such officials.

These two cases, *Glick v. Henderson* and *Judd v. Packard*, left prison administrative decisions on whether to test for AIDS in the hands of prison administrators.

An area still under judicial debate concerns the confidentiality of testing. In *Baez v. Rapping* (1988), a doctor issued a precaution to jailers to avoid contact with Baez's body fluids, as Baez had tested positive for infection with the AIDS virus. Baez sued the physician, claiming a violation of his right to confidential medical treatment. Ruling against Baez, the court stated, "a failure to ensure a warning to prison officials to avoid contact with the body fluids of an AIDS carrier might itself be deemed a failure to perform official duties"(*Baez v. Rapping,* 1988:115). In essence, the doctor had a duty to warn jailers.

By contrast, in *Woods v. White* (1988) the court adopted a different position. Prison officials disclosed that an inmate had tested positive for AIDS, in violation of his Constitutional right to privacy as applied to doctor-patient relationships. The court ruled that this right is not stripped away at the time of incarceration. The court also stated that, "Casual, unjustified dissemination of confidential medical information to non-medical staff and other prisoners can scarcely be said to belong to the sphere of defendant's discretionary functions" (*Woods v. White,* 1988:703).

In the absence of judicial mandate, most states disclose positive test results to the attending physician, medical staff, correctional management in the institution and in the central office. However, states requiring disclosure to other categories of people, such as correctional officers, spouses and sexual partners, victims, and parole agencies are clearly in the minority (Hammet, 1990).

The issue of the right to privacy concerning AIDS test results comes under general privacy rights afforded prisoners. In *Turner v. Safley* (1987), the Supreme Court held that regulations that impinge upon prisoner privacy must be reasonably related to legitimate penological interests. In the case of divulging AIDS test results, the courts must decide whether the interests of the state (prison administrators) outweigh the privacy interests of the infected prisoner. In the final analysis, as we learn more about AIDS and preventing AIDS transmission, test result policies inside prisons will undergo continuous evolution and judicial scrutiny. If the trend toward mainstreaming all prisoners continues and safety procedures treat inmates universally (as though all are capable of transmitting contagious diseases), the courts will mandate the relevance of confidential AIDS test results to more restricted ranges of personnel.

In the meantime, the courts will continue to refrain from micro-managing such policies. For example, in May 1988, Alabama inmates, represented by attorneys from the American Civil Liberties Union, argued that mandatory testing upon prison admission unconstitutionally compelled prisoners to undergo testing against their will and was a violation of their Fourth Amendment rights (*Harris v Thigpen,* 1990). Additionally, the fact that the results were not held confidential abrogated their right to privacy (applied through the Fourteenth Amendment). The suit alleged that prison administrators failed to advise prisoners regarding the "inconclusive and sometimes misleading significance of the results," failed to provide proper counseling and medical care to AIDS-infected prisoners, "forced infected prisoners to live in a segregated unit in conditions resembling a 'leper colony,'" and deprived them of programs available to other inmates (Takas, Hammet & Abt, 1989:4). The Court found against the prisoner plaintiffs on every count, stating that the correctional system's need to prevent the spread of a disease outweighed prisoner constitutional rights (*Correctional Care,* January/February 1990).

Segregation

If testing reveals infection, or an inmate begins to exhibit symptoms of infection, correctional administrators must decide whether to segregate the individual. This has been a difficult dilemma for officials. Officials representing Colorado's prison system have been sued by both noninfected and infected inmates. The noninfected inmate claimed that the policies regarding AIDS-infected inmates were not sufficient to protect him from prisoners who were contagious, despite a policy of segregation. The segregated, infected inmate contended that he was unjustly denied access to educational and recreational programs while in segregation (Wagner, 1987).

The current trend is to "mainstream" rather than routinely segregate those found to be AIDS infected. Such a policy permits all categories of infected inmates to remain in the general population. In 1985, only 4 percent of state and federal correctional facilities practiced mainstreaming. By 1989, 35 percent practiced mainstreaming, making it the most common policy used. On the other hand, 18 percent of the prisons continued to segregate infected inmates whether or not they showed symptoms (Hammet, 1990).

Conditions within AIDS segregation units are usually substandard (Olivero & Roberts, 1989). As stated previously, prisoners have compared AIDS segregation units to "leper colonies" (*Harris v. Thigpen,* 1990). Prisoners have complained that conditions in segregation include prohibitions on eating, exercising or attending religious services with prisoners in the general population (*Lewis v. Prison Health Services, Inc.,* 1988).

There may be health hazards that result from placing AIDS-infected inmates in medical units because of possible exposure to disease (Vaid, 1987). Currently, there appears to be a resurgence of tuberculosis in United States prisons and jails. This rise has been linked to AIDS infection. Inmates with suppressed immune systems are more susceptible to progression from tuberculous infection and conversion to the active disease (Hammet, 1988). As such, their placement in areas where there are numerous sick people may increase their risk of infection or contracting further diseases.

Vaid (1987) reports that infected inmates have been placed in medical observation units that are not suitable for long-term confinement. Furthermore, infected inmates have been confined to segregation cells under 23- or 24-hour lockdown conditions and denied access to law libraries, outdoor exercise, and educational, vocational, and work-release programs. For example, in *Muhammad v. Carlson* (1986), Muhammad contested his placement in disciplinary segregation, without a hearing, when it was found that he was infected with AIDS. The court ruled that a prisoner who tested positive for AIDS had no right to a hearing. The placement was seen as a medical directive, not the result of a discretionary administrative decision. Unfortunately, the inability to participate in such programs prevents a specific group of inmates from earning good-time credit to reduce their periods of incarceration.

Segregating AIDS-infected prisoners compounds existing problems of overcrowding. Segregating another subgroup of prisoners, that is likely to increase in numbers (especially for systems with mandatory testing of all prisoners), may overtax the system (Vaid, 1987). These conditions may be exacerbated by some correctional administrators and judges, who have questioned whether it would be wise to deny early release to infected prisoners out of concern for the supposed threat they hold for illegal intravenous drug users or sexual partners in the community. In essence, they advocate extended confinement of infected prisoners (Takas, Hammet & Abt, 1989). Correctional systems throughout the country could become quarantine facilities if such policies were implemented (Olivero, 1989). City officials in Boston were planning to enforce a statute for preventive detention of arrested prostitutes who indicated they would return to prostitution if released from custody (Takas, Hammet & Abt, 1989).

Correctional administrators cannot rely upon state or federal legislatures to assist in the problem. The get-tough philosophy has resulted in legislators enacting mandatory sentences, revising criminal codes, and establishing lengthy minimum terms and preventive detention policies, while failing to explore alternatives to incarceration (Vaid, 1987). These policies contributed to prison overcrowding even before the AIDS epidemic.

Overcrowding is a by-product of the lack of funds available to correctional administrators. Inadequate appropriations prevent many systems from developing special wards for AIDS patients, and diminish the quality of medical care and the creativity and effectiveness of educational efforts (Vaid, 1987). The government's proclivity to ignore correctional systems may be tolerated by politicians who do not want their names associated with, or who do not want to appear to endorse, the lifestyle of groups with a high risk of contracting AIDS, i.e., homosexuals and illegal intravenous drug users (Olivero, 1990).[6]

In accordance with their reluctance to micro-manage correctional systems, the courts have not intervened on the issue of whether segregation is necessary. Instead, they rely upon the policies provided by correctional administrators. For example, prison administrators in *Lewis v. Prison Health Services, Inc.* (1988), stated that segregation was necessary for a variety of reasons, including:

> (1) to protect noninfected prisoners; (2) to protect the infected prisoner from abuse [by] noninfected prisoners; (3) to limit the contact of those with AIDS with the general population, hence preventing their exposure to diseases found there, such as the common cold; and, (4) to control prison staff exposure to AIDS.

The court agreed with prison administrators, stating that, "any one of these rationales constitutes a legitimate end; in the conglomerate these goals are certainly legitimated" (*Lewis v. Prison Health Services, Inc.,* 1988:5). Furthermore, the court stated that, "so long as there are legitimate governmental ends, and the means are rationally related to the ends, the equal protection clause [of the Constitution] is not violated" (*Lewis v. Prison Health Services, Inc.,* 1988:5). Similarly in *Judd v. Packard* (1987), Judd argued that placement in segregation constituted discrimination based upon a handicap, i.e., being AIDS-infected. The court ruled that there was no "invidious discrimination." The courts have utilized a similar analysis when deciding cases in which inmates have sought to have infected inmates removed from the general population.

However, prison officials are responsible for the transmission of AIDS under certain circumstances. In *Foy v. Owens* (1986), inmate Foy sued prison officials for not segregating AIDS-infected prisoners. The court ruled that the mere presence of AIDS carriers did not amount to a violation of Constitutional rights.[7]

However, in *Foy,* the court also stated that transmission would have to have been proven and the plaintiff would have to demonstrate that officials were somehow negligent and this negligence caused its transmission. In *Cameron v. Metcuz, Broglin, McBride* (1989), inmate Cameron argued that he had been exposed to AIDS as the result of negligence on the part of officials. Cameron was placed in a unit where he was bitten by an infected prisoner who had a violent and promiscuous history. As such, he argued that prison officials had acted with deliberate and callous disregard for his personal safety. He also argued that officials were in violation of state policies that mandated segregation of inmates with contagious diseases upon a verification that their behavior may be "predatory or promiscuous."

The court stated that this case was a precedent builder. It held that correctional administrators have an obligation to take reasonable steps to protect inmates from exposure to AIDS from predatory criminals. This reflects one instance in which the courts have been firm in holding prison officials responsible for the transmission of AIDS. For example, Judge McMillan, in *Glick v. Henderson* (1988), stated that he believed a policy that placed prisoners at high risk for assault or an unreasonable danger of sexual assault by AIDS carriers would be a violation of constitutional rights.

Education

Educating infected prisoners is a viable approach to reducing AIDS transmission. It may also be a way to eliminate fear and hostility about AIDS among noninfected inmates and correctional officers (Vaid, 1987). Most states provide staff and inmates with some general training information and materials on AIDS and the means of transmission. Staff training emphasizes ways to reduce risk during contact with inmates. Inmate training typically explains AIDS transmission behaviors such as sharing hypodermic needles and at-risk sexual activity. Another important component of prison AIDS education is counseling inmates before and after AIDS testing, with specific attention directed toward those who test positive for the HIV virus.

There are numerous approaches to assisting inmates in obtaining information about AIDS. Some prison systems, such as Texas and Oregon, have developed AIDS departments or communicable and infectious disease coordinators. The tasks of these professionals are to stay abreast of new developments, to provide up-to-date information for educational purposes, to offer AIDS education, and to develop an expertise to provide appropriate policy responses to AIDS-related issues (Hammet, 1988). There are also prisoners involved with AIDS self-help groups and inmate-produced informational newsletters (see *Gay Community News* or DJA Inc.). Some of these endeavors were intended to address the perception that prison officials and the government were not doing enough for the inmates infected with AIDS or were unresponsive to the inclusion of AIDS transmission among minorities and prisoners. Finally, in states that have conjugal visits, such as California and Washington, AIDS information and education is provided to wives by counselors.

Education, however, is not without its limitations. The fact that AIDS information is provided does not mean that all inmates will heed the warnings and change their behaviors. Second, some correctional administrators believe that turnover is too great in some prisons and most jails for an adequate educational program. Correctional administrators from California, for example, argued, for an unstated reason, that AIDS education would result in a panic among prisoners and prison personnel (Hammet, 1988).

In addition, they indicated a reluctance to provide inmates with information on how to avoid the risks of AIDS transmission (Hammet, 1988). Prison administrators had problems disseminating information on behavior which is prohibited in prison, such as homosexual conduct or intravenous drug use. They were concerned about giving the appearance of condoning these practices. This may account for the fact that only four states have condoms available to inmates. Vermont was the first state to initiate this practice (Hammet, 1989). Vaid (1987:244) pointed out that, "even though illicit intravenous drug use is common in prisons, inmates receive no information about sterilizing hypodermic needles or 'outfits' as they are called in prison." As such, the nature of AIDS transmission practices, which are usually prohibited by correctional officials, inhibits officials from providing information.

CONCLUSION

Historically, living conditions in prisons and jails throughout the United States have been constitutionally inadequate, especially with regard to medical care (Vaid, 1987). The conservative get-tough approach in criminal justice is related to an intolerance for convicted criminals, and support for harsh and deprived conditions. The prevailing view is that inmates are placed in prison to be punished and to suffer. Moreover, there is little thought given to their eventual return to society (Olivero & Roberts, 1990).

Additionally, there is an intolerance for homosexuals and illegal intravenous drug users, coupled with hysteria about AIDS. For example, religious explanations have been utilized to explain the high incidence of AIDS among homosexuals and illegal intravenous drug users. It is viewed, by some religious leaders, as God's retribution for the perversions and sins committed by addicts, prostitutes, and homosexuals (Black, 1986), despite the fact that AIDS strikes "innocent" people outside of these suspect groups. For others, AIDS has become synonymous with syphilis, leprosy, and the plague. Inciardi (1990:303) stated that AIDS has become a "contemporary metaphor for corruption, decay and consummate evil."

Repulsion to AIDS-infected individuals has ranged from attempts to keep AIDS-infected children out of schools (e.g., see *Chalk v. District Ct. Cent. Dist. of California* (1988), or *Doe v. Boston Elementary School District No. 148* (1988)), and termination of employment (see *Raytheon Co. v. Fair Employment and Housing Commission* (1989), to outright acts of violence or vandalism against the infected (Wagner, 1987).

The future for inmates infected with AIDS does not appear to be bright. Public attitudes have translated into government neglect for conditions inside prisons, especially in regard to prisoners with AIDS. At the same time that elected officials have increased penalties for crime, created mandatory prison sentences, and abolished parole, they have not appropriated funds to permit prison administrators to manage increased numbers of offenders (Vaid, 1987), much less attended to the rising numbers of prisoners infected with AIDS. We can anticipate a future of overcrowded prison facilities, with little governmental attention or public outcry focused on the special needs of AIDS-infected inmates.

The future possibility of help from outside of prisons is even more bleak for AIDS-infected inmates, when their relatively powerless position in society is examined. Those in prison are not likely to have the social or political power to force changes inside the walls of correctional facilities (Olivero, 1990). Those who are sentenced to prison and those who contract AIDS appear to be drawn from the same populations, a group that typically is representative of the American underclass. Most of those infected in prison are disproportionately members of minority groups; they tend to be black and Hispanic.

Not surprisingly then, the racial or ethnic background of prisoners with AIDS is 46 percent black, 27 percent Hispanic and 27 percent white (Hammet, 1989). In the general population, 25 percent of all AIDS victims are black. The disproportionate incidence of AIDS among blacks may be explained by their greater involvement in illegal intravenous drug use (Greaves, 1986). Of the heterosexual intravenous drug users known to have AIDS in the United States, 50 percent were black, 30 percent were Hispanic, and 20 percent were white (De Jarlais, Hunt & Abt, 1988).

The position of AIDS-infected prisoners to demand changes or better treatment of prison administrators is tenuous. The treatment of the AIDS-infected inmates by prison administrators may be related to their power in the prison social hierarchy. The operant (as opposed to official) organization and administration of correctional facilities is the result of political conflict between various groups who seek to secure their diverse interests in prisons (Statsny & Tyrnauer, 1982). It appears that inmates and some prison administrators share society's repulsion of AIDS victims. Prisoners found to be infected by AIDS are an "outgroup" and are stigmatized within the prison community. Noninfected inmates insist on the removal of the infected inmates from their midst and will resort to violence should their demands not be met (Vaid, 1987). Prison officials may be forced to treat AIDS-exposed prisoners according to this outgroup status and force them into segregation, where they are provided less than desirable conditions.

Historically, the courts have stepped in to force prison administrators to provide adequate treatment of prisoners. This may not be the case today or in the future (Olivero & Roberts, 1990). Olivero (1990) argues that in the case of prisoners with AIDS, the courts have allowed prison administrators to victimize prisoners. The courts, in their effort to avoid the practice of micromanaging prisons and establishing medical guidelines for the treatment of prisoners with AIDS, have determined that both segregation and nonsegregation of prisoners are legally justified. Further, the courts have found that conditions of deprivation within segregation units are constitutional. The public's resentment of offenders, society's repulsion for those with AIDS that transcends correctional walls, governmental neglect, and an aversion by the courts to become involved have resulted in treating AIDS-infected inmates with even greater disdain than convicted felons.

NOTES

1   In 1987, the incidence rate for those exposed to AIDS in general society was considered to be 8.6 cases per 100,000 persons. The aggregate rate for state and federal correctional centers was thought to be 54 per 100,000. In jails, it was projected to be 126 cases per 100,000 prisoners (Hammet, 1988).

2   This is not to say that illegal IV drug users are totally unwilling to adjust their behavior as the result of educational messages (Des Jarlais, Friedman & Hopkins, 1985). However, at present, the research in this area appears to be inconclusive (Inciardi, 1990).

3   Whether these cases were acquired in prison or are associated with furloughs is unknown.

4   AIDS-infected inmates among new entrants to Alabama, Colorado, Idaho, Iowa, Maryland, Minnesota, Nebraska, Nevada, South Dakota, and Wisconsin prison systems ranged from 0.0 to 7.4 percent. Higher incidence would be expected from New York and New Jersey where AIDS infection is prevalent among IV drug users (Moran & Peterman, 1989).

5   There are other testing policies. For example, 22 percent of the prisons have screening for "high-risk groups," 14 percent have voluntary testing upon request, 29 percent if there are clinical indications, involvement in an incident or epidemiological studies, and 2 percent have no testing policy or the policy is unknown (Hammet, 1990).

6   In *Gates v. Deukmejian* (1988), a pending case, prisoners housed in an AIDS segregation unit filed suit alleging a low level of care as the result of severe overcrowding and understaffing.

7   In *Muhammad v. Frame* (1987:3), the court corroborated the *Foy* decision by stating, "We find that more than mere presence of AIDS carriers in the prison population is needed to establish a claim."

REFERENCES

Alcabes, P. & C. Braslow (1988). "A Cluster of Cases of Penicillinase-Producing Neisseria Gonorrhoea in an Adolescent Detention Center." *New York State Journal of Medicine,* September:495-96.

Black, D. (1986). *The Plague Years: A Chronicle of AIDS, the Epidemic of Our Times.* New York, NY: Simon and Schuster.

Blumberg, M. (1990). "Issues and Controversies with Respect to the Management of AIDS in Corrections." In M. Blumberg (ed.) *AIDS—the Impact on the Criminal Justice System,* Columbus, OH: Merrill Publishing Company.

Brewer, T. (1988). "Transmission of HIV-1 Within a Statewide Prison System." *AIDS,* 2:363-367.

Clements, C. (1989). "AIDS and Offender Classification: Implications for Management of HIV-Positive Prisoners." *The Prison Journal,* LXVIX (2):19-28.

Correctional Care (January/February, 1990). "Court Supports Prison Policy." 4(I):1,5.

Davis, A. (1968). "Sexual Assault in the Philadelphia Prison System and Sheriff's Vans." *Trans-Action,* 6:8.

De Jarlais, D., S. Friedman & W. Hopkins (1985). "Risk Reduction for the Acquired Immunodeficiency Syndrome Among Intravenous Drug Users." *Annals of Internal Medicine,* 103(5):755-759.

De Jarlais, D., D. Hunt & Abt Associates, Inc. (1988). *AIDS and Intravenous Drug Use.* Washington, DC: National Institute of Justice.

DJA Inc. (1991). *National Prison Group.* Jami Naturalite (#185660), P.O. Box 3003, Jackson, MI, 49204: DJA Inc.

Friedland, G. & R. Klein (1987). "Transmission of the Human Immunodeficiency Virus." *New England Journal of Medicine,* 317:1125-1135.

Gay Community News (1991). *Gay Community News.* 62 Berkeley St., Boston, MA, 02116: *GCN.*

Greaves, W. (1986). "The Black Community." In H. Dalton et al., (eds.) *AIDS and the Law: A Guide For the Public.* New Haven, CT: Yale University Press.

Greenspan, J. (1988). "Statistics on AIDS in Prison." *The National Prison Project,* 16:5-8.

Hammet, T. (1986). *AIDS in Correctional Facilities: Issues and Answers.* Washington, DC: U.S. Department of Justice, National Institute of Justice, Office of Communication and Research Utilization.

_____ (1987). *AIDS in Correctional Facilities: Issues and Answers,* Second Edition. Washington, DC: U.S. Department of Justice, National Institute of Justice, Office of Communication and Research Utilization.

_____ (1988). *AIDS in Correctional Facilities: Issues and Answers*, Third Edition. Washington, DC: U.S. Department of Justice, National Institute of Justice, Office of Communication and Research Utilization.

_____ (1989). *1988 Update: AIDS in Correctional Facilities.* Washington, DC: National Institute of Justice.

Hammet, T., S. Moini & Abt Associates (1990). *Update on AIDS in Prisons and Jails.* Washington, DC: National Institute of Justice.

Inciardi, J. (1990). "AIDS and Drug Use: Implications for Criminal Justice Policy." In R. Weisheit (ed.) *Drugs, Crime and the Criminal Justice System.* Cincinnati, OH: Anderson Publishing Co.

Kelly, P. (1986). "Prevalence and Incidence of HTLV-III Infection in Prison." *Journal of the American Medical Association,* 256:2198-2199.

Lanier, M. & B. McCarthy (1989). "Knowledge and Concern About AIDS Among Incarcerated Juvenile Offenders." *Prison Journal,* LXVIX(1):39-52.

Lockwood, D. (1980). *Prison Sexual Violence.* New York, NY: Elsevier North Holland, Inc.

Miah, M. & J. Olivero (1990). "Inmate Knowledge, Attitudes and Behaviors Concerning AIDS." Unpublished paper presented at the annual meeting of the Academy of Criminal Justice Sciences, Denver, Colorado, March.

McNeil-Lehrer (1989). "AIDS in Prison." *News Hour.* Public Broadcast Stations. Aired May 29, 1989.

Moran, J. & T. Peterman (1989). "Sexually Transmitted Diseases in Prisons and Jails." *The Prison Journal,* LXVIX(1):1-6.

Morgado, A. & J. Olivero (1991). "Mexican Inmate Knowledge and Behavior Concerning AIDS." Unpublished paper presented at the annual meeting of the Academy of Criminal Justice Sciences, Nashville, Tennessee, March.

Olivero, J. (1989). "Intravenous Drug Use and AIDS: A Review and Analysis of Evolving Correctional Policy." *Criminal Justice Policy and Review,* 3(4):360-375.

_____ (1990). "The Treatment of AIDS Behind the Walls of Correctional Facilities." *Social Justice,* 17(1):113-125.

Olivero, J. & J. Roberts (1989). "The Management of AIDS in Correctional Facilities: A View of the Federal Court System." *The Prison Journal,* LXIX(2):7-18.

_____ (1990). "The United States Federal Penitentiary at Marion, Illinois: Alcatraz Revisited." *New England Journal on Criminal and Civil Confinement,* 16(1):21-51.

Statsny, C. & G. Tyrnauer (1982). *Who Rules the Joint?* Lexington, MA: Lexington Books.

Sutton, G. (1990). "Alabama Experience in AIDS Management Within the Department of Corrections." *Correctional Care,* 4(I):15-16.

Takas, N., T. Hammet & Abt Associates (1989). *Legal Issues Affecting Offenders and Staff.* Washington, DC: National Institute of Justice.

Vaid, U. (1987). "Prisons." In H. Dalton, S. Burris & Yale AIDS Law Project (ed.) *AIDS and the Law.* New Haven, CT: Yale University Press.

Wagner, P. (1987). "AIDS and the Criminal Justice System." In W. Dornette (ed.) *AIDS and the Law.* New York, NY: John Wiley and Sons.

TABLE OF CASES

Baez v. Rapping, 680 F. Supp. 112 (S.D.N.Y. 1988)

Cameron v. Metcuz, Broglin, McBride, 705 F. Supp. 454 (N.D. Ind. 1989)

Chalk v. District Ct. Cent. Dist. of California, 840 F.2d 701 (9th Cir. 1988)

Cordero v. Coughlin, 607 F. Supp. 9 (S.D.N.Y. 1984)

Doe v. Boston Elementary School District No. 148, 694 F. Supp. 440 (N.D. Ill. 1988)

Foy v. Owens, No. 85-6909 (E.D. Pa. March 19, 1986)

Gates v. Deukmejian, No. CIV S-87-1636 LKK JFM (E.D. Cal. July 27, 1988)

Glick v. Henderson, 855 F.2d 536 (8th Cir. 1988)

Harris v. Thigpen, 727 F. Supp. 1564 (M.D. Ala. 1990)

Jarret v. Faulkner, 662 F. Supp. 928 (S.D. Ind. 1987)

Judd v. Packard, 669 F. Supp. 741 (D. Md. 1987)

Lewis v. Prison Health Services, Inc., 915 F.2d 1561 (3d Cir. 1988)

Muhammad v. Carlson, 845 F.2d 175 (8th Cir. 1988)

Muhammad v. Frame, No. 87-5282 (E.D. Pa. September 11, 1987)

Noisy v. Bowles, Broward County, No.87-10523-CM (17th Cir. 1987)

Raytheon Co. v Fair Employment and Housing Commission, 212 Cal. App. 3d 1242, 261 Cal. Rptr. 197 (1989).

Smith v. Department of Corrections, No. 87-6412 (U.S.D.C.S.D. Fla. 1987)

Turner v. Safley, 476 U.S. 1139 (1987)

Woods v. White, 689 F. Supp. 874 (W.D. Wis. 1988)

4

Prison Gang Dynamics: A Look Inside the Texas Department of Corrections

Robert S. Fong
California State University—Bakersfield

Ronald E. Vogel
California State University—Long Beach

Salvador Buentello
Texas Department of Criminal Justice

INTRODUCTION

In recent years, American courts have played an important role in the evolution of prisoners' rights (Martin, 1989). Through litigation filed under 42 U.S.C. Section 1983[1] at an annual rate of more than 20,000 cases, prisoners have successfully prosecuted their claims of unconstitutional treatment behind bars (Cole, 1989; Turner, 1979). Today, nearly every prison system has been ordered by the courts to correct inhumane conditions, ranging from overcrowding to poor medical care (The National Prison Project, 1988).

Without a doubt, court-mandated changes have brought about noticeable improvement in the treatment of prisoners. Evidence suggests, however, that judicial intervention in correctional administration has systematically stripped away the authority of prison officials over the discipline of their inmates (Eckland-Olson, 1986; Jacobs, 1977). As a result, a state of lawlessness exists in which many prisoners find it beneficial to organize themselves for the purpose of sharing and eventually dominating, through violent means, the power

57

base once occupied by correctional personnel (Eckland-Olson, 1986; Beaird, 1986; Jacobs, 1977). In Texas, for instance, the sudden chaos created by prison gangs in the mid-1980s was so severe that prison officials almost lost control of their prisons (Fong, 1990; Beaird, 1986).

The uniqueness and relevancy of the Texas experience provides an ideal resource base for understanding prison gangs. Using Texas as a case study, this chapter examines four aspects of prison gangs: (1) the link between judicial reform and the proliferation of prison gangs; (2) the various organizational characteristics of prison gangs; (3) strategies for the management of prison gangs; and (4) strategies for the detection of prison gang development.

JUDICIAL INTERVENTION: A HISTORICAL REVIEW

Historically, prisoners were held to have forfeited all their civil rights; in essence, they were slaves of the state (*Ruffin v. Commonwealth,* 1871; *Price v. Johnson,* 1948). For a long time, this attitude was the subject of substantial criticism (Poltkins, 1975; National Commission on Criminal Justice Standards and Goals, 1973; South Carolina Department of Corrections, 1972). However, very little was done on the part of the courts to change this position.

Although prisoners' rights have been strengthened in the past four decades by various court decisions, progress during the 1950s and 1960s was hampered by the courts' application of the "hands-off" doctrine, which prevented the courts from reviewing cases initiated by prisoners against prison officials (Milleman, 1973). *Banning v. Looney* (1962) exemplified this practice. Specifically, the court in *Banning* stated: "...courts are without power to supervise prison administration or to interfere with the ordinary prison rules or regulations" (1962:290).

This judicial philosophy was reinforced in *Sutton v. Settle* (1962) in which the court held that the supervision of inmates within federal institutions was not the responsibility of the courts with regard to management and disciplinary rules.

As a result of judicial reluctance to review prisoners' suits against prison officials, conditions in prisons were left to the discretion of prison administrators and state legislatures. Needless to say, prison conditions in most jurisdictions were seldom improved. However, changes came swiftly with the civil rights movement in the 1960s when prisoners became more assertive in seeking redress from the courts (Irwin, 1980; Bronstein, 1970).

In *Cooper v. Pate* (1964) and *Wilwording v. Swenson* (1971), the United States Supreme Court clearly established that prisoners were entitled to file complaints against prison administrators under the provision of the Civil Rights Act of 1871, codified as 42 U.S.C. Section 1983. In practice, however, the Court's subsequent decision in *Preiser v. Rodriquez* (1973) substantially reduced the potential for prisoners' petitions under Section 1983 by dismissing all cases alleging wrongful deprivation of good time, arbitrary parole denial or revocation, and other claims in relation to the length of imprisonment (Turner, 1979). One of the reasons for this ruling was the Court's desire to reduce its crowded dockets (Poltkins, 1975).

Despite the limitations imposed by *Preiser,* suits filed under Section 1983 had the effect of instructing the judiciary about what actually occurred behind prison walls and inducing significant changes in the correctional process involving, among other things, access to federal courts (*Cooper v. Pate,* 1964), racial segregation (*Lee v. Washington,* 1968), inmate-to-inmate legal assistance (*Johnson v. Avery,* 1969), equal access to facilities for religious worship regardless of denominations (*Cruz v. Beto,* 1972), mail censorship (*Procunier v. Martinez,* 1974), disciplinary proceedings (*Wolff v. McDonnell,* 1974), access to medical care (*Estelle v. Gamble,* 1976), and access to law libraries (*Bounds v. Smith,* 1977).

Of all prison-related cases heard by the courts, one of the most controversial was *Ruiz v. Estelle* (1982). This case was filed in June 1972 by inmate David Ruiz and was joined with suits of seven other inmates in the spring of 1974, making it a class action suit. After receiving testimony from 349 witnesses and examining approximately 1,600 exhibits, Federal District Judge William Wayne Justice declared that conditions in the Texas prisons constituted a violation of the United States Constitution, specifically the provisions regarding cruel and unusual punishment and due process. Consequently, Judge Justice issued a list of mandates ordering the Texas Department of Corrections to: (1) ease overcrowding, (2) establish a new classification system, (3) eliminate the "building tender" system,[2] (4) increase staffing, (5) establish guidelines for the use of force, (6) provide better medical care, (7) upgrade psychiatric care for inmates, (8) provide care for special needs inmates, (9) improve disciplinary procedures, (10) rewrite vague rules, (11) improve the treatment of inmates in solitary confinement and administrative segregation, (12) provide inmates access to courts, counsel, and public officials, (13) protect inmate witnesses in *Ruiz,* (14) institute certain measures regarding occupational safety and health, and (15) improve death row conditions (Walter, 1984). The State of Texas appealed but was unsuccessful in obtaining a reversal from the Fifth Circuit Court of Appeals. To ensure that his mandates would be effectively carried out, Judge Justice, in an *Amended Order of Reference* issued on July 24, 1981, created the Office of the Special Master and subsequently appointed Vincent Nathan, a native Texan engaged in the practice of law in Toledo, Ohio, to serve as Special Master. To date, the Texas Department of Corrections continues to operate under the watchful eyes of the Special Master and his Special Monitors.

JUDICIAL REFORM AND THE PROLIFERATION OF PRISON GANGS

Despite significant reforms, prisons have not become safer places for inmates to live and correctional personnel to work. On the contrary, more inmate unrest and violence has been recorded. The bloody riot of February 1980 at the Penitentiary at Santa Fe serves as a reminder of the violent nature of institutional life. Nationwide, about 100 inmates and six or seven staff members are killed in prisons every year.

The main reason for the increase in prison violence, as observed by many scholars, is the intrusion of the courts (Eckland-Olson, 1986; Jacobs, 1977). Judicial intervention, which comes in the form of mandated changes consisting of specific guidelines pertaining to the daily operations of prisons, severely undermines the authority of prison officials over the administration of their prisons and the discipline of inmates. Correctional personnel, restricted by court-structured disciplinary procedures and threatened with the possibility of lawsuits, find it difficult, if not impossible, to maintain control over inmates. It is in this context of organizational crisis that prison gangs emerge for self-protection and power dominance. The proliferation of prison gangs in Texas, as argued by some critics, was stimulated by the elimination of the "building tender" system as a result of the *Ruiz* case (Eckland-Olson, 1986; Beaird, 1986).

Table 4.1
When and Where Prison Gangs Began in the United States

Year Formed	Jurisdiction	Name of Gang
1950	Washington	Gypsy Jokers
1957	California	Mexican Mafia
1969	Illinois	Disciples
		Vice Lords
1970	Utah	Aryan Brotherhood
		Nuestra Familia
		Black Guerilla Family
1971	Pennsylvania	Philadelphia Street Gangs
1973	Iowa	Bikers
		Vice Lords
1973	Nevada	Aryan Warriors
1974	North Carolina	Black Panthers
1974	Virginia	Pagans
1974	Arkansas	Ku Klux Klan
1975	Arizona	Mexican Mafia
1975	Texas	Texas Syndicate
1977	Federal System	Aryan Brotherhood
		Mexican Mafia
1978	Wisconsin	Black Disciples
1980	West Virginia	Avengers
1981	Missouri	Moorish Science Temple
1982	Kentucky	Aryan Brotherhood
		Outlaws
1983	Indiana	Black Dragons

Source: G.M. Camp & C.G. Camp (1985). *Prison Gangs: Their Extent, Nature, and Impact on Prisons.* (Grant No. 84-NI-AX-0001). United States Department of Justice, Office of Legal Policy. Washington, DC: U.S. Government Printing Office.

Although the emergence of prison gangs is a recent phenomenon, this trend is of growing concern to many prison administrators. The formation of prison gangs actually began in 1950 when a group of prisoners at the Washington Penitentiary in Walla Walla organized to become known as the Gypsy Jokers. As Table 4.1 reveals, the proliferation of prison gangs continued throughout the 1970s and 1980s.

Table 4.2
Number of Gangs and Gang Members Reported by Correctional Agencies in the United States—1984

Jurisdiction	Prisoners 1-1-1984	Number Gangs	Total Members	Year Started	Percent Gang Members
Arizona	6,889	3	413	1975	6.0
Arkansas	4,089	3	184	1974	4.5
California	38,075	6	2,050	1957	5.5
Connecticut	5,042	2	–	–	–
Federal System	30,147	5	218	1977	0.7
Florida	26,260	3	–	–	–
Georgia	15,232	6	63	–	0.4
Idaho	1,095	3	–	–	–
Illinois	15,437	14	5,300	1969	34.3
Indiana	9,360	3	50	1983	0.5
Iowa	2,814	5	49	1973	1.7
Kentucky	4,754	4	82	1982	1.7
Maryland	12,003	1	100	–	0.8
Massachusetts	4,609	1	3	–	0.1
Michigan	14,972	2	250	–	1.7
Minnesota	2,228	2	87	–	3.9
Missouri	8,212	2	550	1981	6.7
Nevada	3,192	4	120	1973	3.8
New York	30,955	3	–	–	–
North Carolina	15,485	1	14	1974	0.1
Ohio	17,766	2	–	–	–
Oklahoma	7,076	5	–	–	–
Pennsylvania	11,798	15	2,400	1971	20.3
Texas	35,256	6	322	1975	0.9
Utah	1,328	5	90	1970	6.8
Virginia	10,093	2	65	1974	0.6
Washington	6,700	2	114	1950	1.7
West Virginia	1,628	1	50	1980	3.1
Wisconsin	4,894	3	60	1978	1.2
Average Totals		114	12,634		3.0

Source: G.M. Camp & C.G. Camp (1985). *Prison Gangs: Their Extent, Nature, and Impact on Prisons.* (Grant No. 84-NI-AX-0001). United States Department of Justice, Office of Legal Policy. Washington, DC: U.S. Government Printing Office.

A survey conducted by Camp and Camp in 1985 under a grant from the United States Department of Justice revealed that prison gangs were found in 33 prison systems. The total membership was estimated at 12,634 (Camp & Camp, 1985).

Based on the data in Table 4.2, one can quickly see that Illinois and Pennsylvania have the most gangs. Illinois with 14 gangs has a total of 5,300 members; Pennsylvania reports the presence of 15 gangs with a total of 2,400 members. Overall, prison gang members make up about three percent of the total federal and state prison population. However, in most jurisdictions, gang activities are inadequately monitored and intelligence records are poorly maintained.

Despite this fact, some pioneer studies have shown that prison gangs in general share several common characteristics. Prison gangs:

1. are often organized along racial and ethnic lines (Beaird, 1986; Camp & Camp, 1985; Irwin, 1980);

2. have members with similar pre-prison experiences (Buentello, 1986; Beaird, 1986; Camp & Camp, 1985);

3. adhere to a strict code of silence (Buentello, 1986; Camp & Camp, 1985; Irwin, 1980);

4. practice lifetime membership (Fong, 1990; Buentello, 1986; Camp & Camp, 1985);

5. hold a set of values including solidarity and loyalty (Fong, 1990; Buentello, 1986; Camp & Camp, 1985);

6. are hierarchically structured with defined lines of authority and responsibility (Fong, 1990; Buentello, 1986; Camp & Camp, 1985);

7. have clearly defined goals and objectives such as contract murder, extortion, drug trafficking, homosexual prostitution, gambling, and protection (Fong, 1990; Crist, 1986; Beaird, 1986; Camp & Camp, 1985; President's Commission on Organized Crime, 1983);

8. achieve their goals and objectives through brutal and violent means (Fong, 1990; Buentello, 1986; Camp & Camp, 1985; Holt, 1977);

9. are anti-authority (Buentello, 1986; Camp & Camp, 1985);

10. hate and distrust other gangs (Irwin, 1980);

11. perceive themselves as political prisoners and victims of racial, economic, and political inequality (Irwin, 1980; Jacobs, 1974); and

12. are linked to organized criminal activities on the streets (Fong, 1990, Fong & Buentello, 1991; Edwards, 1989; Elizondo & Glass, 1989; Buentello, 1986; Freelander, 1985; Emerson, 1985).

Partly due to poor record-keeping and the reluctance on the part of many prison administrators to recognize the presence of inmate gangs in their prisons, information about prison gangs is limited. Further studies are therefore urgently needed.

TEXAS PRISON GANGS

For several decades, the Texas Department of Corrections was virtually free of inmate gang disruption. It is possible that this condition could be attributed to the introduction of the officially approved "building tender" system. Under the supervision of prison officials, not only did building tenders effectively maintain order among inmates, but more importantly, they served as an intelligence network for prison officials. In fact, as late as mid-1982, the only prison gang in existence was the Texas Syndicate, which was formed by inmates who were members of that gang in the California prison system. Outnumbered and closely monitored by the building tenders, no major disruptions by the Texas Syndicate were recorded. As the "building tender" system began to fade away at the order of the *Ruiz* ruling, prison administrators were faced with two crises: (1) a serious shortage of security staff as evidenced by a pre-*Ruiz* staff-inmate ratio of 1:10 (Beaird, 1986) and (2) the inability of prison administrators to monitor inmate illegal activities due to the lack of inmate informants (Fong, 1990).

It was during this period that inmates actively began to organize themselves to fill this power vacuum. Texas Department of Corrections statistics showed that in March 1982, the Texas Syndicate had 56 members. In 1990, there were eight recognized inmate gangs with a total membership of 1,174.

As these prison gangs competed for power and dominance, the number of serious inmate violent incidents also sharply increased. In 1982, the year the process of eliminating the "building tender" system began, the Texas Syndicate was reportedly responsible for four (33%) of the 12 inmate homicides. In 1983, the Texas Syndicate committed four (50%) of the eight inmate homicides. The most violent period in the history of the Texas Department of Corrections was 1984. In addition to a record number of 25 inmate homicides, 404 non-fatal inmate stabbing incidents were reported. Of the 25 inmate homicides, 20 (80%) were found to be gang-related. Of the 20 gang-related homicides, six (30%) were committed against members of the Mexican Mafia by the Texas Syndicate. In 1985, the prison system recorded 27 inmate homicides of which 23 (85%) were gang-related. Of the 23 gang-related homicides, 13 (56%) were committed against members of the Mexican Mafia by the Texas Syndicate while 10 (44%) were committed against members of the Texas Syndicate by the Mexican Mafia.

Table 4.3
Breakdown of Prison Gangs in Texas 1990

Name of Gang	Racial Composition	Size of Membership	Year Formed
Texas Syndicate	Predominantly Hispanic	289	1975 (CA)* 1978 (TX)*
Texas Mafia	Predominantly White	80	1982
Aryan Brotherhood of Texas	All White	170	1983
Mexican Mafia	All Hispanic	417	1984
Nuestro Carneles	All Hispanic	31	1984
Mandingo Warriors	All Black	36	1985
Self-Defense Family	Predominantly Black	76	1985
Hermanos De Pistolero	All Hispanic	75	1985
TOTAL		1,174	

* CA = California
* TX = Texas

Source: Data provided by the Texas Department of Corrections.

Figure 4.1
Breakdown of Gang-Related Prison Homicides

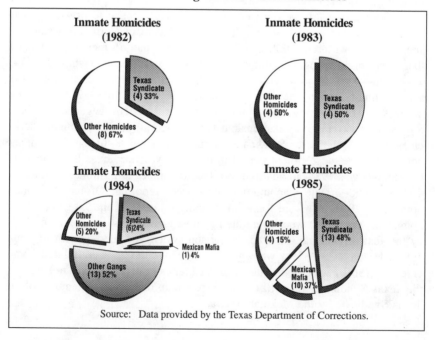

Source: Data provided by the Texas Department of Corrections.

In August 1985, the Texas Syndicate declared war on the Mexican Mafia by killing a Mexican Mafia member at a maximum-security unit near Huntsville, Texas, followed by three homicides at three other prisons in the same month (Buentello, 1986). After considering all available strategies, the Director of the Texas Department of Corrections ordered, in September 1985, the emergency detention of all confirmed and suspected gang members in administrative segregation. These inmates were subsequently assigned to "security detention" group A (assaultive) or group B (non-assaultive) on a permanent basis subject to review for release every 90 days. The continuing process of confining gang members to administrative segregation resulted in a sizeable increase in the administrative segregation population, from 1,860 on September 5, 1985 to 3,055 on January 1987.

Figure 4.2
Texas Department of Corrections
Administrative Segregation Population
(September 1985 - January 1987)

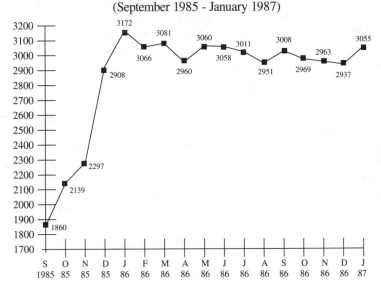

Source: Texas Department of Corrections, *Administrative Segregation Summaries*. (September 5, 1985 to January 29, 1987).

To retake their prisons, Texas prison administrators also launched an aggressive hiring campaign, which boosted the number of security officers from the 1979 level of 2,500 to over 9,000 in 1985 (Crouch & Marquart, 1989).

By far, the two largest prison gangs in Texas are the Texas Syndicate and the Mexican Mafia. The next two sections will focus on the development and structure of these two organizations. Although similarities exist among all of the prison gangs presented in Table 4.3, these two have been chosen to illustrate how prison gangs are structured as well as the rules or constitution that govern them.

The Texas Syndicate

There is very little written information concerning the Texas Syndicate (TS) or Syndicate Tejanos. What is known is that the Texas Syndicate originated at San Quentin in the California prison system in 1975 when a group of predominantly Mexican-American inmates from Texas decided to form their own group for the following reasons: (1) Texas-born inmates were frequent victims of California gangs; (2) Texas-born inmates were not recruited by other California prison gangs; (3) the desire of Texas-born inmates to show that they were brave people; and (4) the belief that a gang would provide personal safety to its members (Buentello, 1986).

To acquire additional information about the Texas Syndicate, one of the authors interviewed an informant who is credited with starting the Texas version of the Syndicate. To protect his identity, the informant will be referred to as inmate TS-1. According to inmate TS-1, the original group at San Quentin consisted of seven members who were all natives of San Antonio, Texas. Initially, the main objectives of the gang were self-protection and to live in harmony with the Mexican Mafia and the Aryan Brotherhood. This nonviolent mission allowed any Texas-born inmate, regardless of his racial identity, to join the gang. Gang membership, however, was a lifetime commitment. During this initial stage, there was no formal hierarchical structure; leadership was informal, and it was based on respect, not fear. As the gang began to grow and different branches formed in other California prisons, the objectives of the gang quickly changed. What used to be a self-protection group had become a violent gang engaged in such illegal activities as drug-trafficking, extortion, and contract murder.

When inmate TS-1 left the California prison system in 1976, the total membership had reached 500. This sizeable membership enabled the Texas Syndicate to participate in serious gang warfare with other gangs, which resulted in several non-fatal violent incidents against members of the Hell's Angels. To date, the Texas Syndicate is recognized as the most-feared prison gang in California (Buentello, 1986).

In 1978, five days after returning to Texas, inmate TS-1 was arrested and sentenced to life in prison for carrying an unloaded rifle. He was assigned to a maximum-security prison near Huntsville, Texas. There, he reunited with several original members of the California Texas Syndicate and subsequently decided to introduce the Texas Syndicate tradition to the Texas prison system. It was at that unit that the Texas version of the Texas Syndicate was formed.

Organizationally, the Texas Syndicate is structured along paramilitary lines.

Figure 4.3
The General Organizational Structure of the Texas Syndicate

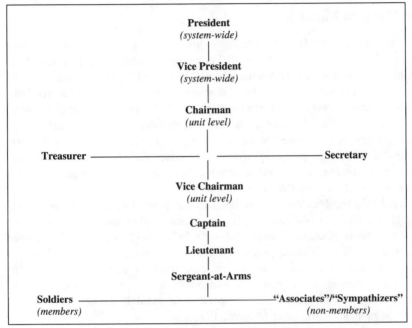

Source: R.S. Fong (1990). "The Organizational Structure of Prison Gangs:
A Texas Case Study." *Federal Probation,* LIV(4):36-43.

Regardless of rank, all members of the Texas Syndicate have to abide by a strict code of conduct known as the Constitution, which includes the following rules (Fong, 1990:40):

1. Be a Texan.

2. Once a member, always a member.

3. The Texas Syndicate comes before anyone and anything.

4. Right or wrong, the Texas Syndicate is right at all times.

5. All members will wear the Texas Syndicate tattoo.

6. Never let a member down.

7. All members will respect each other.

8. Keep all information within the group.

Any violation of these rules, intentionally or unintentionally, results in death. If the killing of a member or nonmember is deemed necessary, volunteers are sought to do the "hit." If there are no volunteers, a number-drawing system is utilized.

The Mexican Mafia

The Mexican Mafia, the second oldest prison gang in America, was formed in 1957 in a cell at the Duell Vocational Institute in California when 13 Chicano inmates, most of whom came from the Chicano barrios in East Los Angeles and had been members of youth gangs, congregated to establish a self-protection group. Soon after, members of the Mexican Mafia actively and violently began to conduct such illegal businesses as drug-trafficking (forcing other weak inmates' wives to smuggle in narcotics), selling weaker inmates as sexual property, extortion, protection rackets, and murders. As members were transferred to other prisons, they opened chapters in their new institutions such as Soledad and Folsom.

By 1967, the Mexican Mafia became the most dominant and powerful gang at San Quentin (Adams, 1977). Gang membership was on a "blood in, blood out" basis (Camp & Camp, 1985). In 1972, 30 (83%) of the 36 inmate homicides in the California prison system were committed by the Mexican Mafia. In addition to terrorizing the prisons, released gang members set up crime bases outside of the prisons to expand the narcotics trafficking network while other released gang members penetrated publicly funded projects to embezzle money for the gang (Adams, 1977).

Unlike the Texas Syndicate that originated in the California prison system, the Mexican Mafia of Texas has absolutely no relationship or connection with the Mexican Mafia in California. Intelligence sources suggest that the Mexican Mafia of Texas selected its name for two reasons: (1) its members are all Mexican-American, and (2) its main objective is to commit illegal acts, thus making "mafia" an appropriately descriptive word. Since its formation in the latter part of 1984, the Mexican Mafia has grown to be the largest prison gang in the Texas prison system.

The Mexican Mafia is organized similarly to the Texas Syndicate; it is hierarchical in nature and has a paramilitary structure.

As is in the case of the Texas Syndicate, all members of the Mexican Mafia are required to live a lifestyle consistent with their constitution, which outlines the following rules (Fong, 1990:40):

1. Membership is for life—"blood in, blood out."

2. Every member must be prepared to sacrifice his life or take a life at any time when necessary.

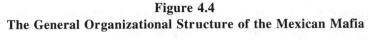

Figure 4.4
The General Organizational Structure of the Mexican Mafia

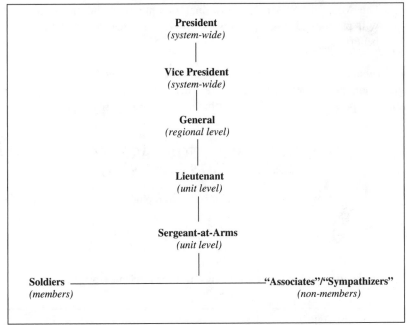

Source: R.S. Fong (1990). "The Organizational Structure of Prison Gangs:
A Texas Case Study." *Federal Probation,* LIV(4):36-43.

3. Every member shall strive to overcome his weakness to achieve discipline within his MEXIKANEMI brotherhood.

4. Never let the MEXIKANEMI down.

5. The sponsoring member is totally responsible for the behavior of the new recruit. If the new recruit turns out to be a traitor, it is the sponsoring member's responsibility to eliminate the recruit.

6. When disrespected by a stranger or a group, all members of the MEXIKANEMI will unite to destroy the person or the other group completely.

7. Always maintain a high level of integrity.

8. Never [reveal] the MEXIKANEMI business to others.

9. Every member has the right to express opinions, ideas, contradictions, and constructive criticisms.

10. Every member has the right to organize, educate, arm, and defend the MEXIKANEMI.

11. Every member has the right to wear the tattoo of the MEXIKANEMI symbol.

12. The MEXIKANEMI is a criminal organization and therefore will participate in all aspects of criminal interest for monetary benefits.

Almost without exception, any violation of the above rules results in death. Even though a unanimous vote is needed before a decision is reached, the lieutenants are able to bypass the process and issue orders without majority approval.

DEMOGRAPHIC INFORMATION:
TEXAS PRISON GANGS

Table 4.4, presented below, provides demographic information on all of the prison gangs in Texas in 1990. This section will briefly discuss the data in this table and provide additional information as needed.

Table 4.4
Demographic Characteristics of Texas Prison Gangs
(1990)

Gang	Gang Size	Mean Age	Race	Mean Years of Education (self-rpt)	Mean IQ	Mean Prior Imprisonment in TDC	Mean Prior Times in Juvenile Custody (self-rpt)	Mean Terms of Imprisonment in Yrs.
Texas Syndicate	289	32.7	H	8.60	88.57	1.15	.64	43.08
Texas Mafia	80	31.8	W	10.64	94.46	1.03	.53	49.53
Aryan Brother-hood of Texas	170	33.6	W	11.16	94.61	.97	.50	51.97
Mexican Mafia	417	31.0	H	9.05	88.51	.97	.39	31.67
Nuestro Carneles	31	34.9	H	9.82	91.03	1.63	.64	37.58
Mandingo Warriors	36	35.8	B	12.97	82.33	1.25	.77	70.72
Self-Defense Family	76	33.0	B	10.12	82.06	1.10	.46	49.56
Hermanos De Pistolero	75	29.4	H	7.8	85.28	.76	.49	32.52

Source: Data provided by the Texas Department of Corrections.

The first variable in the table, "gang size," reveals the total number of identified gang members in the Texas prison system. As discussed earlier, the Mexican Mafia is the largest prison gang, followed by the Texas Syndicate. The smallest documented prison gang is the Nuestro Carneles.

The demographic variables, age and race, are represented in the second and third categories of the table. Note that the combined mean age for all eight gangs is 32.8 years. The third variable, the predominant race of prison gang members, is self-evident. Overall, prison gangs are extremely homogeneous.

The "mean years of education" is a self-report variable not verified by Texas prison officials. It is likely that this variable is inflated by individuals who respond in a socially desirable manner.

The fifth variable in the table shows the "mean IQ" scores, which are the result of testing by the Corrections Department. These scores should be interpreted cautiously due to the cultural diversity and educational level of the population, as well as the willingness of inmates to be tested.

The "mean prior imprisonment in TDC" reveals the average number of times that members of these gangs were returned to the Texas prison system. This variable does not take into account incarcerations in other states. However, this variable reveals that, with the exception of one gang, over 30 percent of the membership of each gang has been sentenced to the Texas prisons only once: Texas Syndicate, 32.5 percent (n=94); Texas Mafia, 36.2 percent (n=29); Aryan Brotherhood of Texas, 38.2 percent (n=65); Mexican Mafia, 41.5 percent (n=173); Nuestro Carneles, 25.8 percent (n=8); Mandingo Warriors, 30.6 percent (n=117); Self-Defense Family, 31.6 percent (n=27); and Hermanos De Pistolero, 53.3 percent (n=40).

The seventh variable in the table is "mean prior times in juvenile custody," another self-report variable. Because these data are not verified by Texas prison officials, they only represent a rough measure of juvenile commitments.

The last variable in Table 4.4 reveals the "mean terms of imprisonment in years," which refers to the average years gang members have been sentenced to prisons. These numbers reflect the most serious charge for which the average gang member is serving time. The table reveals that the Mandingo Warriors on average are serving more time when compared to all other gangs. It is worth noting that the most-feared gang, the Mexican Mafia, is serving an average of 31.67 years, which is the lowest average number of years of imprisonment among these gangs.

STRATEGIES FOR THE MANAGEMENT OF PRISON GANGS

As the newest and most dangerous organized crime syndicates, prison gangs have added a new dimension to the crisis of the American correctional process. Although prison gangs only account for three percent of the total U.S. prison population, they are responsible for 50 percent or more of all prison violence and problems (Camp & Camp, 1985). Yet the lack of knowledge about prison gangs has made it difficult, if not impossible, for correctional officials to channel their efforts toward the effective management of prison gangs despite the fact that bringing them under control is a top priority in many jurisdictions.

In their study of five gang-infested prisons in three states, Camp and Camp suggested the following management options for combating prison gang violence (1988:7-55):

1. Develop an agency policy dealing with prison gangs;

2. Establish a well-protected gang intelligence network to be staffed by designated personnel;

3. Tailor a classification system to thwart gangs at time of reception and place gang members in high-security institutions;

4. Create special programs for gang members;

5. Lock up gang members in special housing units;

6. Crack down on weapons and drugs;

7. Develop special response capability to combat critical gang situations; and

8. Design a set of gang-combating strategies within constitutional boundaries.

Thus far, the most successful strategy in controlling prison gang growth and activities has been the use of lockup, either wholesale or in isolated instances (Camp & Camp, 1985). The rapid decrease in the number of inmate violent incidents, particularly inmate gang-related homicides in the Texas prison system, since the total lockup of gang members in September 1985, is indicative of the effectiveness of this practice (1986, two gang-related homicides; 1987, four gang-related homicides; 1988, two gang-related homicides; 1989, zero gang-related homicides; and 1990, two gang-related homicides).

STRATEGIES FOR THE DETECTION
OF PRISON GANG DEVELOPMENT

Until recently, correctional administrators have generally ignored or downplayed the presence of prison gangs. Their hope was that by refusing to acknowledge their existence, prison gangs would eventually disappear. Evidence suggests that such is not the case. Not only have prison gangs not vanished, they have grown to become the most dangerous organized crime syndicates in America. The economic reality of organized crime dictates that prison gangs are here to stay. Still, many prison administrators take a reactive approach to prison gangs. In most instances, the presence of prison gangs is realized only after it has reached crisis proportions. What normally follows thereafter is a costly combat process. The lesson to be learned, particularly for those prison administrators in jurisdictions free of prison gang disruptions, is that prison gangs must be dealt with proactively. In other words, identify and control them before they become a problem.

In an effort to provide a proactive management model for the detection of prison gang development, Fong and Buentello (1991) surveyed a group of 196 Texas prison officials (ranging from sergeants to senior wardens) who were selected in an identification process as having had extensive experiences dealing with Texas prison gangs since their inception. In that study, each participant was hand-delivered a questionnaire containing a list of 23 prison activities. Survey participants were asked to select the activities that they perceived to be "indicators" of prison gang development. At the end of the study, 181 (92%) had responded to the survey. Based on the results, Fong and Buentello constructed a proactive management model consisting of 11 activities that were identified by survey participants as "indicators" of prison gang development. Those 11 activities include "unusually frequent" (1991:47):

1. inmate requests for protective custody;

2. discovery of gang-related tattoos on inmate bodies;

3. inmate disciplinary violations or contraband possession;

4. secret racial groupings of inmates;

5. inmate informants reporting emergence of inmate cliques;

6. inmate physical assaults on other inmates;

7. police agencies reporting gang activities on the streets;

8. inmate requests for inter-unit transfers;

9. inmate families reporting extortion by inmate cliques;

10. verbal threats made to staff by inmates; and

11. physical assaults on staff by inmates.

While this empirically verified model is not a guarantee for absolute success, it should serve as an important aid to prison administrators in their efforts to detect prison gang development.

CONCLUSION

Controlling prison populations has always been a monumental task and the administration of correctional facilities an arcane process. With scarce resources, prison officials have often been forced to implement questionable policies that have maximized control over inmates while sacrificing constitutional rights. However, the extent of prisoners' rights has been a temporal issue framed by the magnitude of judicial intervention. It was not until the courts began to scrutinize the administrative practices of specific prisons that reforms were introduced and abuses eliminated. Unexpectedly, the "hands-on" approach of the courts also complicated prison management. With mandated court reform came rapid changes and unanticipated results. Unforeseen consequences included rapidly rising inmate costs, the loss of discipline over inmates, and the upsurge of violence created by the development and proliferation of prison gangs.

When Texas inmate David Ruiz filed his lawsuit against the Texas Department of Corrections in 1972, the average cost per inmate was $3.31 per day or $1,209.55 per year. The changes ordered by the *Ruiz* court increased the cost to $32.66 per day or $11,920.45 per year in 1988 (TDC 1988 Fiscal Year Statistical Report, 1989). Nationwide, it has been estimated that over $10 billion must be spent to bring existing conditions into compliance with minimum constitutional standards (Andersen, 1982).

In the Texas prison system where inmates have been afforded greater rights and the "building tender" system eliminated, improvements were found to be Janus-faced. As constitutional rights of inmates increased and traditional practices of inmate control were dismantled, prison officials found it exceedingly difficult, if not impossible, to maintain order among their inmates. As administrative control weakened, prison violence immediately increased and inmates quickly organized to protect themselves, dominate others, and establish a power base for illegal activities.

The development and proliferation of prison gangs have created a great deal of concern for those who are interested in the future of corrections. The seriousness of this problem is reflected by Emerson, who wrote:

> ...unless there is a movement in the United States to reestablish law and order, and to crush the (prison) gangs, organizations, and syndicates, the country has no chance for survival (1985:61).

Although Emerson's reaction is extreme, it reveals the intensity of feelings exhibited by prison officials who confront gang violence on a daily basis.

The secretive nature of prison gangs and the reluctance of prison administrators to acknowledge their presence have hindered research on these groups. Still, a few researchers have managed to study prison gang development and organizational structure (Fong & Buentello, 1991; Fong, 1990; Camp & Camp, 1988, 1985; Eckland-Olson, 1986; Buentello, 1986; Emerson, 1985). These researchers have penetrated the surface and found prison gangs to be vicious, ruthless, dangerous, terroristic, anti-authority, and extremely well-organized. Nevertheless, few empirical studies exist and more research is necessary to better understand the nature and function of prison gangs in America.

NOTES

1   "Every person who, under color of any statute, ordinance, regulation, custom, or usage, of any State or Territory, subjects, or causes to be subjected, any citizen of the United States or other person within the jurisdiction thereof to the deprivation of any laws, privileges, or immunities secured by the Constitution and laws, shall be liable to the party injured in action at law, suit in equity, or other proper proceeding for redress."

2   "Building Tenders" were inmates selected by prison administrators to perform staff functions such as maintaining order among other inmates, often through the use of force. In addition, building tenders served as inmate informants for prison officials. The majority of the inmates chosen to serve as building tenders were serving long prison terms for violent criminal offenses. This system was extensively utilized prior to being ruled unconstitutional by the *Ruiz* court.

REFERENCES

Adams, N.M. (1977). "America's Newest Crime Syndicate—The Mexican Mafia." *Reader's Digest,* 3(November):97-102.

Andersen, K. (1982). "The Inmate Nation: What Are Prisons For?" *Time,* 120(11): 38-41.

Beaird, L.H. (1986). "Prison Gangs: Texas." *Corrections Today,* 18:22.

Bronstein, A.J. (1977). "Reform Without Change: The Future of Prisoners' Rights." *Civil Liberty Review,* pp. 27-28.

Buentello, S. (1986). *Texas Syndicate: A Review of Its Inception, Growth in Violence and Continued Threat to The Texas Department of Corrections.* Unpublished manuscript, Texas Department of Corrections, Huntsville, Texas.

Camp, G.M. & C.G. Camp (1985). *Prison Gangs: Their Extent, Nature and Impact on Prisons.* (Grant No. 84-NI-AX-0001). United States Department of Justice, Office of Legal Policy. Washington, DC: U.S. Government Printing Office.

_____ (1988). *Management Strategies for Combatting Prison Gang Violence.* South Salem, NY: Criminal Justice Institute.

Cole, G.F. (1989). *The American System of Criminal Justice.* Pacific Grove, CA: Brooks/Cole Publishing Company.

Crist, R.W. (1986). "Prison Gangs: Arizona." *Corrections Today,* 18:25-27.

Crouch, B.M. & J.W. Marquart (1989). *An Appeal To Justice: Litigated Reform of Texas Prisons.* Austin, TX: University of Texas Press.

Eckland-Olson, S. (1986). *Judicial Decision and Social Order of Prison Violence: Evidence From Post-Ruiz Years Texas.* Unpublished manuscript. The University of Texas at Austin, Department of Sociology.

Edwards, T. (1985). "Prison Gang Violence Spilling Into Streets." *San Antonio Express News,* 19(July):A1.

Elizondo, D. & S. Glass (1989). "Murder Spree Sends Police Scrambling." *San Antonio Light,* 9(November):A2.

Emerson, R.Q. (1985). "Black/White/Latino: Prison Gangs." *American Survival Guide,* (August):14-19, 61.

Fong, R.S. (1990). "The Organizational Structure of Prison Gangs: A Texas Case Study." *Federal Probation,* LIV(4):36-43.

Fong, R.S. & S. Buentello (1991). "The Detection of Prison Gang Development: An Empirical Assessment." *Federal Probation,* LV(1):66-69.

Freelander, D. (1985). "Warfare Spreading to Streets: McCotter." *The Houston Post,* 10(September):A3.

Holt, N. (1977). "Prison Management in The Next Decade." *The Prison Journal,* 57:17-19.

Irwin, J. (1980). *Prison in Turmoil.* Boston: Little, Brown and Company.

Jacobs, J.B. (1974). "Street Gangs Behind Bars." *Social Problems,* 21(4):395-409.

————— (1977). *Stateville.* Chicago: University of Chicago Press.

Martin, S.J. (1989). "Prisoners' Rights." *Texas Tech Law Review,* pp. 1-14.

Milleman, M.A. (1973). "Protected Inmate Liberties: a Case for Judicial Responsibility." *Oregon Law Review,* 53:29-31.

National Commission on Criminal Justice Standards and Goals (1973). *Report on The Task Force on Corrections.* Washington, DC: U.S. Government Printing Office.

Poltkins, R. (1975). "Recent Development in The Law of Prisoners' Rights." *Criminal Law Bulletin,* 11:405.

President's Commission on Organized Crime (1983). *Organized Crime: Federal Law Enforcement Perspective.* Record of Hearing 1, November 29. Washington, DC: U.S. Government Printing Office.

South Carolina Department of Corrections (1972). *Emerging Rights of the Confined.*

Texas Department of Corrections (1989). *1988 Fiscal Year Statistical Report.*

Texas Department of Corrections. *Administrative Segregation Summaries,* September 5, 1985 to January 29, 1987.

The National Prison Project (1988). *Status Report: The Courts and Prisons.* December 1.

Turner, W.B. (1979). "When Prisoners Sue: A Study of Prisoner Section 1983 Suits in Federal Courts." *Harvard Law Review,* 92:600-637.

Walter, M. (1984). *Overview of Ruiz v. Procunier: A Summary of Relevant Orders, Stipulations, Reports and Issues.* Office of the Special Master, United States District Court, Southern District of Texas.

TABLE OF CASES

Banning v. Looney, 213 F.2d 771 (10th Cir. 1954)

Bounds v. Smith, 430 U.S. 817 (1977)

Cooper v. Pate, 378 U.S. 546 (1964)

Cruz v. Beto, 405 U.S. 319 (1972)

Estelle v. Gamble, 429 U.S. 97 (1976)

Johnson v. Avery, 393 U.S. 483 (1969)

Lee v. Washington, 390 U.S. 333 (1968)

Preiser v. Rodriguez, 411 U.S. 475 (1973)

Price v. Johnson, 334 U.S. 266 (1948)

Procunier v. Martinez, 416 U.S. 396 (1974)

Ruffin v. Commonwealth, 62 Va. 790 (1871)

Ruiz v. Estelle, 666 F.2d 854 (5th Cir. 1982)

Sutton v. Settle, 302 F.2d 286 (8th Cir. 1962)

Wilwording v. Swenson, 404 U.S. 249 (1971)

Wolff v. McDonnell, 418 U.S. 539 (1974)

5

Women in Prison:
Why Are Their Numbers Increasing?

Joycelyn M. Pollock-Byrne
University of Houston—Downtown

INTRODUCTION

In 1990 there were over 32,000 women incarcerated in state prisons (Crawford, 1990). This represents a more than 130 percent increase in the 10-year period between 1980 and 1990. When federal facilities are included, the number rises to 40,556 (Bureau of Justice Statistics, 1991). In this chapter, we will explore the increasing use of imprisonment for women offenders, what these women experience in prison, and why it is imperative that this trend be recognized and evaluated before any more new construction is completed.

Although in 1989 women still comprised only 5.7 percent of the total prison population, and the number of men in prison had also increased dramatically, the percentage increase in the number of women incarcerated has been greater than that for men every year since 1981 (Bureau of Justice Statistics, 1988 and 1989). Obviously, percentage increases are drastically influenced by the size of the base number. The number of women in prison has been, until recently, extremely small; therefore, large percentage increases have not represented huge numerical increases. For instance, between 1980 and 1989, the percentage increase of women in federal and state prisons was about double that of males (202.2% increase compared to 111.6% increase for men). In actual numbers, however, this represented an increase of 27,136 female inmates compared to 353,097 male inmates (Bureau of Justice Statistics, 1991). However, the percentage increases have continued to be much higher for women than men in recent years, even with larger base numbers. Further, women's percentage of the total number of incarcerated offenders is increasing. Also, the increase in women prisoners is especially problematic because there is no place to house these new female inmates except to build new facilities at record rates. The greater use of incarceration is no more apparent than when one looks at prison construction. Several states such as South Carolina, Oklahoma, and Washington did not even have a prison for women until the 1970s. Many other states built their first separate women's prison in the 1960s (Freedman, 1981). Yet only 20 years later, these prisons were already bursting at the seams; in the 1980s, 34 states built new prisons or units for women inmates (Rafter, 1985). Now over 50 percent of all states are planning new construction (Crawford, 1990).

One argument for this increase in the percentage of incarcerated women is that the increases are due to corresponding increases in the number of crimes committed by women. The Uniform Crime Reports indicate that there are large increases in certain crime areas. For instance, the percentage increase of women arrested for embezzlement from 1981 through 1990 was 164.1 percent, and for "other assaults" there was an increase of 125.6 percent. On the other hand, a few crimes showed percentage decreases for those years. For instance, murder and non-negligent manslaughter showed a decrease of 3.6 percent. Most crime categories showed much lower increases for a total crime index increase of 34.6 percent (Uniform Crime Reports, 1990) This compares to the 130 percent increase in state prison commitments for roughly the same period. These figures suggest, therefore, that the rise in female incarceration rates is not due to an increase in the rate of female criminality. The percentage of women incarcerated for violent crime has actually decreased from 49 percent of all inmates in 1979 to 41 percent of all inmates in 1986 (Bureau of Justice Statistics, 1991).

The rate of incarceration is the highest it has ever been. Compared to a rate of 6 women per 100,000 in 1925, the rate of incarceration for women in 1983 was 14 per 100,000, and in 1989, that rate climbed to 31 per 100,000 (Bureau of Justice Statistics, 1991). The trend to incarcerate more women has been fairly recent. In 1970 the rate for women was 5 per 100,000—less than that of 1925, although there had been fluctuations up to 10 per 100,000 in 1939-1940. Of course this is still miniscule compared to the increase for males. From 149 per 100,000 in 1925, the rate has more than tripled to 352 per 100,000 in 1983 and increased again to 549 per 100,000 in 1989 (Sourcebook, 1989; Bureau of Justice Statistics, 1991).

Some research finds that women are more likely to be sentenced to prison for crime today than they have in the past. Simon and Landis (1991) present unpublished data from California, New York, and Pennsylvania that demonstrate that the percentage of women sentenced to prison is greater today than in 1982 for almost every crime category. For instance, in California in 1982, 29.5 percent of women who were convicted of burglary were sentenced to prison; in 1987, 39.7 percent were sentenced to prison. The biggest increase was in theft—in 1982 only 9.8 percent of women were sentenced to prison; in 1987 that percentage doubled to 18.4 percent. In New York and Pennsylvania, the same trend occurred. Except for very few crimes that showed little difference, the offender was more likely to end up in prison in 1987. For instance, in Pennsylvania, only 17.4 percent of women convicted of drug law violations were sent to prison in 1982, compared to 33 percent of them in 1987 (Simon & Landis, 1991). Of course, males are more likely to be sent to prison for almost all crime categories as well. Overall, the rate of commitment to prison for women increased 100 percent from 136 per 1,000 arrests in 1980 to 272 per 1,000 arrests in 1989. Males experienced a 67 percent increase (from 203 per 1,000 arrests to 339 per 1,000 arrests) (Bureau of Justice Statistics, 1991).

There seems to be no doubt that women are more likely to be sentenced to prison today than in the past. One reason is probably the public and political pressure on judges to impose harsher sentences. Fear of crime has increased and there is frustration and intolerance toward crime and criminals. More public cries are heard for "victim's rights" and harsher sentencing. This public pressure has perhaps influenced the sentencing of women as well as men. Another factor may be that several states have determinate sentencing laws that remove the discretion from the judge or jury to "go easy" on a female offender even if they are so inclined. A third factor may be that public perception of women's equality has encouraged equal treatment in punishment. That is, judges may be more likely to sentence women offenders to prison today because they would sentence men to prison for the same crime. Finally, the nation's "war on drugs" has undoubtedly influenced the sentences of both female and male offenders.

WOMEN'S CRIMES

Female criminality has increased, but the pattern of crime is still similar to earlier years. The most typical crimes women commit continue to be larceny/theft (women account for 32% of total arrests) and other property crimes, such as forgery (34.6% of total arrests), fraud (44.2%), and embezzlement (41.2%) (Uniform Crime Reports, 1990). As previously mentioned, large increases are reported in embezzlement (164.1%), offenses against family and children (130.1%), and drug abuse violations (111.6%) (Uniform Crime Reports, 1990). However, these large percentage increases represent fairly small actual numbers as compared to the raw numbers reported for crimes committed by men. Although the percentage increase in women offenders involved in violent crime (61.8%) was fairly high, most of that is accounted for by aggravated assault, which showed an increase of 79.1 percent. This represents roughly 17,794 arrests compared to the 65 percent increase in male arrests which represents 106,455. One must be cautious when comparing percentage increases of males and females because the base numbers are so disproportionate.

A substantial portion of the increase in prison commitments seems to be for drug arrests. Between 1980 and 1989 there was a 30 percent increase in drug arrests of women (possession, manufacturing, and sales) (Bureau of Justice Statistics, 1991). There is evidence that women are more likely to be sentenced to prison for drug offenses today than in the past, and the percentage increases in prison commitments for female drug offenders outstrips that of males (Chesney-Lind, 1991).

In some crime categories, women are approaching equal representation with men. For instance, women now represent 41.2 percent of all arrests for embezzlement and 44.2 percent of all arrests for fraud. In other crime categories, however, there are still large differences. Women continue to commit only about 10-12 percent of all violent crime (as measured by arrest rates) (Uniform Crime Reports, 1990).

In 1987, a survey of women offenders was conducted under the auspices of the American Correctional Association. The sample consisted of 2,090 inmates in over 400 institutions. These women reported that their first arrest occurred most often between the ages of 15 and 24 (58.2%). While about one-quarter of them have been arrested only once (26.3%), over 55 percent have been arrested between two and nine times. The rest have been arrested over nine times. About 45 percent of the women have only experienced one incarceration. However, approximately 40 percent have experienced two to four prison terms. The remainder have received more than four prison sentences. The crimes of conviction are typically drug abuse violations (20.7%) followed by murder and non-negligent manslaughter (15%); and larceny/theft (11.9%) (Crawford, 1990:68). About one-quarter of the women surveyed reported that they committed their crime to "pay for drugs" and another 19.9 percent cited "economic pressures" as the reason for their crime (Crawford, 1990).

There is increasing evidence that a number of women sentenced to prison on a homicide conviction may have been victims of domestic abuse (Browne, 1987; Mann, 1988; Ewing, 1987). Several researchers have explored case histories and discovered that at least some of these women endured years of serious abuse at the hands of their spouse without any help from the system until, in desperation, they killed him. Then, ironically, they were prosecuted and sent to prison by the same system that was unable to protect them. Browne found that abused women were more likely to kill their abuser when he used drugs or alcohol, when he used more threats and had assaulted her more often, sexually assaulted her, and when he threatened the children as well (Browne, 1987:182).

As a result of these findings and lobbying by advocates, several states have started reviews of all women convicted for murder or non-negligent manslaughter when there was evidence of prior battering. Recently, Governor Richard Celeste of Ohio granted clemency to 25 women after reviewing 100 files of women sentenced to prison for homicide with histories of being victimized by battering (Wilkerson, 1990).

In another area, public attention may result in greater incarceration for women. The problem of drug-addicted newborns has reached such proportions that several states are contemplating new criminal or civil sanctions against women who use drugs during pregnancy. These states are considering redefining "child" in "injury to a child" or criminal neglect statutes to include the fetus, or they may propose new fetal endangerment laws. In the past several years, 48 women in 15 states have been arrested for fetal abuse. Women in South Carolina, Colorado, Connecticut, Illinois, Indiana, Massachusetts, Michigan, Ohio, and Florida have been arrested for delivery, child endangerment or manslaughter because of drug use during pregnancy (American Civil Liberties Union, 1990). Although most courts have refused to extend the legal definitions in place to include the fetus; state legislators are responding by proposing new laws or rewriting the existing statutes (Pollock-Byrne, 1991; Merlo, 1991). Despite the grave constitutional problems with such discriminatory laws, many support them in a misguided belief that prison will "cure" the pregnant woman's addiction and prevent injury to the infant.

There also have been instances in which women have received prison sentences solely because of pregnancy and indications of drug use. In one case reported by the American Civil Liberties Union, a woman was sentenced to prison instead of probation solely because the judge found out that she was pregnant and addicted. He stated that he was sending her to prison to protect the baby (*United States v. Vaughn*, 1988).

THE FEMALE OFFENDER IN PRISON

The American Correctional Association survey shows that women prisoners are disproportionately minority (56.6%), with blacks making up 36 percent of the prison population. They are usually in their late twenties and early thirties (51.3 percent of the population is between the ages of 25 and 34). Over one-third of these women have never been married and another one-third are either divorced, widowed, or separated. Almost all have children (80%). Most had their children when they were between the ages of 16 and 20 (55.2%). Most have legal custody of their children (72.3%). Typically, the offenders' mothers or grandparents take care of the children while they are in prison (47.6%) (Crawford, 1990).

A substantial number of women in prison have experienced physical abuse (53%) or sexual abuse (35.6%). Typically, the first physical abuse occurred in her teens and the first sexual abuse occurred quite a bit earlier

(56.6% who reported sexual abuse said it occurred between the ages of 5 and 14). The perpetrator of physical abuse was typically a husband, boyfriend, or parent, and the perpetrator of sexual abuse was typically an unknown abuser, father, or stepfather. Many of these women in prison have attempted suicide (27.9%) and one-third reported that the reason they took drugs was to make themselves feel better. Almost one-half of the women have other family members who are also incarcerated (48.4%). These family members are usually the woman's brother (39.8%), sister (15%), father (11.8%) or husband (12.8%) (Crawford, 1990).

A large number of these women abused drugs before incarceration. Almost one-half reported either using alcohol daily or several times a week (41.1%); 24.7 percent reported using heroin that frequently, 33.3 percent reported using marijuana as frequently and 32.4 percent reported using cocaine with that level of frequency. Smaller percentages of women reported frequent use of crack, prescription drugs, or speed (Crawford, 1990:59-60).

Only 39 percent of the women in prison have completed high school or achieved an equivalency certificate. Over one-third of those who did not finish high school quit because of pregnancy (Crawford, 1990:61-63). Yet only about 17 percent of correctional institutions require enrollment in a General Education Development (GED) program (Crawford, 1990:36). Women in prison typically have only held service or clerical jobs (58%); and about 60 percent have received welfare in the past (Crawford, 1990).

Despite these figures, vocational programs in prison are not numerous enough or large enough to meet the needs of female inmates. Weisheit's 1985 study indicates that although 83 percent of responding states had educational programs, fewer had a variety of vocational programs, especially those considered nontraditional such as electrical (22% of states reported having a program), plumbing (9%), or computer (20%). On the other hand, most states have sewing (53%) and secretarial programs (45%) (Weisheit, 1985).

By 1989, 38 percent of 37 institutions responding to another survey reported having computer training available. Twenty-seven percent provided training in building trades; 24 percent in carpentry and plumbing; 19 percent in printing and welding; and 16 percent in masonry. Also, 22 percent reported that training in graphics was available (Simon & Landis, 1991).

Thus, although some gains have been made in the number and quality of vocational programs, it is still doubtful whether female prisoners are able to learn a vocation in prison that will provide financial security. There are a number of factors that help to explain training programs that are under-enrolled, limited and/or obsolete: (1) many women may not have the educational background to qualify for some programs; (2) there are few programs available and consequently those that do exist often have long waiting lists; (3) a woman's sentence may be too short to take advantage of programs that lead to a certificate; and (4) it may be necessary for the woman to choose prison work that pays rather than training that usually does not, so she can buy the few luxuries that are available from the prison commissary.

Life in Prison

While prisons for women do not present the same grim façade and pervasive undercurrent of violence that one experiences in penitentiaries for men, there is no mistaking the fact that these facilities are indeed prisons. Rules govern everything from the number of minutes one may shower, to gumchewing, to touching. Women report that prison staff control is perhaps more extreme in prisons for women; for instance, women may be held to higher standards of grooming than male inmates. Movement is restricted, of course, and individuals travel alone only on a tightly controlled pass system.

One of the differences between men's and women's facilities is that all types of female offenders are found in a single institution. Older women complain about the noise and violent behavior of younger offenders. Minor drug or property offenders may share a cell or dorm room with women who are firmly entrenched in a criminal lifestyle and may use violence to intimidate other inmates. The drug culture is present in women's prisons, although there is not the extensive black market one finds in prisons for men (Pollock-Byrne, 1990). Women inmates complain that a number of inmates have psychological problems that cause them to exhibit bizarre and sometimes dangerous behaviors. There is a greater problem with attempted suicides and mutilations in women's prisons. Many women succumb to feelings of depression and despair by engaging in self-injury (Pollock-Byrne, 1990). Rule violations are more numerous in women's institutions, although some evidence indicates women inmates are written up for less serious infractions than male inmates, and, in fact, these higher numbers indicate the tighter controls placed upon women (Pollock-Byrne, 1990).

Each day proceeds very much like another. Women are expected to rise early and be dressed, washed, and ready to go to the mess hall for breakfast, usually before 7:00 a.m. Some women who work in the kitchen are roused as early as 4:00 a.m. After breakfast, women are usually ordered back to their cells until "count" clears. Count is taken between four to six times a day depending on the institution. All movement freezes during this time while tallies of the number of inmates in each building are collected and compared to the total number for the institution. If there are problems, everyone stays where they are (sometimes for hours) while the numbers are reconciled. After morning count the women are escorted to their morning assignments.

Almost all women in many institutions work or go to school. Groups of women are escorted to the education building or other locations for GED classes, high school courses, or vocational programs. Others will go to work assignments in the laundry, administration building, grounds, or other places. Those who put their name in for sick call may be escorted at this time to the infirmary. The number remaining on the tier or in the dormitory may be quite small. These women will be between assignments, awaiting transfer, on bedrest, or punitive "daylock." Those not on "daylock" are often free to watch television, shower, read, play card games or otherwise amuse themselves.

At lunchtime, all women are returned to their living unit to be escorted to the mess hall together. Count is taken again—sometimes before, but usually after lunch. In the afternoon the process is repeated with women going back to their assignments or switching assignments—that is, some women will go to school or a vocational program in the morning and will go to a job assignment in the afternoon or vice versa. Often counselors have submitted slips instructing the correctional officers to send certain inmates to the administration building to meet with them. Some women may have visitors.

In the evening, after a relatively early dinner (between 4:30 and 6:00 p.m.), there may be more classes, e.g., college classes are typically offered in the evenings. There may also be rehabilitation programs with community volunteers, club meetings, movies, and usually an opportunity for outdoor exercise in the yard. Many women choose to stay in their cells for reading, writing, or listening to the radio. In the dayroom there is the television, which is on constantly, as well as card games, dancing, and other entertainment. Once the routine is established, the biggest problem is boredom, especially in those institutions where women offenders have a great deal of free time. Most women gain weight in prison; partly because of the starchy, institutional food, but also because meals form the high point of every day.

Some women choose to avoid prison life for a solitary existence largely confined to their cells. In most institutions women are not forced to go to mess hall or to assignments. Jean Harris writes of her life in Bedford Hills as one of minimal interaction with other inmates (Harris, 1988). Other women are heavily involved in the prisoner subculture, which may include participating in homosexual relationships and/or pseudofamilies.

Subcultural Adaptations

The subculture of a prison includes the inmate "code," social roles, and social groupings. It is clear that subcultural adaptations in the women's prison are very different from those found in institutions for men. For instance, while "snitches" are hated in both institutions, the sanctions against informers employed by women are relatively minor. There does not seem to be a strong prohibition against inmate-staff contact in institutions for women, unlike that found in institutions for men. Women do not "do their own time" and do not hesitate to get involved with each other.

Leaders are not as obvious in prisons for women. There are no gangs as such. Women seem to prefer smaller cliques, including pseudofamilies, that utilize the familial roles found on the outside. Social roles are different in women's prisons, although research indicates some types of inmates may be present in both types of institutions, i.e., snitches, squares, and homies.

In women's institutions, homosexuality tends to be consensual and most women participate not only for sexual satisfaction, but for the emotional components of a relationship. Women voluntarily take on the "male" role of "stud broad." Prison homosexuality, with its exaggerated role portrayals and open displays of possession, is distinguished from true homosexuality in which the individuals involved are committed to a lesbian lifestyle before institutionalization and tend to keep their sexual orientation and any relationships they may be involved in hidden. Male homosexuality, on the other hand, has been described as coercive, involving elements of power, subjugation, and violence. The "punk" role is often forced upon young males. Sex may be more of a commodity in prisons for men—to be bought, sold, or traded (Pollock-Byrne, 1990).

Inmate Mothers and Their Children

There is no doubt that the biggest difference in the "pains of imprisonment" between men and women in prison is children. Women consistently report that the most important people to them are their children (Crawford, 1990). They overwhelmingly experience or relate feelings of despair, frustration, and depression related to their imprisonment, and to their separation from and inability to care for their children. This is true even though many women were not good mothers before they were in prison. Drugs or lifestyle often resulted in the mother/offender abdicating her role to her mother or other caregivers. Once in prison, however, she has time to think about her children and her failings. No research indicates that children create the same emotions for men in prison or constitute the same feelings of deprivation.

Effects of maternal incarceration on children can be severe. Baunach reports that children may experience physical, emotional or psychological, and academic problems, including hypertension, aggressive behavior, withdrawal, and academic difficulties (Baunach, 1979). Little is known of the long-term effects of incarceration on children, but from the statistics indicating that many men and women in prison also have family members in prison, one cannot be too optimistic about the future of these children unless some type of intervention counteracts the negative impact of maternal incarceration.

Visitation between mother and child preserves the bond between them and makes readjustment less difficult. All prisons for women allow visiting by children. Only a few, however, make special efforts to encourage such visitation. Because prisons are often long distances from metropolitan areas, often caregivers cannot or will not make the trip and consequently some women never see their children. This is especially problematic for women prisoners because most states have only one facility for women, usually far away from where their families live. Because most states have several facilities for men, it is possible to place men closer to their families. One 1980 study found that only 37 percent of responding women's institutions had special allowances for those who could not make the regular visiting time periods (Neto & Rainier, 1983:125).

Some prisons do pay special attention to the needs of children whose mothers are incarcerated. Bedford Hills in New York has a *Sesame Street Program* for children visiting their mothers that helps to make the visit less threatening and more enjoyable by providing a children's playroom in the adult visiting room. There are arrangements for child care so adults can take care of family matters while the children are adequately cared for (Haley, 1977). A survey of women's prisons found, however, that only 12.2 percent had on-site child care available for visitors (Crawford, 1990:31). Some prisons allow visitation by children for a period of several days, either in special housing or in the women's cell/room. Weisheit reported in his study that 25 of 36 responding institutions allowed weekend visits with children. Twenty of these provided transportation (Weisheit, 1985).

Crawford's study reports that nationally, 6 percent of women are pregnant when committed to prison (1990:32). Women who give birth while in prison encounter special difficulties. Most prisons have no arrangements for postnatal nurseries (one exception is Bedford Hills, where women might be able to keep their newborns with them for up to one year at the discretion of prison administrators). This means that women who give birth ordinarily must immediately give up custody to the state or make arrangements for relatives to care for the infant. Often the woman is permitted only a short visit in the hospital before the baby is taken away and she is returned to prison (Pollock-Byrne, 1990).

The American Civil Liberties Union reports that pregnant prisoners are sometimes pressured to abort. In *Morales v. Turman* (1974), a pregnant woman testified that prison officials instructed her to take 10 unidentified pills and exercise. Other prisoners told her that it would lead to a miscarriage and, indeed, she later aborted. The court, in this case, found that pregnant women were routinely denied adequate medical care (Leonard, 1983). Most prisons do not have hospitals and often when a woman goes into labor, the delay in transporting her to an outside hospital poses medical risks for both the mother and the baby.

When a woman with children is released, the problems of readjustment are severe. A working woman may not be the best caregiver because she must make arrangements for her children to be placed in daycare. On the other hand, if the mother is unemployed, she may be considered an inadequate provider for her children and may not be able to get them back from state custody. Often the woman must depend on family to help with child care and these environments may not be ideal. If the child has been in foster care or state custody it is even more difficult for her to show she is able to take care of her child adequately. Prerelease, work-release, and halfway houses almost never have accommodations for children, even if they do accept women. There are few community placements for women in general, and almost none at all for women with children.

WOMEN'S PRISONS TODAY

Women who enter prison today experience the legacy of the past. From the earliest separate institutions built for women, these prisons have had different goals and different environments from the prisons designed and run for male prisoners. The early institutions built in the late 1800s and early 1900s were designed to teach women inmates "how to be women." Attention was given to wifely and domestic skills, and proper feminine traits such as purity, chastity, and temperance were encouraged. This view that women inmates would be released to a household run by a husband bore no more resemblance to reality at that time than it does today (Rafter, 1985; Freedman, 1981; Pollock-Byrne, 1990). By and large, women then and now will be released from prison to make it on their own, often with children to support. Yet even today, the misconception of women as simply wives and mothers, rather than sole providers, has meant that vocational programs are deficient and when women are released, they are unable to economically support their families.

Although they have been largely ignored for several decades, recently changes have occurred in prisons for women, including more and better vocational programs. These changes have come about largely as a result of lawsuits filed by women prisoners. Women prisoners have not been as active in the courts as have male prisoners, and the actual number of lawsuits filed by women is small in comparison to the number of suits filed by men (Gabel, 1982; Aylward & Thomas, 1984). In recent years, however, women have won several lawsuits alleging unconstitutional conditions in prison in the areas of health care, program services, and visitation.

The two constitutional sources for such lawsuits are the Fourteenth Amendment and the Eighth Amendment. The Fourteenth Amendment prohibits states from arbitrary classification and discrimination in treatment. Although sex has not been accorded the same strict scrutiny standard that is employed against differential treatment by race, the U.S. Supreme Court has recognized an intermediate standard of review so that states must show "an important state interest" and a "substantial relationship" between the state interest and the challenged action. Using this standard, several courts have written that states may not provide fewer programs to women inmates, even under a cost-benefit rationale (Pollock-Byrne, 1990).

The Fourteenth Amendment was used in *Glover v. Johnson* (1979), in which women alleged the state discriminated against them by having 22 vocational programs for men, but only three available to women. Although no court case has yet held that prisoners have a constitutional right to vocational programs, to provide disparate opportunities based on sex for no important state interest (other than economics) was ruled unconstitutional. States have also been unable to use the economics argument for their exclusion of women from work-release programs. Nationwide, there are very few placements for women in work release facilities and some courts have forced states to provide openings for women despite the cost and inconvenience created (Pollock-Byrne, 1990).

The Eighth Amendment prohibits cruel and unusual punishment. Thus, some cases have alleged that certain conditions, such as no provision for prenatal care or lack of sufficient medical services in general, are cruel and unusual in that the pain inflicted by such deprivations is arbitrary and unnecessary.

The Eighth Amendment is more often used in suits alleging unconstitutional conditions existing in the medical services area. In *Todaro v. Ward* (1977), for instance, women in Bedford Hills alleged deficiencies in the availability of physicians, failure to perform laboratory tests, long delays in the return of lab reports, an inadequate system for keeping medical records, lack of adequate supervision over patients in the sick wing, and medical personnel who ignored gynecological concerns. The court agreed and ordered better access, better nurse screening, prompt access to a doctor during sick call, better follow-up care, and periodic self-audits.

Equal Treatment vs. Differential Needs

There are two positions taken by advocates for women's prisoners' rights that are inconsistent and compete for legitimacy. This controversy is reflected in the writings and positions taken by advocates of women's legal rights. The first position is that under the Fourteenth Amendment, women must be treated equally to men. Thus, if men have a certain number of programs, women should have them also. If men have certain visitation or telephone privileges, women should have them also. This "equality" stance basically advocates equal treatment of men and women across the board. Any different treatment is suspect and probably unconstitutional. This argument supports those situations in which women prisoners have been shortchanged in the past because of lack of attention and small numbers. Equalization would mean that benefits for women would increase, but only if their position was "less equal" to begin with.

The second approach rejects the equalization argument and offers a "differential needs" analysis. That is, women and men are not the same, therefore equalization would not be helpful if certain needs were different. For instance, if it is true that women are less likely to desire certain recreational equipment, such as weightlifting apparatus and basketball equipment, it would be ridiculous to force the state to provide them. Women may have different needs, for instance, other types of recreational equipment not seen in the prison—such as swimming pools or aerobics instructors.

The equalization approach is a comparison to a male standard through which women may not always benefit. In fact, other writers have noted that this equalization approach may be the reason for the greater numbers of women in prison, and is used as an argument to build even more prisons (Chesney-Lind, 1991). In some respects, women receive certain privileges in prison that men do not. For instance, women may enjoy more privacy in prison than men because of the view that women need more privacy than men. They often have separate rooms rather than cells and dormitories. They may also have more amenities in prison, such as kitchens on the floors and separate washing machines. Women's prisons have better staff-to-inmate ratios. They may benefit from special children's visitation programs, such as weekend visits. These privileges may be lost if a strict equalization standard is upheld because, typically, these are not found in prisons for men. Indeed, men may legitimately ask that because women demand equal programs and services, male prisoners deserve the visitation and architectural luxuries found in prisons for women. The danger is that prison administrators, when faced with court decisions that demand equal services and programs, will meet the demand by decreasing services for all. Unfortunately today, when overcrowding forces crisis management in corrections, this is not an idle concern.

It is clear that women and men have different needs. Women need more and different medical services. Obstetrical and gynecological needs would not be met by a pure equalization standard. There is every indication that children are more important to female prisoners than to male prisoners. This is not to say that male prisoners do not love their children, but they may not be the priority in their lives that they are to women. It is certainly true that women inmates are more important to their children because they will be the primary child care providers when they are released. These realities should support differential programming. Some differences may be illusory—women's need for privacy may be more stereotypical than real. Others are probably, even if purely induced by socialization, real nevertheless. The need for emotional support, for instance, has been documented as a high priority for women in prison (Toch, 1975).

There has been a definite trend in equalization between men's and women's prisons in the last decade or so, brought on by the type of lawsuits mentioned above, as well as other reasons, such as increased cross-sex supervision. In this move to make women's prisons come into some standard of conformity, major differences are overlooked or minimized. There is a story about one women's prison that had only a cyclone fence around it as security. When a new male captain was transferred to "shape up" the prison, he immediately began making plans for razor wire and more extensive perimeter security. Not only did he neglect to ask, but only a few observers thought to mention that there had not been any escapes from the prison in over six years. Evidently because it was a prison, he thought it ought to look like a male prison, whether or not the same features were required for legitimate security reasons. In Crawford's survey she reports that over 80 percent of the facilities responding reported no major disturbances in the previous five years. Almost one-half reported no escapes in the previous year (1990:31). This illustrates the tendency to push and pull women's institutions into a male standard.

IS NEW CONSTRUCTION NECESSARY?

With an average yearly cost of housing female offenders in prison as high as $35,000 in some regions, it seems imperative that we examine closely the trend of incarcerating more women (Crawford, 1990:30). One of the most intriguing differences between men and women is the different rate of participation in crime. Even though they have reached virtual parity in some areas and seem to be increasing their numbers in others, it is still true that women do not commit as much crime as men. Even those who did may not have been sent to prison. Most statistics indicate that some type of chivalry did operate to divert women from prison. Although findings are somewhat mixed, it seems that women recidivate less than males. If deterrence theory is correct, we should have had more female criminals, because they could be relatively sure that they would escape serious punishment. Yet women's crime figures remained miniscule compared to men's.

Although many justifications may be given for sending a woman (or a man for that matter) to prison, the likelihood of the prison sentence deterring future crime or rehabilitating the individual cannot seriously be presented as a viable justification. Every evaluation indicates that prison, while it may serve to punish, does little or nothing to rehabilitate. Indeed, the prison stay may make it much harder for the individual to salvage any part of his/her life as it was before incarceration once that individual is released from prison. It is at least possible that part of the reason women have not seemed to participate in crime to the same extent or to the same degree as males might be that we have, up until recently, been less likely to place women in prisons where their criminality can be solidified.

Control theory tells us that it is "ties to the community" that insulate against deviance. This is one of the few theories of deviance that seems to explain the male/female differential in crime figures. Women, who have always had primary care for children and family and who do seem to need more familial ties than males (even to the extent of creating artificial families in prison), may be less likely to risk criminality. By treating women criminals equally, in some misguided sense of justice, we may be destroying those ties and making it impossible for the woman to maintain those bonds that make her care what happens to her, thereby creating the very problem we have not had to deal with in times past—large numbers of women criminals.

It is arguable whether the increased number of men sent to prison today benefit from such imprisonment (or indeed, whether society benefits in the long run). That question is left to others to debate. What seems to be very clear is that diversion choices—that had traditionally been used for women—are now increasingly being replaced with prison sentences, even though there is no indication whatsoever that other alternatives do not work; that is, that they do not deter many women offenders from a life of crime. Women are especially suited to community placements. The public is less fearful of women offenders, the crimes women commit are less likely to pose great risk to the public, their rates of recidivism tend to be lower, and they have a myriad of economic, social, and medical needs that can best be met in a community placement. Many community placement alternatives show measures of success that we should not, nor can we afford to, ignore (Chesney-Lind, 1991).

The most productive treatment/punishment option for a woman offender may be a halfway house where she can keep her children with her. In this community setting, she may learn better parenting skills and be assured of good child care while she trains for a vocation, works, or gets an education. Community service or restitution could be used to meet the public's demand for punishment. Because women offenders do not raise the same level of fear in the public, these halfway houses should be viable options to prison construction. These facilities would provide a setting where women can learn a skill, become drug-free, learn to be better mothers, and develop responsibility. These facilities would be cheaper than prisons and, more importantly, will benefit the lives of the mother and her children, rather than further deteriorate them. One thing is certain, the choices we make now will affect us for generations.

REFERENCES

American Civil Liberties Union (1990). *Reproduction Freedom Project Newsletter,* April 20, 1990.

Aylward, A. & J. Thomas (1984). "Quiescence in Women's Prisons Litigation: Some Exploratory Issues." *Justice Quarterly,* 1,2:253-276.

Baunach, P. (1979). "Mothering Behind Prison Walls," Paper presented at the American Society of Criminology conference, Philadelphia, Pennsylvania.

Browne, A. (1987). *When Battered Women Kill.* New York, NY: The Free Press.

Bureau of Justice Statistics (1988). *Prisoners in 1987.* Washington, DC: U.S. Department of Justice.

_____ (1989). *Prisoners in 1988.* Washington, DC: U.S. Department of Justice.

_____ (1991). *Women in Prison. Special Report.* Washington, DC: U.S. Department of Justice.

Chesney-Lind, M. (1991). "Patriarchy, Prisons and Jails: A Critical Look at Trends in Women's Incarceration." *The Prison Journal,* 71, 1:51-67.

Crawford, J. (1990). *The Female Offender: What Does the Future Hold.* Washington, DC: American Correctional Association.

Ewing, C. (1987). *Battered Women Who Kill*. Lexington, MA: Lexington Books.

Freedman, E. (1981). *Their Sister's Keepers: Women's Prison Reform in America, 1830-1930*. Ann Arbor, MI: University of Michigan Press.

Gabel, K. (1982). *Legal Issues of Female Inmates*. Northampton, MA: Smith College School of Social Work.

Haley, K. (1977). "Mothers Behind Bars: A Look at the Parental Rights of Incarcerated Women." *New England Journal of Prison Law,* 4,1:141-155.

Harris, J. (1988). *They Always Call Us Ladies*. New York: Scribner's.

Immarigeon, R. & M. Chesney-Lind (1991). *Women's Prisons: Overcrowded and Overused*. San Francisco, CA: National Council of Crime and Delinquency.

Leonard, E. (1983). "Judicial Decisions and Prison Reform: The Impact of Litigation on Women Prisoners." *Social Problems,* 31,1:45-58.

Mann, C. (1988). "Getting Even? Women Who Kill in Domestic Encounters." *Justice Quarterly,* 5,1:33-53.

Merlo, A. (1991). "Perspectives on and Policy Implications of the Prosecution of Pregnant Women. " Paper delivered at the Academy of Criminal Justice Sciences annual meeting, Nashville, Tennessee, March.

Neto, V. & L. Ranier (1983). "Mother and Wife Locked Up: A Day with the Family." *The Prison Journal,* 63,2:124-141.

Pollock-Byrne, J. (1990). *Women, Prison and Crime*. Pacific Grove, CA: Brooks/Cole.

_____ (1991). "The Criminalization of Maternal Drug Abuse." Paper presented at the Academy of Criminal Justices Sciences annual meeting, Baltimore, Maryland.

Rafter, N. (1985). *Partial Justice: State Prisons and Their Inmates, 1800-1935*. Boston, MA: Northeastern University Press.

Simon, R. & J. Landis (1991). *The Crimes Women Commit, The Punishments They Receive*. Lexington, MA: Lexington Books.

Sourcebook of Criminal Justice Statistics (1989). Washington, DC: U.S. Department of Justice.

Toch, H. (1975). *Men in Crisis*. Chicago, IL: Aldine-Atherton.

Uniform Crime Reports (1990). Washington, DC: Federal Bureau of Investigation.

Weisheit, R. (1985). "Trends in Programs for Female Offenders: The Use of Private Agencies as Service Providers." *International Journal of Offender Therapy and Comparative Criminology,* 29,1:35-42.

Wilkerson, I. (1990). "Clemency Granted to 25 Women Convicted for Assault or Murder." *New York Times,* (December 22):A 1, 11.

TABLE OF CASES

Glover v. Johnson, 478 F. Supp. 1075 (E.D. Mich. 1979)

Morales v. Turman, 383 F. Supp. 53 (E.D. Texas 1974)

Todaro v. Ward, 431 F. Supp. 1129 (S.D.N.Y. 1977), *aff'd,* 652 F.2d 54 (2d Cir. 1981)

United States v. Vaughn, No. F-2172-88B (D.C. Super. Ct., August 23, 1988)

6

Professionalism Among Correctional Officers: A Longitudinal Analysis of Individual and Structural Determinants*

Robert Blair
The College of Wooster

Peter C. Kratcoski
Kent State University

INTRODUCTION

Correctional officers in American institutions today operate in an atmosphere that requires a high degree of professional expertise. The research described here explored the individual and structural factors that affected the development of professionalism among correctional officers in state prisons over an eight-year period. This longitudinal study explored the influence of individual characteristics of the officers and the work environment on the levels of professionalism they achieved.

Like other criminal justice and social service occupations, corrections has been in a state of transition. Improving the image of correctional work and becoming more effective are goals that have motivated the desire to change. These efforts at self-improvement, which may include requiring more basic education and specialized training and the use of more sophisticated equipment on the job, are often equated with the concept of professionalism.

* A version of this paper was presented at the annual meeting of the Midwestern Criminal Justice Association, Chicago, IL, October 1990.

Unfortunately, because of a shift toward a philosophy of punishment, resulting in a tremendous increase in the number of inmates housed in state, federal, and local correctional facilities, the role of the correctional officer is less clearly defined than in the past. Consequently, the correctional officer may experience considerable role conflict.

The inmate population in the United States has doubled since 1980, and over one million inmates are housed each year at an annual cost of $20 billion. Economists tag prison employment—especially the occupation of front-line correction officers—as a growth industry (Silvestri & Lukasiewicz, 1989). Although the number of correctional officers increased at a fraction of the rate of increase for inmates, records are being set in employment as well. The correctional officer occupation ranks among the top 20 occupations in growth rates. Using 1988 as a base, by 2000 the officer force is projected to increase by 41 percent. By 2000, it is estimated that there will be over 180,000 officers. In a national survey sponsored by the National Institute of Corrections (Benton, 1988) it was predicted that there would be a shortage of qualified and motivated personnel in corrections during the 1990s, and corrections administrators will have to offer increased compensation and benefits, and will have to make correctional work more satisfying, stimulating, and professional if this shortage of personnel is to be avoided.

The boom in the prison business comes at a time when the criminal justice system is undergoing a major paradigmatic shift in philosophies of punishment. The determinist view of crime, premised upon the positivist belief in the perfectibility of man and the application of scientific principles for ameliorating social problems, is in decline. Officers in the system who were trained during the past two decades when the positivist reform model was in vogue received training that complemented liberal programs with a rehabilitative ideal.

On the ascendancy is a competing view of criminal behavior based upon utilitarian principles that hold the individual responsible for criminal acts and advocate punishment proportionate to the seriousness of the crime. Hence the resurgence of such punishment philosophies as deterrence, retribution, and just deserts. It is not yet clear whether correctional officers currently entering the field of correctional work accept these philosophies of punishment or if they adhere to the rehabilitation ideal. Nor is it clear whether experienced officers will shift their orientations toward a more custodial style, as recently legislated get-tough prison policies become institutional realities.

PROFESSIONALISM

Definitions of professionalism in corrections rely heavily upon ideal types developed by investigators of professionalism in complex organizations (Hall, 1968). Hall defines a profession as containing both structural and attitudinal components. Structural components include full-time status, specialized training, a professional reference group, and a formal code of ethics. Attitudinal components of professionalism include loyalty to a professional association, viewing the occupation as a public service, having autonomy in determining role performance, self-regulation, and a sense of calling to the profession. Adaptations of Hall's categories to corrections personnel were first attempted by Williams and Thomas (1976) and Poole and Regoli (1980).

Professionalism is generally viewed as a matter of degree and as varying along a continuum. Correctional officers have been typed as "emerging" professionals (Frank, 1966) whose arrested movement on the continuum fails to qualify them as fully recognized or "established" professionals (Williamson, 1990).

Some writers have been willing to extend the concept of professional to "case workers...engaged in the process of counseling and rehabilitating offenders" (Roebuck & Zelhart, 1965:45) but not to those who simply supervise and manage the everyday living experiences of inmates (Weber, 1957). One of the difficulties associated with using a typology to determine professionalism is establishing how far along the continuum any given professional falls. A second problem is the tendency for ideal-type indicators to proliferate over time (Vogel & Adams, 1983). A third problem is deriving adequate measures that meet standards of formal replication (Whitehead & Lindquist, 1989). An additional problem concerns measuring professionalism when it is conceived as an ideal type, because there is a notable lack of consensus among researchers on what constitutes the critical variables of the concept (Regoli, Poole & Lotz, 1981). The typical procedure is for researchers to select one component of the typology and to inflate the value of that component as an indicator of the concept. In studies of correctional personnel, for example, attitudes and "orientations" are usually targeted as the critical indicators of professionalism (Whitehead, Lindquist & Klofas, 1987; Cullen, Lutze, Link & Wolfe, 1989).

The definition of professionalism in the present study reflects the structural and attitudinal dimensions that Hall (1968) and others used in studies of professional groups. Professionals have the following characteristics. They work at full-time positions, have specialized training, a professional reference group, subscribe to and read journals in the profession, and use a professional group as a referent for role ideas and training needs. In addition, they view their roles as useful for society and view their occupation as a career rather than as just a temporary job. Professionals also have attitudes that reflect service values.

While there is general agreement about the criteria used to define "professional," there is not agreement on the most useful techniques for operationalizing these criteria, particularly in regard to the professional status of the correctional officer. Quantitative measurement has the advantage of easier categorization and statistical manipulation of the data. However, some have questioned whether quantitative measurements really capture the essence of the correctional officer's work. Some of the intangible criteria used to define a professional, such as autonomy at work, dedication to service, and even having the knowledge or skill to perform the operations of the job, are difficult to measure with quantitative techniques.

The present study builds upon research that examines the relative importance of individual and organizational predictors of professionalism among correctional officers. Under a liberal punishment milieu there were serious debates about whether correctional officers could move toward a greater custody orientation and away from a rehabilitation orientation and still claim legitimacy as a professionalizing occupation.

Our study also annotates the efforts of researchers who have attempted to isolate meaningful predictors of professional orientation in officers. Much of the research published so far has yielded little toward explaining determinants of professional orientations (Jurik, 1985; Cullen, Lutze, Link & Wolfe, 1989).

Using previous investigations of professional orientations and their predictors as a touchstone, our analysis proceeds as follows. First, we test for professionalism as a phenomenon with structural and attitudinal components; second, we isolate organizational and individual predictors of levels of professionalism; and third, we compare the findings of this empirical analysis of professionalism with insights derived from qualitative field techniques.

REVIEW OF LITERATURE

Williamson (1990) believes the dramatic expansion of the officer force under a more punitive system may constitute a setback in professionalization, causing the occupation to slide still farther toward marginal status on an ideal professionalism continuum. On the other hand, Cullen et al. (1989) investigated orientations of correctional officers and found that the rehabilitative ideal was alive and well and that officers defined their roles closer to "correcting" than to "guarding."

Recent investigations of professionalism among correctional staff study it as a function of either individual attributes brought to the position or as an outcome of structural effects of correctional settings (Jurik, Halemba, Musheno & Boyle, 1987; Whitehead & Lindquist, 1989). Our study builds on this tradition with a few notable exceptions. We approach professionalism as a multidimensional phenomenon. We categorize predictors of professionalism as individual and structural variables, but we include psychological variables among our individual attributes. Finally, our study diverges from others in that we focus on two units of analysis; for individual variables the unit of analysis is the individual; the institution is the unit of analysis for structural variables.

Individual and structural characteristics were selected on the basis of their established importance in previous literature. Ten individual characteristics were selected, including background variables of seniority, entry age, sex, race, education, and community size. Two psychological variables, authoritarianism and anomie, are included as individual properties of the officer role, and a test for job-related alienation is also included. Structural characteristics that are distinct attributes of employing institutions include crowding, employee absenteeism rates, institutional security ranking, and misconducts written for inmate physical assaults.

Individual Characteristics

Seniority and age of entry are two variables that have received attention as predictors of orientations in correctional officers. Cullen et al. (1989) found a weak but positive relationship between years of tenure and support for a rehabilitation orientation. However, Whitehead and Lindquist (1989) found no significant relationship between tenure and indicators of professionalism. Age at time of entry into the occupation was found to be a significant predictor of a rehabilitation orientation by Cullen et al. (1989). Whitehead and Lindquist (1989) also studied entry age for white and nonwhite officers and found that white officers who entered the profession relatively later in life tended to desire closer contact with inmates, were less punitive, and less concerned for corruption of their authority than nonwhite officers.

When testing for the effects of gender, race, education, and community size on outcome variables, researchers report mixed findings. Gender has not been a significant predictor of orientations of officers, although its relation to professionalism has received limited attention in the literature (Philliber, 1987). Studies that test for race of officers report mixed effects. Jacobs and Kraft (1978) were among the first to show that race was not a predictor of rapprochement between officers and inmates. In their recent study of professional orientations, Whitehead and Lindquist (1989) reported that white officers expressed a desire for less distance from inmates than did black officers. Two other studies, however, contradict these findings. Jurik (1985) discovered that minority officers had more favorable attitudes toward inmates than did white officers; similar patterns were found by Cullen et al. (1989) in their recent study of a group of southern correctional officers.

In more than a dozen studies in which effects of education were examined for a variety of dependent variables, researchers found little support for education as a significant predictor of outcomes (Philliber, 1987). Jurik (1987) reported negative effects of education, suggesting that high levels of education lead to status inconsistency and alienation. Poole and Regoli (1980), however, reported that education was inversely related to a custody orientation. This argument supports the earlier finding of Kassebaum, Ward,

and Wilner (1964:104) who reported a "steady decrease in traditional attitudes with increasing education."

Size of community of origin is another individual characteristic of officers that has received limited attention in social science research, although the
rural/urban dichotomy is given considerable attention in official reports that
analyze the causes of prison disturbances. Conflicts are explained as logical
outcomes when predominantly rural officers interact with a culturally distinct,
urban inmate population (McKay Commission Report, 1972). Toch and
Klofas (1982) found, however, that officers from urban areas were more alienated than those from nonurban areas.

Researchers have encouraged greater exploration of the interaction
between psychological characteristics of officers and various attitudinal and
structural outcomes (Vogel & Adams, 1983:482). Others suggest that psychological variables should be examined for their utility as predictors of professional orientations (Whitehead & Lindquist, 1989). Two personality
attributes—authoritarianism and anomie—are particularly relevant as individual attributes affecting levels of professionalism.

Finally, alienation as a job-related phenomenon is viewed as one of the
hazards of working in corrections. Toch and Klofas (1982) examined its
effects on officers in four prisons and found more experienced officers and
the urban or "metro-access" officers were more alienated than their "back-
woods" counterparts.

Poole and Regoli (1981) found that alienation was particularly prevalent
in officers who reported negative relationships with colleagues.

Structural Characteristics

Arguments for the efficacy of individual characteristics as predictors of
professionalism are compelling, but the prevailing explanation is that professionalism is primarily a function of organizational factors, and is determined
by such institutional variables as security classification, crowding, environ-
mental stress, conduct of inmates, and the degree to which administrative
policies allow correction officers to perform in a manner comparable to how
they perceive the role should be played. Those who assign this determinate
status to structural characteristics argue that the attributes an individual brings
to a correctional officer position will eventually "fade" as the amount of time
spent on the job increases.

Administrators cite crowding as the most salient institutional characteristic of jails (Klofas, 1990:94) and prisons (U.S. Department of Justice, 1980).
Crowding was observed to generate "hard-nosed" vigilance and aggressive-
ness among officers (Jacobs & Retsky, 1975) and selective nonenforcement of
rules (Poole & Regoli, 1980). When combined with role conflict, crowding
triggers laxity in enforcement of rules (Sykes, 1958).

Another organizational variable of importance to the structuralist analysis of correctional officers' professionalism is absenteeism or extensive use and abuse of sick leave. Officers frequently interpret sick leave as a "benefit" or as "earned" time. Wynne (1977) found that officers have a disproportionately high incidence of heart attacks in comparison to other groups. Cheek and Miller (1983) found an excessively high incidence of hypertension that could not be attributed to chance. Differential rates of sick leave use, or abuse, have negative impacts on the development of professionalism.

Security classification level is another structural variable receiving attention in the literature on correctional officers. In an early investigation (Kassebaum et al., 1964) it was found to be positively related to high levels of authoritarian attitudes. However, two recent studies (Whitehead & Lindquist, 1989:80; Cullen et al., 1989:39) found inappreciable effects of security status upon measures of professionalism.

Inmate misconduct is another structural characteristic found to relate negatively to the development of professionalism among correctional officers. The officers who work with aggressive inmates were observed to adapt "macho denial" postures and perceived their colleagues to be aggressive and hostile (Cheek & Miller, 1983).

Role autonomy is measured by the ability to make decisions and affect the outcome of situations. An indication of the degree to which the correctional officer has role autonomy is his/her feelings of powerlessness. The fact that the correctional officer must consistently shift between correctional philosophies oriented toward custody and those oriented toward rehabilitation may lead to feelings of powerlessness, in that his/her behavior cannot determine the outcome of a situation (Poole & Regoli, 1980; Hepburn & Albonetti, 1980).

Even those who are strongly committed to the punishment model may still feel that they lack power because, as Wicks (1981:61-62) observed, even though some correctional officers resort to physical force to exert power over inmates, it is normally illegally used and not sanctioned by the administration. Walters (1988) found six variables related to powerlessness in correctional officers. They were:

1. Having a belief that the public has a negative view of the correctional officer role.

2. Having experienced a career turning point resulting from having a negative experience with the administration or by realizing that decision-making powers are lacking and that the administration is not likely to be supportive of attempts to exert power.

3. Having a high custody orientation toward the job.

4. Being disappointed with the field of corrections in general.

5. Being younger.

6. Being disappointed with the correctional officer role.

He found that officers oriented toward high custody also had great feelings of powerlessness while low-custody-oriented officers had fewer feelings of powerlessness.

It is interesting to note that older correctional officers felt far less powerless than young correctional officers. The maturation process appears to help in the correctional officers' becoming more positive about their work and the feeling that they can control their own life on the job. Increased education did not significantly lead to greater feelings of power. Also, education did not appear to lead to more control of one's work situations. In addition, length of service had no impact on feelings of powerlessness. Those with a greater length of service (54 months or more) did not feel more powerful than those with low service (24 months or less) or medium service (28-54 months). Increased rank also fails to affect levels of powerlessness. Neither the security level of the institution in which the correctional officers worked nor the hours of contact with the inmates affected feelings of powerlessness.

A summary of the related literature on professionalism among correctional officers reveals an array of individual and organizational variables that are isolated as determinants of professionalism. The focus of this study is on the relative impact of several individual and structural factors on professionalism.

Individual factors selected as predictors of professionalism include correctional experience, age at entry to the occupation, sex, race, education, size of community of origin, job-related levels of alienation, and two psychological variables, authoritarianism and anomie. Organizational characteristics of the prison believed to have an impact upon professionalism are crowding, absenteeism, institutional security classification, and serious misconduct.

METHODOLOGY

Design and Sample

Cross-sectional designs are generally employed, often in trying to understand phenomena that, of necessity, demands longitudinal data (Philliber, 1987). In attempting to understand professionalism, for example, researchers compare experienced officers with new officers or young with old, but this is not the same as tracing out changes in attitudes in the same group of correctional officers over time. This study has the advantage of a longitudinal design in which determinants of scores on a measure of professionalism are examined over an 8-year period for state correctional officers. The design is necessarily exploratory, given the nature of the sampling technique.

The analysis is based upon responses to an interviewer-administered questionnaire for 78 officers who were initially part of a larger group of 150 officers selected randomly for a training evaluation study sponsored by the

Pennsylvania Bureau of Corrections in 1976 (Now, the Pennsylvania Department of Corrections.). Eight years later, contact was reestablished with the original group of officers while the senior author was conducting a participant observation study of state prisons. Eighty-three of the original 150 officers were available for a follow-up interview. Of the 83 officers interviewed for the two testing times, 78 submitted two complete sets of usable responses. The ages of officers included in the sample ($\overline{X}$=36.21) are representative of officers in the state ($\overline{X}$=37.41). A potential source of internal invalidity is experimental mortality (Campbell & Stanley, 1963); those not available for the second test may differ in statistically significant ways from retested subjects. Efforts to control for this source of error included making sure that the post-test sample reflected the first sample in ratio of officers from facilities at all levels of security classification, and calculating differences between those included and omitted in the follow-up tests. Nevertheless, because the final analysis is not based upon representation of all officers in the study for both tests, we preset the design as exploratory and suggest caution in generalizing results.

Dependent Variable

Meeting conventional criteria for standardization of instruments is a formidable challenge (Whitehead et al., 1987); however, success in validation of measures does not necessarily improve predictability, leading some to suggest experimentation with alternative measures (Whitehead & Lindquist, 1989). When the first set of interviews was conducted for this longitudinal study, no standardized measures of professionalism in the criminal justice literature were available. Moreover, Miller and Fry (1976) expressed skepticism about the adoptability of Hall's (1968) attitudinal measures for correctional personnel, suggesting that the "collective self-image" of officers derived from the scale may occur "independent of objective professionalism;" hence the decision to include behavioral-driven dimensions in our operational definition of professional behavior of officers. Haga, Graen, and Dansereau (1974:125) tested related questions that measured professionalism as it was conceptualized at the time of the initial investigation. Seven questions comprise the professionalism scale: training received, beliefs about who should provide training, sources of ideas about the job, whether the position is viewed as a career, subscriptions to professional magazines, extensiveness of reading professional literature, and whether job is perceived as useful to the larger community.

Independent Variables

The two measures for personality traits of authoritarianism and anomie were measured with standardized Likert-type scales. The ten-item authoritarian scale measures two components of the authoritarian syndrome: "authoritarian submission" and "power and toughness" (Robinson & Shaver, 1973:346). Respondents were asked to indicate levels of agreement with such statements as: "What young people need most of all is strict discipline by their parents." Anomie was measured by the Srole (1956) five-item scale as a psychological phenomena revealing "self-to-others alienation" (Srole, 1956:711). One of the five statements is: "Nowadays a person has to live pretty much for today and let tomorrow take care of itself."

Education was measured with a closed-ended question requesting officers to check ordinal categories that ranged from "less than eighth grade" through a "post-graduate degree." Length of service was selected instead of age after examining for the independent effects of age and multicollinearity. Officers were asked how long they worked at their present position and the number of years they were employed in corrections. In addition they were asked to indicate the size of the place lived in for most of their lives; six ordinal categories were provided, ranging from "open country" to a city with a population in excess of 250,000.

Finally, a set of 17 questions was included from a larger battery of 77 items developed as part of a training evaluation study. The test was designed to measure retention of knowledge pertaining to awareness of basic practitioner skills in counseling and security, reflecting training received at training academies for officer recruits. The construction of the knowledge test was based upon an examination of literature on correctional service training, interviews with three directors of training in three states, reviews of handouts given by academy instructors, observation of all academy classes, and examination of tests administered by federal and state training academies (Long & Blair, 1978).

The initial set of 77 questions was administered in a pretest to 277 correctional employees, and the results were subjected to reliability tests, leading to the selection of 17 (alpha=.63) items for the current study. Seven of the 17 items in the knowledge test address elementary counseling techniques and 10 explore security-related knowledge. One counseling-related question was the multiple-choice item requesting that respondents indicate the meaning of "A helpful response": (1) "takes into account the person's prison record; (2) lets the person know you care about how he feels about his problem; (3) always offers a solution to the problem; (4) can only be made by a professional counselor." Questions pertaining to institutional security related to such topics as proper techniques of observation, causes of riots, and the proper sequence of steps to follow when handcuffing.

Four structural characteristics of the state prisons were included in the analysis. Crowding was measured for each prison by dividing the average number of inmates for a given year by the capacity intended at time of construction; the quotient was multiplied by 100. Absenteeism was measured by calculating the mean hours of absenteeism for each officer complement for each prison. Security classification was determined by the Bureau of

Corrections administrative staff; a rank of 1, designates minimum security; a rank of 6, maximum. The measure for misconduct was acquired by tallying the total number of serious misconduct reports in each institution for each year that the tests were administered.

Relationships between variables selected for the statistical analysis were examined to determine whether they violated symmetry and linearity assumption of multivariate analysis. The regression equations were computed with and without log transformation, and paired comparison t-tests were calculated for each set of variables. The professionalism scale was then regressed on each set of individual and structural variables; restricted and simultaneous models were employed to determine combined and separate effects of individual and organizational variables.

FINDINGS

One objective of the study was to determine whether changes occurred over time in individual and structural characteristics believed to be important predictors of professionalism. Table 6.1 contains the scale ranges, means, stan-

Table 6.1
Comparisons of Correctional Officers' Characteristics,
1976 (I) and 1984 (II).

Variables	Range	Mean	S.D.	t-values	Sig.[b]
Professionalism I	1-12	6.45	.254		
Professionalism II	2-11	6.38	.267	−.21	.832
Knowledge I	23-40	34.23	.351		
Knowledge II	28-42	32.54	.481	−3.08	.003
Authoritarianism I	6-22	12.63	.491		
Authoritarianism II	5-25	13.59	.503	1.95	.055
Anomie I	0-4	1.38	.136		
Anomie II	0-4	1.64	.154	1.60	.144
Size of Community I[a]	1-6				
Size of Community II					
Education I[a]	2-8				
Education II					
Experience I[a]	1-21	7.75	.58		
Experience II					
Crowding I	66-110	85.78	1.85		
Crowding II	98-143	124.75	1.64	19.33	.001
Sick Leave I	9.90-12.41	10.98	.085		
Sick Leave II	11.49-12.65	11.92	.041	19.33	.001
Security Level I[a]	1-6				
Security Level II					
Misconduct I	872-1004	938.20	5.34		
Misconduct II	1280-1485	1380.89	9.04	73.18	.001

[a] Data not reported because values are constants for both tests
[b] 2-tailed test of significance

dard deviations, and t-values for variables for the tests administrated. The values for size of community, education, experience, and security classification were constants in the two sets of data, and therefore measures of central tendency were omitted from the table. A comparison of mean scores on the two sets of data shows that five of the seven variables that were examined between time one and time two experienced statistically significant changes. Knowledge retention declined, and authoritarian values increased slightly, although the difference was statistically significant. There were precipitously sharp increases in crowding and serious misconduct reports. Absenteeism also rose significantly during the period of the test. The mean scores for professionalism and anomie reflect slight changes in the direction of lower scores for each, but changes for both were not statistically significant.

Table 6.2
Zero-Order Correlations, 1976 (N=78)

Variables	1	2	3	4	5	6	7	8	9	10
Individuals										
1 Authoritarianism										
2 Anomie	.352a									
3 Education	-.366a	-.56								
4 Experience	.184c	.007	-.424a							
5 Size of Town	-.217c	.021	-.027	-.079						
6 Knowledge	-.187c	-.048	.118	-.047	.158					
Structural										
7 Crowding	-.137	-.120	-.251b	.355a	.188c	.107				
8 Absenteeism	.079	-.010	.227c	-.284b	.101	-.180c	-.294b			
9 Security Level	.143	.114	-.057	.034	.217b	-.131	.129	.220c		
10 Misconduct	.154	-.143	-.047	.248b	-.108	.548a	.168c	-.021		
Dependant Variable										
11 Professionalism	-.295b	-.239b	.092	.075	.104	.091	.197c	.004	.139	.356a

ap=<.001
bp=>.01
cp=<.05

Tables 6.2 and 6.3 present correlational information on all of the variables for the two tests. The data in Table 6.2 indicate that four of the correlations between professionalism and its independent variables were statistically significant for the 1976 data. Two antecedent personality traits, authoritarism (-.295, p<.01) and anomie (-.239, p<.01), reveal an inverse relationship to scores on the professionalism measure; the two structural characteristics, crowding (.197, p<.05) and incidence of serious misconduct reports (.356, p<.001), were positively correlated to professionalism scores. The correlated background variables of education, years of experience, size of community, and knowledge retention yielded weak and non-significant relationships to professionalism scores. The r-values for the structural characteristics, absenteeism and security status, also revealed weak nonsignificant statistical correlations with professionalism.

Table 6.3
Zero-Order Correlations, 1984 (N=78)

Variables	1	2	3	4	5	6	7	8	9	10
Individuals										
1 Authoritarianism										
2 Anomie	.341a									
3 Education	-.341a	-.231b								
4 Experience	.072c	.085	-.424a							
5 Size of Town	-.204c	-.028	-.027	-.079						
6 Knowledge	-.266b	-.195c	.363	-.144	-.025					
Structural										
7 Crowding	-.100	-.235b	-.210c	.344a	.044	-.038				
8 Absenteeism	.071	.123	.259b	-.366a	.119	.123	-.490a			
9 Security Level	.091	.180c	-.057	.034	.217b	-.081	.096	.120		
10 Misconduct	-.013	-.181c	-.231c	.286b	-.223c	-.134	.411a	-.421a	.061	
Dependant Variable										
11 Professionalism	-.202c	-.342a	.023	.189c	.037	.097	.270b	-.369a	-.209b	.331b

ap=<.001
bp=>.01
cp=<.05

Table 6.3 shows correlations between the variables for the measure completed in 1984. In the row of values for professionalism the data reveal that seven of the 10 independent variables have r-values that are statistically significant. Authoritarianism (-.202, p<.05) and anomie (-.342, p<.001) reflect a similar relationship to that found in 1976, although the inverse relationship between professionalism and anomie is more pronounced in the 1984 data. Experience (.189, p<.05) was the only background variable in either test that showed any relationship with professionalism.

The two structural factors that were positively related to professionalism in 1976, crowding and misconduct, were similarly related in the data for 1984. Crowding (.270, p<.01) showed a more pronounced positive relationship, and misconduct showed about the same relationship for both years (.331, p<.01). The remaining two structural variables, absenteeism (-.369, p<.001), and security classification (-.209, p<.01), also showed statistically significant relationships with professionalism, suggesting that measures for these factors are negatively related to professionalism scores. Again, the weak relationships found in 1976 between professionalism and education, size of community, and knowledge retention were also found in 1984.

In summary, two of the six individual attributes (authoritarianism and anomie) showed the same relationship with professionalism in both tests; one individual attribute (experience) was significantly associated with professionalism in the second test. Two of the structural variables (crowding and misconduct) were positively related to professionalism in the first test; all four of the structural variables (crowding, absenteeism, security status, and misconduct) were correlated in statistically significant ways with professionalism in 1984, although absenteeism and security classification were inversely related to professionalism.

In addition to exploring how values of individual and structural characteristics affected professionalism, another objective was to determine what variables would prove to be the most salient for predicting variation in professionalism scores at two points in time.

Table 6.4

Beta Coefficients, t-Statistics and R^2 Change for Individual and Structural Predictors of Professionalism Values, 1976 and 1984 (N=78)

Variable (t-statistic)	1976	1984
Individual		
1 Authoritarianism	-.242	-.045
	(-1.873)[c]	(-.375)
2 Anomie	-.136	-.207
	(-1.218)	(-1.744)[c]
3 Education	(.052)	.082
	(.409)	(.639)
4 Experience	.159	.123
	(1.305)	(1.006)
5 Size of Town	-.082	.056
	(-.707)	(.491)
6 Knowledge	.148	.073
	(1.321)	(.648)
Structural		
7 Crowding	-.242	.022
	(-1.526)[c]	(.176)
8 Absenteeism	-.128	-.369
	(-.990)	(-1.714)[c]
9 Security Level	.294	-.160
	(2.498)[a]	(-1.452)
10 Misconduct	.493	.179
	(3.375)[a]	(1.426)
R^2	.2934	.1991
F(10,77)	(2.827)[b]	(2.790)[b]

[a]p=<.001
[b]p=<.01
[c]p=<.05

Table 6.4 contains the standardized beta coefficients, t-statistics, and R^2 changes for the simultaneous regression of professionalism on individual and structural predictors for the two sets of data. This table shows that authoritarianism (t= -1.873, p <.05) is inversely related to professionalism in both years and is a statistically significant predictor of the professionalism score for 1976, but not for 1984. Similarly, controlling for the effects of other variables, anomie (t= -1.744, p<.05) was also inversely related to professionalism for both years, and was a statistically significant predictor for 1984. These are the only individual attributes in the two equations that were statistically significant predictors of professionalism. Three structural variables were found to have statistically significant relationships to professionalism for the 1976 data: crowding (t= -1.526, p<.05), security status (t= 2.498, p<.001), and misconduct (t= 3.375, p<.001). However, the effects of these three structural variables on professionalism diminished in the second test as revealed in Table 6.4; absenteeism (t= -1.714, p<.05) was the only meaningful structural predictor of professionalism in the second regression equation. The total variance explained by the regression of all the independent variables on professionalism in a simultaneous model was approximately 30 percent for the 1976 data and twenty percent for 1984.

Another objective was to determine whether individual characteristics of officers are better predictors of professionalism scores than characteristics of the prisons where they work. Given the theoretical importance attached to the

Table 6.5
Restricted Model Comparisons

Variables	R^2 Changes		F-Values	
Individual	1976	1984	1976	1984
(1,2,3,4,5,6)	.1303	.0792	2.061c	1.257c
Structural				
(7,8,9,10)	.1631	.1199	3.869a	2.856b
R^2	.2934	.1991		
R(10,77)		2.790a	2.827a	

ap=<.01
bp=<.05
cp=<.10

salience of the organization for determining orientations of officers, the block of organizational variables was allowed to enter the hierarchical regression equation first. The block of structural characteristics proved to be the best set of predictors of professionalism scores, as reported in Table 6.5. Sixteen percent (F4,77=3.869, p<.01) of the total variance was explained by the structural variables in the hierarchical model for the 1976 data; this diminished to

12 percent ($F4,77=2.856$, $p<.05$) in the restricted model for the 1984 equation. The R^2 for the combined effects of the individual variables on professionalism was 13 percent ($F6,77=2.061$, $p<.10$) for the 1976 test and eight percent ($F6,77=1.257$, $p<.10$) for the 1984 test.

DISCUSSION

Several tentative conclusions are suggested by this exploratory longitudinal investigation of individual and structural determinants of professionalism. First, it reveals, albeit only as a modest tendency, that structural characteristics of prisons are more important (statistically significant) than individual attributes for explaining professionalism scores over time. Second, professionalism levels did not change appreciably, but statistically significant changes did occur in two of the individual variables (knowledge retention and authoritarian values) and in three organizational characteristics (crowding, serious misconduct, and absenteeism). Third, during the eight-year interval, the impact of given variables on professionalism changed. And fourth, for the two simultaneous models, the percent of the variance explained by all the independent variables declined from 30 percent in 1976 to 20 percent in 1984. How can these findings be interpreted in the light of recent trends in studies of professionalism, and what implications are suggested for officer training and education?

The study complements findings of others who have investigated the link between professionalism and various individual and structural attributes. The study indicates that professionalism, as measured by the indicators selected for this study, did not decline appreciably over the eight-year period for individual officers, reflecting an enduring commitment to professionalism. Cullen et al. (1989) and Whitehead and Lindquist (1989), among others, discovered similar patterns for different indicators of professionalism in cross-sectional studies, although they reported lower estimates of the combined effects of independent variables.

Because of their salience over time in predicting professionalism, the effects of general psychological measures of both authoritarianism and anomie are worth pursuing in future investigations. Our findings complemented tests of those who studied the effects of authoritarian attitudes in law enforcement officers.

We therefore encourage further examination of the link between personality traits and other indicators of professionalism (Smith, Lock & Fenster, 1970; Vogel & Adams, 1983). Also, further attention needs to be given to the temporal and causal relationship of these two personality measures with other outcome variables, such as institutional anomie as operationalized by Hepburn and Albonetti (1980).

Because few of the independent variables proved to be significant predictors of professionalism over time, it is suggested that either other factors not included in the investigation have become important, or that some degree of homogenization has taken place among officers over time. This could be due to role immersion or the development of consensus on goals of imprisonment (Cullen et al., 1989:40).

It was shown that the impact of indirect structural variables changed over time, that structural characteristics of the correctional facilities had more impact on professionalism in both sets of measures, and that both individual and structural variables have declined in impact over time. In future research, more attention needs to be given to the specific characteristics of the institutions in which the research is being conducted, because it appears that the input of these characteristics will vary, depending on the specific correctional facility situations at the time the research is being completed. Furthermore, because the variables included in the study explained between 20 and 30 percent of the variance in professionalism scores, one can conclude that either the more important factors affecting professionalism were not included in the study, or the measurements used were not valid because they did not capture the essence of the concept. Probably both statements are true to some degree. There is a need to conduct additional tests of reliability and validity for the instruments used in this study and to incorporate both attitudinal and behavioral components of professionalism in longitudinal studies.

While there is an obvious need for the standardization of professionalism measurements, there is also a need for conceptual clarity with respect to the meaning of "structural determinants." Variables included as "structural" or "organizational" in the present study were measurements acquired independently of the subjects being studied. When structural determinants were examined in empirical research on correctional officers in the past, a variety of concepts were used, including "institutional attributes" (Walters, 1989:12), "organizational influences" (Jurik, 1985:523), "organizational conditions" (Whitehead & Lindquist, 1989:72), and "work conditions" (Cullen et al., 1989:36). Similarly, a wide variety of indicators was used as proxies for structural variables, including attitudes of subjects. Using measurements of subjects as proxies for structural variables is conceptually problematic and reflects the paucity of theory development related to the correctional officer role.

Looking at the research from a practitioner's perspective, correctional administrators or supervisors might respond to our findings and other similar research on correctional officer's professionalism with a sarcastic "so what?."

They might also ask if there is anything in the research that is useful— something that can help them administer or supervise. They might comment that we could have saved ourselves a lot of time and money by simply asking them what makes a correctional officer effective or "professional."

Interestingly enough, many of their responses to the interview questions pertaining to professional correctional officers conformed to the criteria given as important for being a professional. As mentioned in the introduction to this chapter, important elements of a profession include structural components such as specialized training, having a code of ethics, and adhering to the standards of a professional reference group, and attitudinal components such as showing loyalty to a professional association, having autonomy at work, self-regulation, a sense of calling, and perceiving one's work as providing a public service. The following excerpts from a number of interviews with correctional officers that were completed during the course of this study illustrate this point.

For example, autonomy at work is emphasized in the remarks of an interviewee who described a professional officer in this way:

> He learns how to differentiate fiction from non-fiction. You have to have your own mind and know how to deal with a problem, face it and don't push it off. You have to deal with each guy as an individual. When something comes up you have to ask yourself: what can I do about it? What hat will I wear in this situation? Do I have to refer this? For example, I had a guy on the block, he was a little rowdy and I was the only one there. I wasn't the cause of his problem, but all his frustration and anger was coming out on me. He went off and I had to either walk away from him, or punish him. That is where rapport with other inmates comes in. As I was walking away, I could tell I wouldn't get jumped from behind because the other inmates protected me.
>
> (Interview by Robert Blair with anonymous correctional officer.)

An example of being influenced by a professional reference group is related in the interview excerpt below:

> We are correction officers and it's our function. We do counseling, we're chaplains, fathers, big brothers, and the word guard takes away from the professional role we play. I resent the references the [Philadelphia] Inquirer reporter made to us as guards. The inmates from Philadelphia County call us Correction Officers. Upstate (Dallas?) they refer to the officers as guards. Seldom do you ever hear hack or screw.
>
> We're from high crime areas (we black officers) and we can identify with these guys. There are some differences,

of course, but we understand why they resort to crime. If they are fortunate to have a T.V. and can experience the American dream, then chances are they won't get into trouble. But if not, they are going to get it. The ghetto area guys have special problems and even if they come from the ghetto I'm a believer that not everyone will be a bank robber or a thief. An officer from the area understands it and they can talk to black inmates (I can call black inmates mother fucker and they can call us the same and we understand the language.)

(Interview by Robert Blair with anonymous correctional officer.)

An example of self-regulation was given by another officer.

The professional officer also takes the time to read the OMs, the operations manuals. When he is around inmates on the inside he carries himself erect, has good eye contact, is curt, but not rude, forceful, but not abusive or antagonizing. The professional officer learns to read the inmates. He deals with problems as they occur and is able to determine what items are important. An inmate came up to me one time with a broken shoelace. Now, just that insignificant event can be a catastrophe. It would have been easy to turn away and tell him to come back later. It can mean a lot to an inmate, just to get his shoelace replaced; a guy could flip out over something like that. Just a simple thing, but you have to deal with it. You have so many different hats to wear; you have to be sympathetic, a good listener...it's like driving a car: stop, look and listen all the time.

(Interview by Robert Blair with anonymous correctional officer.)

The socialization process involved in becoming a correctional officer is illustrated by this officer's comments:

The biggest pressure on you, especially when you first come, and it's hard on you, is that you're constantly in gear. You can't relax, you have to be constantly alert, and it's very hard to go home and turn off.

It's a mind job and it drains you. You have to be thinking constantly. Each man has to be dealt with personally. The job has taught me to assess each person and each situation and do it fast and get the words out and say the right thing. My maturity helps me on the job. They can walk around in their birthday suit, but I'm not a giggly kid. I'm a professional correctional officer. I can detect when things start getting tense, it's like a sixth sense. I feel the tension ahead of time and I'm psychologically tuned to it. I can feel a negative change in the inmates. When the pressure gets too heavy I give it all to my maker. I've taken the written test, the stress test, and I am a born-again Christian, but I don't care what other people's religion is.

(Interview by Robert Blair with anonymous correctional officer.)

Other officers' comments illustrate dedication to public service and the difficulties surrounding professional development in correctional work. In reference to the inadequacy of training of correctional officers, this officer observed:

It's mostly socializing and there is not enough information on techniques. So I worked on training on the job for officers, and designed it for places where the need was maximal. Where? Weapons, corridor duty, cell search, and packing. We also designed courses on first aid, fire, and CPR. The Training Coordinators have fallen apart; they are lazy. I had to go all the way to the superintendent to enact this training. I tried to build teamwork. The whole training thing was "hands-off" at first. So the training effort could have failed, or people would jump on the bandwagon of training if it worked. I used volunteers and I looked around and tried to find the most knowledgeable officer for that given topic. I would ask him to type up something and then go over it with the Captain and make suggestions. Then after the first two classes we would revise the program.

(Interview by Robert Blair with anonymous correctional officer.)

Officer turnover was also mentioned:

There is always the problem of keeping them. There has been a record of high turnover, and now they are attracting more officers with high school degrees from the rural area. The guys are good workers, dependable, and they are staying. The college guys are good, but they just aren't staying. Back in the 70s they worked at getting more blacks, but they didn't stay.

(Interview by Robert Blair with anonymous correctional officer.)

Various administrators, supervisors, correctional officers, and inmates offered the names of specific officers who were considered "good." On probing into what makes them good, we received comments like "he has the experience," "he knows how to handle himself," "he knows how to keep the place running smoothly," "you know where you stand with him," "he's fair," "he works at his job," "he's steady, dependable," and many more similar kinds of responses were given. These descriptions of the "good" correctional officer seem to be tapping into the more subjective facets of correctional work. While everyone directly involved in the correctional institutional experience seems to be able to differentiate the effective workers from the mediocre and ineffective workers, finding a way to measure the traits that account for the difference is a task for those interested in pursuing additional research on this matter.

Veteran correctional officers report that there is nothing new in corrections. They tell you, "What goes around, comes around," and "I have seen it all." Of course, they are referring to the fact that during their careers they were expected to be both counselors and disciplinarians. They have worked under administrators who asked for a rigid enforcement of rules and regulations by correctional officers and under those who were satisfied with a loose compliance with rules and regulations. They have worked under conditions in which the inmate population was far above capacity and when it was below capacity, when treatment programs were plentiful and when they were rarities. Even the types of prisoners have varied in racial and ethnic group composition and types of offenses committed before incarceration.

The officer who is flexible, who adapts to the various situations, who can change from authority figure to counselor, depending on the type of interaction required, who has the good judgment to realize which rules and regulations need to be rigidly enforced and which ones can be bent, who really believes his/her work is important and contributes to the welfare of the community, approximates the image of a professional. To discover the determinants of such an orientation, qualitative measures, in addition to the measurements used in this study, must be developed. It would appear that we should rely more on the practitioners for help in developing the indicators of professionalism. Also, more structural observation of the correctional officer at work is needed.

The findings suggest the need for more longitudinal investigations, presumably with greater attention to minimizing the design errors evident in this study. Moreover, in future longitudinal research greater attention should be devoted to interaction effects attributable to change itself; this proposed analysis suggests the need for more elaborate designs. However, preliminary to establishing more sophisticated designs and measurement models is the need to radically expand the knowledge base of the correctional officer role, including extensive field observations of structural, behavioral, and attitudinal determinants of the officer role.

REFERENCES

Benton, N. (1988). "Personal Management: Strategies for Staff Development." *Corrections Today,* 50(5)(August):102-106.

Campbell, D. & J. Stanley (1963). *Experimental and Quasi-Experimental Designs for Research.* Chicago, IL: Rand-McNally.

Cheek, F.E. & M.D. Miller (1983). "The Experience of Stress for Correction Officers: A Double-Blind Theory of Correctional Stress." *Journal of Criminal Justice,* 11(2):105-112.

Cullen, F.T., F.E. Lutze, B.G. Link & N.T. Wolfe (1989). "The Correctional Orientation of Prison Guards: Do Officers Support Rehabilitation?" *Federal Probation,* 53:33-41.

Frank, B. (1966). "The Emerging Professionalism of the Correctional Officer." *Crime and Delinquency,* 12:272-276.

Haga, W., G. Graen & F. Dansereau, Jr. (1974). "Professionalism and Role Making in a Service Organization: A Longitudinal Investigation." *American Sociological Review,* 39:122-133.

Hall, R.H. (1968). "Professionalization and Bureaucratization." *American Sociological Review,* 33:92-104.

Hepburn, J.R. & C. Albonetti (1980). "Role Conflict in Correctional Institutions: An Empirical Examination of the Treatment-Custody Dilemma Among Correctional Staff." *Criminology,* 17(4)(February):445-459.

Jacobs, J.B. & L.J. Kraft (1978). "Integrating the Keepers: A Comparison of Black and White Prison Guards in Illinois." *Social Problems,* 25:304-318.

Jacobs, J.B. & H.G. Retsky (1975). "Prison Guards." *Urban Life,* 4(April):5-29.

Jurik, N.C. (1985). "Individual and Organizational Determinants of Correctional Officer Attitudes Toward Inmates." *Criminology,* 23:523-539.

Jurik, N.C., G.J. Halemba, M.C. Musheno & B.V. Boyle (1987). "Educational Attainment, Job Satisfaction, and the Professionalization of Correctional Officers." *Work and Occupations,* 14:106-125.

Kassebaum, G., D. Ward & D. Wilner (1964). "Some Correlates of Staff Ideology in the Prison." *Journal of Research in Crime and Delinquency,* 1:96-109.

Klofas, J. (1990). "Review Essay: The Jail and the Community." *Justice Quarterly,* 7(1)(March):69-102.

Long, H. & R. Blair (1978). "Evaluating the Impact of Training on Correctional Officers in the Pennsylvania Bureau of Corrections." Governor's Justice Commission and Bureau of Correction, Harrisburg, Pennsylvania.

McKay Commission Report (1972). *Attica: The Official Report of the New York State Special Commission on Attica.* New York, NY: Bantam Books.

Miller, J. & L. Fry (1976). "Measuring Professionalism in Law Enforcement." *Criminology,* 14:401-412.

Philliber, S. (1987). "Thy Brother's Keeper: A Review of the Literature on Correctional Officers." *Justice Quarterly,* 4(March):9-37.

Poole, E.D. & R.M. Regoli (1980). "Examining the Impact of Professionalism on Cynicism, Role Conflict, and Work Alienation Among Prison Guards." *Criminal Justice Review,* 5:57-65.

_____ (1981). "Alienation in Prison: An Examination of the Work Relations of Prison Guards." *Criminology,* 19:251-270.

Regoli, R.M., E.D. Poole & R. Lotz (1981). "An Empirical Assessment of the Effect of Professionalism on Cynicism Among Prison Guards." *Sociological Spectrum,* 1:53-65.

Robinson, J. & P. Shaver (1973). *Measures of Social Psychological Attitudes.* Ann Arbor, MI: Survey Research Center Institute for Social Research.

Roebuck, J. & P. Zelhart (1965). "The Problem of Educating the Correctional Practitioner." *Journal of Criminal Law, Criminology, and Police Science,* 56:45-53.

Silvestri, G. & J. Lukasiewicz (1989). "Projections of Occupational Employment, 1988-2000." *Monthly Labor Review,* 112:42-65.

Smith, A., B. Lock & A. Fenster (1970). "Authoritarianism in Policemen Who Are College Graduates and Noncollege Police." *Journal of Criminal Law, Criminology and Police Science,* 61(2):313-315.

Srole, L. (1956). "Social Integration and Certain Corollaries: An Exploratory Study." *American Sociological Review,* 21:709-716.

Sykes, G. (1958). *The Society of Captives.* Princeton, NJ: Princeton University Press.

Toch, H. & J. Klofas (1982). "Alienation and Desire for Job Enrichment Among Correction Officers." *Federal Probation,* 46:35-44.

U.S. Department of Justice (1980). *American Prisons and Jails: Summary and Policy Implications of a National Survey, Vol. 1.* Washington, DC: U.S. Government Printing Office/National Institute of Justice.

Vogel, R. & R. Adams (1983). "Police Professionalism: A Longitudinal Cohort Study." *Journal of Police Science and Administration,* 11:474-484.

Walters, S. (1988). "One Hundred Twenty-Six Correctional Officers Used Dean's Alienation Scale to Measure Powerlessness." *Journal of Crime and Justice,* 11:2(Fall):47-58.

_____ (1989). "Factors Affecting the Acceptance of Female Prison Guards by their Male Counterparts." Paper presented for annual meeting of Academy of Criminal Justice Sciences, Denver, Colorado.

Weber, G. (1957). "Conflicts Between Professional and NonProfessional Personnel in Institutional Delinquency Treatment." *Journal of Criminal Law, Criminology and Police Science,* 48(May-June):26-43.

Whitehead, J.T. & C.A. Lindquist (1989). "Determinants of Correctional Officers' Professional Orientation." *Justice Quarterly,* 6:69-87.

Whitehead, J.T., C.A. Lindquist & J. Klofas (1987). "Correctional Officer Professional Orientation: A Replication of the Klofas-Toch Measure." *Criminal Justice and Behavior,* 14(December):468-486.

Wicks, R.J. (1981). *Guards: Society's Professional Prisoner.* Houston, TX: Gulf Publishing Company.

Williams, S.J. & C.W. Thomas (1976). "Attitudinal Correlates of Professionalism: The Correctional Worker." *Criminal Justice Review,* 1:120-125.

Williamson, H.E. (1990). *The Corrections Profession.* Newbury Park, CA: Sage Publications.

Wynne, J.M., Jr., (1977). *Prison Employee Unionism: The Impact on Correctional Administration and Program.* Sacramento, CA: American Justice Institute.

7

Shock Incarceration: The Military Model in Corrections

Peter J. Benekos
Mercyhurst College

INTRODUCTION

As prison populations continue to increase beyond the legitimate capacity to confine, the pressure on policymakers and corrections administrators to "do something" about overcrowding has resulted in several "reforms" and initiatives. While the continuum of community corrections sanctions has been expanded to include "alternative sentencing" (Klein, 1988) and "intermediate punishments" (Morris & Tonry, 1990), the practice of incarcerative punishment is also being reexamined. Shock incarceration, as an alternative to "standard" prison sentences, is one such effort attracting considerable interest (MacKenzie & Shaw, 1990).

This chapter examines the development of the military approach to incarceration and reviews the characteristics, assumptions, and outcomes of shock incarceration (SI) programs. Thus far, these programs appear to be receiving popular support while conforming to the contemporary context of conservative ideology and get-tough political rhetoric. The "boot camp" model of prison, however, is viewed by many as an alternative—capable of simultaneously achieving several goals. These observations suggest that SI may be raising false expectations while serving political exigencies to deal with crime and criminals.

DEVELOPMENT OF SHOCK INCARCERATION

The belief that discipline, hard work, and military training are good regimens for the body and soul is not new to corrections. In the late 1800s, Elmira Reformatory, under the stewardship of Zebulon Brockway, practiced a penology based on disciplinary training (Burns, 1991:8). In describing the salient elements of the Elmira model, Hawkins and Alpert (1989) note the emphasis on military drill, active inmate involvement, education, and early release contingent on an inmate's progress. The objectives included "the improvement of both body and mind" for first-time, youthful offenders (1989:51).

A century later in Georgia and Oklahoma, the "boot camp" model reemerged and since then has been planned for or adopted in various forms by departments of corrections across the country (MacKenzie & Shaw, 1990; MacKenzie, 1990). MacKenzie reported that by the end of 1989, 14 states had programs on-line and 13 were in the process of establishing them (1990:44). The basic elements of these programs "emphasize strict rules and discipline and require physical training and drills" (MacKenzie, 1990:50). Programs are generally targeted for youthful, first-time, nonviolent offenders.

A contemporary forerunner of boot camp prisons was "shock probation" (Burns, 1991). This form of split sentence was predicated on giving the first-time, prison-bound offender a "short, sharp, shock" of incarceration that would serve to "scare" or deter the offender by exposing him/her to the realities of prison prior to receiving probationary status and community supervision. The "scared straight" phenomenon for juveniles also reflected this approach (Finckenauer, 1982).

While shock probation reflects elements of a rehabilitative-reintegrative era of corrections, shock incarceration emphasizes the punitive-retributive objectives of corrections. In supporting alternatives such as shock incarceration, policymakers and administrators are responding to the prevailing social and political environments. They recognize that in order to be "acceptable" responses to crime, criminals, and prison overcrowding, the alternatives must be safe for the community, relatively inexpensive to operate, and tough on the offenders (Corrigan, cited in Gordon, 1990). This expectation to be safe, inexpensive, and tough (the "SIT" standard) requires that new programs be less expensive than incarceration without adding to the community's risk or without having the appearance of being a nonpunitive intervention.

Description

The shock incarceration sanction is modeled on the military boot camp and incorporates its essential elements: military drill, discipline, physical training, hard work, and regimentation (MacKenzie & Shaw, 1990). In addition, a rehabilitation component is incorporated into the shock experience.

This includes education, vocational training, and a variety of treatments (Parent, 1989).

The SI programs target less serious, nonviolent offenders who meet eligibility requirements and qualify for a comparatively short term of incarceration generally lasting 90 to 180 days. Successful completion of the program results in parole and community supervision.

Boot Camp Components

In a comprehensive review of SI programs, Parent found that most of the physical training was based on exercises from the United States Army Field Manual (1989:23). While program regimens vary, two daily physical training sessions are generally conducted and the training requirements are gradually increased as inmates become conditioned and more fit. Marching and running are also characteristic of the military model and inmates run from three to five miles (New York) to 12 miles (Orleans Parish) per day (Parent, 1989:23).

Based on observations of the physical training, Parent found that the intensity was comparable to "a well-run high school football program and slightly less intense than in real military recruit training" (1989:23). In addition to drills and exercises, SI inmates are assigned hard labor doing such things as forestry conservation (New York) and construction and maintenance projects (Georgia). The work details are designed to provide labor-intensive experiences that "exact maximum physical effort" and structure inmate time (Parent, 1989:24).

The physical training and labor are both conducted according to regulations and strict discipline. Inmates are expected to comply with authority and to demonstrate appropriate obedience and respect. This intense discipline appears to be the essence of the boot camp model and the image that is emphasized when promoting SI programs. By marching, drilling, confronting, and punishing SI inmates, advocates maintain that the programs can create positive experiences and graduate offenders who are less likely to recidivate (MacKenzie & Shaw, 1990:126).

Rehabilitative Component

The emphasis on the militaristic and physical aspects of SI does not negate the importance of efforts to provide some rehabilitative interventions for inmates. Programs that deal with substance abuse, lack of job skills, illiteracy, and inadequate social skills are "prudent" responses to inmates' needs and problems (Parent, 1989:27). In addition to education programs, vocational training, and various treatments such as relaxation therapy, therapeutic community, and reality therapy, Parent found that "all SI programs" give inmates basic health instruction and information on "sexually transmitted diseases, including AIDS" (1989:28).

Treatment philosophies and program components vary depending on the state's goals but the "largest difference among SI programs is the amount of time spent in rehabilitation activities" (MacKenzie & Shaw, 1990:128). In her study of 14 states, MacKenzie (1990) compared the amount of time inmates spent in rehabilitation activities with the time spent working. She found three states (Alabama, Arizona, and Mississippi) in which rehabilitation activities equaled or exceeded the amount of time scheduled for work routines. She concluded that in almost all programs, SI inmates as compared to those in regular prisons, "spend a fairly large amount of time in rehabilitation-type activities" (1990:45).

Table 7.1
Shock Incarceration Treatment Components

Jurisdiction	Program Length	Treatment					
		Drug/ Alcohol Counseling	Reality Therapy	Relaxation Therapy	Individual Counseling	Recreation Therapy	Therapeutic Community
Georgia	90 days						
Oklahoma	120 days	X	X	X	X	X	
Mississippi	90 days		X	X	X		
Orleans Parish	120 days	X			X		
Louisiana	90-180 days	X	X		X		
South Carolina	90 days	X				X	
New York	180 days	X	X		X	X	X
Florida	90-120 days	X	X	X			

Source: D. Parent (1989). *Shock Incarceration: An Overview of Existing Programs,* p. 21. Washington, DC: U.S. Department of Justice.

In his survey of the SI treatment components in eight states, Parent found that six offered drug and alcohol counseling while only one, New York State, used the therapeutic community (see Table 7.1) (1989:21).

Release

At the end of the shock experience, inmates are released to some form of community supervision. As with other components of SI, the nature and intensity of this phase also vary among programs. Parent (1989) found that most of the programs in his study had "intensive" levels of supervision and offered some reentry services.

For example, Mississippi used a "community volunteer" concept to assist SI inmates in their readjustment. Problems with the implementation and administration, however, seemed to indicate that this effort would be discontinued (Parent, 1989). In the New York State program, a new supervision program was created by the Division of Parole for SI graduates (New York State

Department of Correctional Services, 1991). This program reflects an effort to provide better cooperation between institutional and community staff and to enhance reintegrative success (NYSDOCS, 1991).

The transition to a less-structured environment for SI graduates, however, does not appear to present unique management problems. In his assessment, Parent observed that intensive supervision did not seem warranted in all cases and, therefore, he recommended a more selective use of this "scarce resource" (1989:33).

Goals

The descriptions provided by Burns (1991), Courtright (1991), MacKenzie (1990), MacKenzie and Shaw (1990), Osler (1991), and Parent (1989) suggest that SI programs have similar components and characteristics. While the differences do not appear to be significant, they do indicate different program goals. Alabama, for example, tends to emphasize "a chance for rehabilitation" (Burns, 1991:20) while others such as New York State stress a reduction in prison crowding (NYSDOCS, 1991).

As expected, SI programs have designated goals that are essentially similar to those for criminal justice: "deterrence; rehabilitation; punishment; incapacitation; and (to) reduce crowding/cut costs" (Parent, 1989:11-12). The specific, announced goal or goals, however, determine the program components and their duration and intensity. For example, if the specific goal is to provide immediate relief for crowded conditions, the duration would be "relatively brief." By comparison, an SI program with a rehabilitative goal would be longer (Parent, 1989:12).

SHOCK INCARCERATION IN NEW YORK STATE

The largest and most comprehensive shock incarceration program is administered by the New York State Department of Correctional Services (Parent, 1989; Courtright, 1991; NYSDOCS, 1991). Not only is the NYS-DOCS program a model for other states but its staff also consults with and trains other SI personnel. Because of its comprehensive nature, and in an effort to further examine the potential of SI, this section summarizes some salient dimensions of the New York State program.

Eligibility

The first NYSDOCS SI facility opened in 1987. The number of facilities has since grown to five with an annual maximum capacity of 3,000 individuals, 1,500 per six-month cycles (NYSDOCS, 1991:1). Inmates who meet the legal criteria of age (16 to 30 years of age), offense type (less serious, nonviolent, nonsexual), time to parole eligibility (indeterminate sentence with three years to eligibility), and first-time commitment are sent to one institution (Lakeview Shock Incarceration Correctional Facility) for further screening. These inmates receive medical and psychological assessments and are also screened for criminal histories, security classification, and psychiatric suitability. Those who are approved then have to volunteer for the program (NYSDOCS, 1991:11-13; 24-26).

The *Third Annual Report of Shock Incarceration in New York State* reports that of 13,008 shock eligible inmates who were reviewed between July 13, 1987, and October 19, 1990, 5,938 inmates (45.6%) were sent to SI (NYSDOCS, 1991:24). Of the 7,070 inmates not admitted, 4,965 (70.2%) were disqualified for mainly medical/psychiatric and criminal history reasons. Another 1,737 (24.6%) refused the program and 368 (5.2%) were pending.

In addition to the legislative criteria, the NYSDOCS has established specific screening standards to "carefully restrict" the inmates who are selected for SI (1991:13). These criteria and the introduction of an institution with a "dedicated screening and orientation process" have resulted in a decline in "the proportion of inmates refusing the program" (1991:3). This screening process reflects the specific nature and goals of the New York Shock facilities.

Goals

The New York program has established two goals (NYSDOCS, 1991:22):

- to reduce the demand for bedspace;
- to treat and release specifically selected state prisoners earlier than their court-mandated periods of incarceration without compromising the community protection rights of the citizenry.

In order to increase available bedspace, the program offers sentence reductions for inmates who complete the SI requirements. To protect the community, a "treatment-oriented program" and a "strong intensive Parole Supervision program" have been developed (1991:23).

Programs

In addition to the military milieu and boot camp regimen, New York's SI has two distinguishing program components: a therapeutic community and substance abuse services.

Based on the theoretical model of "control theory," a therapeutic community called Network has been designed "to establish living/learning units" (NYSDOCS, 1991:17). The objective of this "total learning environment" is to foster "involvement, self-direction, and individual responsibility" and to instill "a sense of self-worth and personal pride" (1991:18). Specially trained staff work with inmates to develop personal goals and to meet community standards. Confrontation groups are also used to deal with attitudes and behaviors, and to encourage learning experiences that will promote conformity, attachment, and prosocial behavior (1991:19).

Because most SI inmates have histories of drug and/or alcohol abuse, substance abuse treatment is strongly emphasized. All inmates, regardless of drug or alcohol histories, must attend classes that include 546 hours of "the therapeutic approach to treating addiction," 260 hours of academic education, and 650 hours of hard labor (1991:21). These components are in addition to 500 hours of physical training, drill, and ceremony. The stringent therapeutic programs are unique to New York and reflect commitment to a comprehensive incarceration program and to efforts to increase the success of SI graduates.

Parole

Inmates who complete the 180-day SI program are eligible for early release to an intensive parole supervision program specifically created by the Division of Parole for SI graduates. The Division of Parole reports a 99 percent release rate for SI inmates who successfully complete the program (NYS-DOP, 1991:3). This "after-shock" supervision includes reduced caseloads, i.e., one officer for about 15 parolees, to insure adequate home visits, curfew checks, and random drug testing. In addition, several community service agencies are involved in providing support for job placement, education, counseling, and "relapse prevention" (NYSDOCS, 1991:22). In New York City, additional efforts and programs have been undertaken to provide housing, temporary employment, and a continuation of the Network milieu. Parolees are also supervised by a two-parole officer team for each thirty shock parolees (NYSDOP, 1991:5).

The New York model provides for a cooperative and complementary effort between SI staff and the Division of Parole. The two agencies recognize that after eight months of shock incarceration (two months in processing and orientation and six months in SI programming), inmates need aftercare and support to improve reintegration and to enhance the chances for success (NYSDOCS, 1991:54). As a result, prerelease planning, coordination of resources, and assistance from community service providers "have been effective in helping most graduates make a successful transition" (1991:54).

Another important element of the New York parole program is the loss of incarceration time for graduates who violate parole and are returned to prison. In other words, the six months of shock incarceration are not credited toward completion of the original sentence for SI graduates who fail during their parole (NYSDOP, 1991:27). This is viewed as an added incentive for SI parolees to succeed in the reintegrative phase of the SI program (Courtright, 1991:62).

Evaluation

As stated above, the goals of the NYSDOCS are to reduce the demand for bedspace and to treat and release SI inmates without compromising community safety. The success in meeting these goals has been evaluated by using both a "fiscal" analysis of SI and a "follow-up" study of SI graduates.

Fiscal

The fiscal analysis focuses on two primary considerations: per diem cost for SI compared to minimum- and medium-security facilities and the capital savings by not constructing additional prisons/bed space. Because of the staffing patterns and the military and therapeutic programming in SI facilities, the average daily operating cost is 43.6 percent higher than for medium-security facilities and 71.9 percent higher than for minimum-security ones: $80.52 per day for SI as compared to $56.07 for medium and $46.85 for minimum (NYSDOCS, 1991:30). Because SI inmates spend fewer days incarcerated, however, the cost per inmate is less than if he/she served until the regular parole eligibility date. As a result, based on 2,783 shock inmates released as of October, 1990, NYSDOCS reports that the net savings for each graduate was 319.1 days. This reflects an estimated savings of $49.3 million in operational costs (NYSDOCS, 1991:31).

In addition, by releasing these 2,783 SI inmates after 180 days of incarceration (excluding 43 days of screening and orientation), the NYSDOCS estimates a savings of 1,214 beds and $80.35 million in construction costs (1991:33). Based on these fiscal considerations for 2,783 SI graduates, the NYSDOCS reports a total savings of $129.65 million (1991:34).

In summary, the Shock Incarceration Program is capable of reducing demand for bedspace and saving the state money, this despite the fact that it is more expensive to provide this intensive level of incarcerative programming.

Recidivism

Using "return to custody" as a measure of the SI outcome, data comparing three groups of inmates for an 18-month follow-up indicate that SI graduates had "comparable" rates of return. One comparison group consisted of inmates who would have been eligible for SI but the program was not yet available ("PreShock"). The inmates in the other group were eligible for SI but were not selected ("Considered") (NYSDOCS, 1991:83-84).

During the follow-up period (18 months), 34.6 percent of the SI graduates were returned to custody. The rate for "PreShock" inmates was 34.7 percent and it was 41.5 percent for the "Considered" inmates (1991:8). Based on these data, the NYSDOCS concluded that (1991:88):

> despite being incarcerated for shorter periods of time, the
> Shock graduates appear to be returning at a rate similar to
> a carefully selected, comparable group of inmates.

The results of these two dimensions of evaluation, fiscal and inmate success, offer support for New York State's SI program. Selected inmates can be incarcerated, punished, treated, and released within a short period of time (120 days), thus reducing operating costs and making bedspace available for other inmates. In addition, this relatively inexpensive and tough program that releases inmates "early" does not increase risk to the community. Therefore, shock incarceration appears to meet the SIT standard for correctional reform and alternatives to prison incarceration: safe, inexpensive, and tough.

DISCUSSION

As with many correctional reforms, the perceptions and assessments of SI are mixed. Some researchers are skeptical (Morash & Rucker, 1990; MacKenzie, 1990; Sechrest, 1989) while others are cautiously optimistic (Burns, 1991; Osler, 1991; MacKenzie, Gould, Riechers & Shaw, 1989). There are, however, some basic concerns that are indicative of the assessments of the shock incarceration phenomenon.

Program Goals

One concern, for example, is that without substantial empirical evidence, it is difficult to determine whether the goals of SI are actually being achieved. As a result, questions about the effectiveness of boot camp punishment, regimented therapeutic programming, and decisions regarding which components to emphasize are not consistently resolved. Osler (1991) concludes that the only proven goal is that SI is a "cheap punishment" that provides cost savings due to shorter terms of incarceration. Joseph Lehman, the Commissioner of Corrections in Pennsylvania, is "unconvinced" that SI has any rehabilitative effect but he recognizes it as a "less expensive punishment" (1991:7).

Based on his review of the Alabama program, however, Burns concludes that the boot camp "concept" can be successful and can "serve a useful rehabilitative purpose" (1991:29). MacKenzie et al. (1989) evaluated the Louisiana motivational program and identified components that are "associated with successful rehabilitation;" i.e., program intensity; volunteer nature; and structured aftercare (1990:39). These and other program elements, however, need to be "examined for therapeutic integrity" (1990:39) and for the potential of abuse (1990:35). In this regard, Morash and Rucker (1990) present a critical assessment of the boot camp assumptions and share concern that inconsistent standards and authoritarian environments create the potential for abuse of power and negative program outcomes.

Public Opinion

Ironically, the perception of this authoritarian environment is an important basis of public support for the boot camp alternative. Several journalistic accounts have emphasized the "boot" image of SI programs and have described the militaristic, disciplinary, and physical nature of the boot camp experience (Morash & Rucker, 1990; Michelmore, 1991a; Cuneo, 1991).

In a survey of public reaction to the boot camp phenomenon, Gauthier and Reichel (1989) found that the most prevalent reason for supporting shock incarceration was the provision for "authority" over inmates. This public support is consistent with a get-tough ideology and the belief that a military regimen can maintain order and instill self-discipline and prosocial behavior in offenders. A major public concern, however, was that boot camp incarceration was not long enough (Gauthier & Reichel, 1989).

Although SI programs continue to be developed with similar basic features, the goals of this short, sharp shock of structured incarceration vary. For some policymakers it is a panacea for punishment and deterrence, and the problems of rising prison costs and institutional crowding. For others, it is a correctional program aimed at rehabilitation and reintegration (Osler, 1991). As a reform that has received both political and public support, and one that appears to be "all things to all people," a more realistic view of SI is that the military model is "unlikely to provide a panacea" for the problems facing corrections (Morash & Rucker, 1990:218).

At worst, shock incarceration is a cheap illusion of punishment that has gained political popularity because of the punitive image that has been portrayed. It is a *sop for Cerberus* that is consistent with a conservative agenda and responsive to the need to do something about the costs of incarceration and the rising prison population. It gets tough with offenders in return for sentence reductions and it offers images that demonstrate a punitive sanction. Prison reform efforts such as boot camp "are nearly always well-intentioned and nearly always leave a legacy of failure (Haas & Alpert, 1991:ix). In an effort to crack down on crime, SI offers a crackdown on criminals. With this emphasis on punishment, however, the potential for abuse of authority requires close monitoring of SI programs.

As a ruse to reduce crowding, this popular indulgence in shock prisons postpones serious and substantive initiatives to confront the issues and problems of prisons and the rising prison populations. Shock incarceration programs only affect a small number of inmates. For example, in the largest state program, which has an annual capacity of 3,000 inmates, New York's SI programs reach 5.8 percent of the state's prison population (Bureau of Justice Statistics, 1990). In seven states studied by Parent, using 1987 data, the annual maximum SI capacity represented only 3.4 percent of these states' prison populations. Even though cost savings can be substantial as reported by the NYSDOCS, a larger proportion of inmates would need to be included in order to significantly affect prison populations and correctional costs.

At best, SI offers reduced prison sentences to selected prisoners in return for "voluntary" participation in various "treatment" programs. The model acknowledges rehabilitative goals and justifies efforts to provide skills and aftercare support to prisoners. As a correctional reform, it attempts to integrate retributive and rehabilitative goals and to give prison administrators a structured environment in which to control inmate behavior.

And although SI is still relatively new, data do indicate that SI graduates present no greater threat to the community than parolees who have not received the SI experience. This is an important lesson that suggests selected offenders can serve shorter sentences and still receive just deserts without risk to the community: SI is no better, but it is no worse, than regular prison sentences.

It is not evident, however, why SI has these outcomes. Does a shorter sentence minimize the negative impacts of prison or does a structured, controlled environment instill self-discipline and improve self-esteem? Does rehabilitative programming in prison improve reintegration or are intensive parole supervision and community support more crucial to success? For example, could SI programs be as effective *without* the boot camp milieu? Marc Mauer, assistant director of The Sentencing Project, believes "that if we show inmates we care, that we want them to change, and that we're willing to put money into it, the military part may not be necessary" (cited in Michelmore, 1991b:7).

It is disconcerting that shock incarceration programs are being developed and promoted as "quick-fix" solutions to complex problems. They are reflective of the "scared straight" panacea phenomenon (Finckenauer, 1982) and offer politicians and bureaucrats a program to "look good" (Michelmore, 1991b). Pennsylvania Corrections Commissioner Lehman expresses concern that "boot camp is just another fad" (cited in Michelmore, 1991b:7):

> The history of corrections is replete with examples of the
> public's and everyone else's desire to find simplistic solu-
> tions. There are no simple solutions in corrections.

Osler also recognizes the complex nature of crime and corrections, and observes that "generally, programs like these will not erase the social conditions under which these people must live upon release" (1989:19). When public, and therefore political, support for shock incarceration wanes and resources are reduced, it is conceivable that programs will regress to more punitive, disciplinary, and repressive environments in which retribution and punishment serve to justify abusive practices. As Cullen and Gilbert (1982) reviewed the demise of rehabilitation, they observed that when humanitarian and rehabilitative goals are rejected, prisons become hopeless environments to warehouse society's criminals. With the contemporary emphasis on punishment, the "new" boot camp warehouses have the potential to personify the abuse of authority.

The problems of crime are real and frightening but politicalization of corrections and military discipline of inmates do not address the crime problem: giving the appearance of getting tougher with some prisoners is not the reality of getting tougher with the problems of crime. The shock incarceration model appears to be the "new kid on the correctional block." However, without clear understanding of its legitimate capabilities and limitations, public expectations will be unrealistic and resources to maintain the therapeutic integrity of SI programming will become scarce.

As Osler's (1991) discussion suggests, it is too soon to conclude too much. As a result, efforts to develop SI programs should proceed with caution. In addition, resources such as those committed to shock programs might be better concentrated in the community and with residential initiatives.

REFERENCES

Bureau of Justice Statistics (1990). "Prisoners in 1989." Washington, DC: U.S. Department of Justice.

Burns, J.C. (1991). "A Comparative Evaluation of the Alabama Department of Corrections' Boot Camp Program." Presented at the 1991 annual meeting of the Academy of Criminal Justice Sciences, Nashville, Tennessee.

Courtright, K. (1991). "An Overview and Evaluation of Shock Incarceration" in New York State. Unpublished manuscript, Mercyhurst College, Erie, Pennsylvania.

Cullen, F.T. & K.E. Gilbert (1982). *Reaffirming Rehabilitation.* Cincinnati, OH: Anderson Publishing Co.

Cuneo, R. (1991). "N.Y. Prison's Paramilitary 'Shock' Program Viewed as a Model in Rehabilitation." *Erie Daily Times,* (June 23):B, 1.

Finckenauer, J.O. (1982). *Scared Straight and the Panacea Phenomenon.* Englewood Cliffs, NJ: Prentice-Hall.

Gauthier, A.K. & P.L. Reichel (1989). "Boot Camp Corrections: A Public Reaction." Presented at the 1989 annual meeting of the Academy of Criminal Justice Sciences, Washington, DC.

Gordon, D.R. (1990). *The Justice Juggernaut: Fighting Street Crime, Controlling Citizens.* New Brunswick, NJ: Rutgers University Press.

Haas, K.C. & G.P. Albert (eds.) (1991). *The Dilemmas of Corrections.* Prospect Heights, IL: Waveland Press.

Hawkins, R. & G.P. Alpert (1989). *American Prison Systems: Punishment and Justice.* Englewood Cliffs, NJ: Prentice-Hall.

Klein, A.R. (1988). *Alternative Sentencing: A Practitioner's Guide.* Cincinnati, OH: Anderson Publishing Co.

Lehman, J. (1991). "Pennsylvania To Open Boot Camp." *Correctional Forum,* (June):7.

MacKenzie, D.L. (1990). "Boot Camp Prisons: Components, Evaluations, and Empirical Issues." *Federal Probation,* 54(3)(September):44-52.

MacKenzie, D.L. & D.B. Ballow (1989). "Shock Incarceration Programs in State Correctional Jurisdictions-An Update." *National Institute of Justice Research in Action,* (May/June) Washington, DC: U.S. Department of Justice.

MacKenzie, D.L. & J.W. Shaw (1990). "Inmate Adjustment and Change During Shock Incarceration: The Impact of Correctional Boot Camp Programs." *Justice Quarterly,* 7(1):125-147.

MacKenzie, D.L., L.A. Gould, L.M. Riechers & J.W. Shaw (1989). "Shock Incarceration: Rehabilitation or Retribution?" *Journal of Offender Counseling, Services & Rehabilitation,* 14(2):25-40.

Michelmore, D.L. (1991a). "Camp with an Emphasis on the Boot." *Pittsburgh Post-Gazette,* (June 10):A, 1.

———— (1991b). "PA Boot Camp Plan Draws Skepticism." *Pittsburgh Post-Gazette.* (June 10):A7.

Morash, M. & L. Rucker (1990). "A Critical Look at the Idea of Boot Camp as a Correctional Reform." *Crime and Delinquency,* 36(2)(April):204-222.

Morris, N. & M. Tonry (1990). *Between Prison and Probation: Intermediate Punishments in a Rational Sentencing System.* New York, NY: Oxford University Press.

New York State Department of Correctional Services (1991). *The Third Annual Report to the Legislature: Shock Incarceration in New York State.* Albany, NY: Division of Program Planning, Research, and Evaluation.

New York State Division of Parole (1991). *Legislative Report: Shock Parole Supervision Program.* Albany, NY: Office of Policy Analysis and Information.

Osler, M.W. (1991). "Shock Incarceration: Hard Realities and Real Possibilities." *Federal Probation,* 55(1)(March):34-42.

Parent, D.G. (1989). "Shock Incarceration: An Overview of Existing Programs." *National Institute of Justice Issues and Practice Report.* Washington, DC: U.S. Department of Justice.

Sechrest, D.K. (1989). "Prison 'Boot Camps' Do Not Measure Up." *Federal Probation,* 53(3)(September):15-20.

8

Probation at the Crossroads: Decrementalism and Organizational Reform

Edward W. Sieh
Niagara University

There is a new mood evident throughout the land, and it manifests itself increasingly in restrictions placed on public spending and growing expectations for accountability in government...We now must learn to make do with less, or find new and more resource-conscious ways of providing the services we have come to expect from government (Harlow & Nelson, 1990:165).

INTRODUCTION

As the nation experiences fiscal conservatism and economic recession, it becomes evident that economic and social inequalities in our society have a number of negative consequences for the quality of life in America (Cochran, 1989:17). "Paralleling other changes in America's political environment, there has been a growing dissatisfaction with government programs dealing with the nation's marginal or deviant populations (i.e., the poor, the criminal, the uneducated)" (O'Leary, 1987:8). This attitude has led to program cuts and a reduced sense of concern for the poor and the miscreant.

Many states, including Connecticut, Maine, Texas, Michigan, and New York, are facing severe budget deficits. During such periods states are reluctant to vote for expensive new prisons (Allen, Eskridge, Latessa & Vito, 1985:262). While probation is considered one of the most likely alternatives to prison sentences, some states are planning to cut support for probation. Financial support for probation agencies has not kept pace with the growing number of probationers. Indeed, since the mid-1970s, probation has fallen on hard times. The mood of the country has grown more punitive, and the public has increasingly demanded consistent, harsher sentencing, not "lenient" probation (Petersilia, Turner, Kahan & Peterson, 1985:9).

Probation is the most frequently used sanction: "About four times as many offenders are placed on probation as are sent to prison" (McCarthy & McCarthy, 1991:95). The probation population has been growing at a more rapid rate than the rate of prison populations. Between 1984 and 1989 there was a 35.4 percent increase in the national probation population. In the state of New York there were 112,000 persons on probation on January 1, 1989. This amounted to a 7.4 percent increase over the previous year (Kline, 1989:1-2). "To date, no alternative sentence seems to offer as much flexibility and potential for both offender control and offender change" (McCarthy & McCarthy, 1991:129). There is little reason to believe that the number of persons placed on probation will decrease any time soon.

In the context of these developments, the purpose of this chapter is to examine the impact of reduced funding and increased caseloads on a sample of probation officers, and to identify their perceptions of probation as a component of the criminal justice system. It is apparent that various developments have begun to change the level of offender control and supervision in the community. These factors include: more offenders on probation, larger caseloads, reduced employment opportunities, economic recession, unrealistic expectations of becoming successful in a society requiring social and educational skills, the judiciary's perception of public demands for punishment, and the reduced service resources to manage offenders (Allen et al., 1985:273).

CENTRAL ISSUES

Most probation and parole caseloads are large; some officers in New York City have caseloads of 250 clients. Larger caseloads are believed to be associated with less supervision, and less assistance to offenders, but more recidivism (Allen et al., 1985:272). Probation officers have long advocated a decrease in caseload size as a means of increasing the effectiveness of community supervision. Experiments have been conducted in which smaller caseloads (usually 35) were created and the characteristics of the clients were matched with clients on normal, larger caseloads. Adams (1975) reported some improvement in the behavior of youthful offenders on smaller caseloads, but not adults (Lauen, 1988:31).

> Fifty probationers used to be regarded as the maximum number for one officer to supervise (American Correctional Association, 1977). However, the current trend is not to suggest an optimum caseload, but rather, to determine appropriate caseload size within a context of the types of probationers being supervised. For example, probation officers may not be able to adequately supervise more than 20 'maximum-supervision' cases; 'medium caseloads' might consist of 50 offenders; and 'low-supervision caseloads' might contain as many as 200 offenders (Petersilia et al., 1985:10, n.6).

Staff limitations invariably reduce the quality and quantity of services and an otherwise well-designed correctional program may easily fail for lack of sufficient staffing levels. Monetary conservatism and reduced funding make this problem particularly acute (McCarthy & McCarthy, 1991:373).

In states such as California, that have a large number of presentence investigations, there is the feeling that the quality of these reports has deteriorated. With so many reports to prepare, probation officers have limited time to obtain or verify criminal record information, sometimes relying on the offender's version of his criminal history (Petersilia et al., 1985:85).

Traditionally, probation was not intended to handle serious offenders. However, probation officers are now supervising caseloads with higher numbers of serious offenders needing additional attention, while the nonviolent first offender and the petty thief are shunted aside and left unsupervised. This means petty offenders can act with impunity, feeling that nothing will happen if they break the law because the officer must focus attention on the serious offender. There is reason to believe this could lead to more career criminals and a rising recidivism rate (Petersilia et al., 1985:x).

With the reduced resources and greater caseloads, probation officers cannot be required to closely monitor their probationer's behavior. Overloaded probation systems combined with impractical and naive expectations of programs that promise constant surveillance and strong public safety limit probation systems to reactive supervision strategies. This results in probation being viewed as both a foremost cause and the primary solution to prison crowding (Cochran, 1989:16).

During the past two decades the field of probation has been exposed to considerable scrutiny both from within the field and from external agencies. Most studies indicate that the major focus has been on the offender as the "client," and whether the role of the probation officer in his/her relationship with the "client" is one of *surveillance* or *rehabilitation*. From a management perspective, the studies do not address the issue of how a probation system could operate more effectively (Cochran, 1982:102).

When the war on drugs escalated in the 1980s, it was evident that while it was possible to increase arrests, convictions, and sentences to prison, "the end product was not a reduction in crime but a system in chaos" (McCarthy & McCarthy, 1991:12). Based on the conclusions of Petersilia et al. (1985), Cochran (1989), and Harlow and Nelson (1990), one could argue that the problems plaguing probation are serious. The questions in this study are: How are these problems perceived by probation officers? and What impact do social, economic, and political changes have on probation as an organization as well as a service? These questions are addressed in order to understand and recommend how probation systems can confront the problems that will be referred to here as decrementalism.

DECREMENTALISM

The early 1980s were difficult times for most criminal justice agencies. After a decade of unprecedented government expenditure, the major funding sources were no longer available. "In the mid-1980s, the growing gap between rising demand for service and scarce resources has forced many top police managers to rethink their role and the role of their department in local affairs" (Levine, 1985:691). This resource-demand gap is called decrementalism (Levine, 1985:691).

> For the most part they have been balancing their budgets by making marginal adjustments in their operating procedures and expenditures. In doing so, they have been essentially pursuing a strategy of decrementalism; that is, they have made short-term adjustments in their operating arrangements that have yielded some cost saving without a corresponding loss of visible operating effectiveness (Levine, 1985:692).

So far, most agencies have been successful at coping with the problems of revenue reductions. One of the major reasons for this success can be called "the spending-service cliché." That is, revenues, expenditures, service delivered, and actual public problems solved or alleviated are loosely linked in most administrative systems. Another way of thinking about this is that a dollar spent does not equate with service delivered or a problem solved in any direct way. Because of this loose linkage, most government agencies have been able to compensate gradually and institute administrative efficiencies with a minimal erosion of services (Levine, 1984:251).

Rational decision-making is impossible in the political environment of public administration due to the complexity, uncertainty, and differences of opinion over means and ends. Therefore, disagreements about priorities result. Moreover, there are few transferable assets that can be shifted from one program to another because of court or legislative requirements. As a result, there is a clear preference for familiar, short-run, incremental, and piecemeal solutions. This strategy proves ineffective when dealing with the long-range effects of retrenchment. The problem is mistakenly viewed as cyclic with the belief that funding will be restored when, in fact, the changes may be permanent (Levine, 1984:252).

Furthermore, although decremental strategies usually include some improvement in productivity and devices that have potential long-term value to the department, tactics intended to maximize resources such as across-the-board budget reductions, hiring freezes, reduction-by-attrition, deferred maintenance, and freezing and rationing operating expenses cause problems to accumulate that may compound if funding is not restored and increased (Levine, 1985:692). In terms of cost, this practice may eventually require additional expenditures to improve services if serious erosion in the levels and quality of public services are to be prevented.

METHODOLOGY

According to the U.S. Department of Labor (1972) a "job analysis" identifies what the worker does in relation to data, people, and things; the methodologies and techniques used on the job; the machines, tools, equipment, and work aids; the materials, products, subject matters, or services that result; and the traits required of the worker.

Job analysis is a principal way of studying workers in the criminal justice system. While earlier works have extensively studied the police, seldom has job analysis been used to assess the tasks and duties of probation officers (Colley, Culbertson & Latessa, 1986:67).

This chapter discusses "problems at work" as part of a job analysis conducted on a sample population of probation officers in 1990. The major focus is what officers do and how they do it. The sample included 43 respondents of a possible 87 self-selected probation officers (49%) who worked for an urban county probation department in a northeastern state. These officers included both men and women who worked in the Intake Unit, the Investigation Unit conducting presentence reports, the Adult Supervision Unit, the Juvenile Supervision Unit, and the Intensive Supervision Unit, as well as unit supervisors and administrators. Most of the respondents (37), were line probation officers; 4 were unit supervisors. Of this group, 30 percent worked with juveniles, 58 percent worked with adults, 10 percent were unit supervisors and the rest were administrators. All of the subjects, except one, were white men and women with a mean age of 44 years. On average they had 12 years of experience in the department.

In a fashion similar to McCleary's (1978) study of the parole bureaucracy, the officers in this study agreed to be interviewed in their offices with some sessions lasting as long as four hours. As part of this open-ended discussion of their work functions, the officers were asked to comment on the problems they encountered at work. Specific questions were asked about the department's recently identified budgetary problems, and whether there were any problems with administrative support, training, reward structure, public image, personnel practices, ability to care for the clients, and any other areas of concern. The officers were also questioned about what they thought the department should do about these problems. As each interview was transcribed for analysis, each respondent was given a number and the response was coded accordingly. Key responses were incorporated into the text of the article.

FINDINGS

Based on interviews with 43 officers, the responses suggested that certain issues and developments were problematic for the department. Two major concerns were the workload and the administration and organization of the department.

Workload

In this department, the number of offenders on probation has risen by 16 percent in five years (*Directors Report*, 1984-1989). While the number of cases under supervision increased by only 4 percent, the number of investigations increased by 25 percent during this same period (*Directors Report*, 1984-1989).

The state oversight agency recommended that, based on this workload, the department should have 30 additional officers. While investigators do 18 investigations a month, the recommended number is 15. For adult POs with caseloads of 95, the recommended caseload is 70. The juvenile POs should have 35, not 50 cases (Respondent 44). The problems in the department affect most of the units, including those working with juvenile status offenders and the most serious adult offenders.

For at least the last three years, the department has been subject to funding limits, either in the form of reduced appropriations or a continuation of established levels due to shortfalls in the county's or state's budgets. Eight positions, not including an inactive diversion program, have remained vacant. As retrenchment occurs, staff burnout sets in, morale falls, and the work becomes very stressful, particularly for junior officers who have to worry about being laid off. Even senior officers are uneasy about being given a portion of the laid-off officers' caseloads.

As caseloads grow there is a heightened sense of a "siege mentality." This perspective evolves into a self-fulfilling prophecy (Respondent 27). As work-related stress increases, the officers believe the job has become impossible, and that they are incapable of doing anything about it. They place self-imposed restrictions on their efforts and initiatives, leading to the belief that the only way to deal with this problem is through an emphasis on control, not on casework. Clients with drug and alcohol problems who are required to seek counseling receive it outside the department and this means that the officers' principal concern is not that the clients improve their behaviors but that they fulfill their program requirements and therefore satisfy the conditions of probation. It also means that officers are recommending earlier discharges in order to keep their caseloads at a manageable level. In addition, other officers carry cases that should be discharged but they want to appear to have a high volume for the sake of reminding others of their heavy workload.

Some officers recognized the interrelated nature of their problems. They expressed concerns that the increase in the number of officers has not coincided with the increase in court personnel. They believed that historically they have been overlooked in manpower needs and salary and that, while there has been an increase in the number of district attorneys and judges, there has not been a corresponding increase in the number of probation officers.

Some officers attribute their problems to the court's sentencing practices.

> If there were fewer cases then you could be more effective. We need to convince judges that they don't have to put some people at either end of the spectrum on probation, either the dangerous or the B misdemeanors who shoplifted. We are used as a dumping ground. They put people on probation who are bad risks and this makes us look bad (Respondent 36).

In response to the demands of the court, the number one priority in the probation department is to see that the presentence investigations (PSIs) are done on time. The officers who do investigations are expected to do 20 per month. This means an investigator is expected to do one investigation every work day. Some officers have as many as 11 investigations awaiting completion. These problems are compounded by the necessity to do custody investigations which take twice as much time to complete because the officer must investigate two households and not one, as occurs with a juvenile petition. Juvenile officers cannot devote the time to helping the juvenile offenders if they must do 10 or 11 PSIs per month in addition to their own work obligations.

Adhering to risk-assessment supervision guidelines and providing time to meet with the adult client are also important. Guidelines are among the first things sacrificed because of heavy caseloads. So much of the work is seen as "managing a workload" that some officers felt they did not have enough time to provide anything but the minimal level of supervision, particularly when trying to help dysfunctional families. This was particularly true in the Intake Unit where officers felt they did not have time to do follow-up interviews. The officers believed their professional standards were reduced. More importantly, it was assumed that probationers sensed a reduced level of officer supervision, and took advantage of this by violating the law which contributes to more paperwork for the officer and a further reduction in the level of supervision.

Organizational/Structural Concerns

The other major area of concern among the officers was the administration and organization of the department. Besides concerns with the administration in general, officers responses also suggested problems with planning and evaluation, communication in the department, and the system of rewards.

> They have two people to oversee all the special programs
> and that is not enough. These people are tied up in the
> budget three-fourths of the year (Respondent 30).

Ordinarily the department would have several staff levels including assistant probation officers, probation officers, senior probation officers, supervisors, chief probation officers, two deputy directors, and one director. Over the years, as a cost-saving measure, many of these levels were eliminated, leaving only probation officers, unit supervisors, deputy director, and director positions. With a flat organizational hierarchical structure, the director's position carries disproportionate authority but may be overly sensitive to shifting political interests that require too much political posturing. This may explain why the director was considered too passive in the face of mounting pressures at work. (With the latest budget cuts, however, the director has taken a more "aggressive" position.) This flat organizational structure was an issue of concern for everyone, including members of the administration. "It leads to a morale problem in the department" (Respondent 28).

Some officers felt there was too little guidance, structure, cohesion, and progressive planning, and that more should be made of grants available to the department. Changes were perceived to occur independently of the direction of the administration, or did not occur at all. The officers wanted the administration to lead more by example, be more visible, and more involved.

There was a feeling that there was too little communication from the administration, particularly when the department is in a state of flux. The department has "never asked for much input from the staff on programs, program changes, and direction" (Respondent 6). The monthly staff meetings apparently were held for the purpose of disseminating information downward but not upward. When any communication was directed upward, officers assumed that the deputy director would tell them only what they wanted to hear but that nothing would really happen to any proposals brought forward from lower staff.

A related problem is the perceived lack of effective evaluation. The problem exists in two areas. Quarterly reports are required by the state and intended to alert the unit supervisor or anyone else who needs to read the file as to the progress of cases. The officers felt quarterly reports were purposeless and that state officials were insensitive to officer complaints (Respondent 33).

> My quarterlies are meaningless but at least if you don't put down something you can't be sued for what you didn't say. I am meeting minimum state requirements (Respondent 17).

The officers also felt that there were no adequate performance evaluations for the department. There was a belief that the union was not interested in evaluations and the administration just wanted to know the job was done. Officers believed the administration was interested in form over content.

> When the inventory is not done the person is told to not go out into the field until it is but the officer is not going out into the field as it is...Some of the state regulations are not feasible with 100 cases (Respondent 8).

Even when the officers were evaluated according to the quarterly reports, or whatever measure employed, the officers felt they were not properly understood.

> One officer was good with clients but was not a good paper pusher, so they thought that he was not a good officer. He held them accountable and they changed but they wanted it down in writing so they could critique it (Respondent 36).

The department had two officers who never saw their clients. "We do not hold ourselves accountable but we hold other people accountable. There are people here who don't spend two minutes with the clients" (Respondent 27). Unit supervisors rarely accompanied officers on a field visit or observed an officer during office visits.

County budgetary constraints have limited the use of overtime, which has meant inadequate intensive supervision of those likely to commit crimes at times other than during regular hours. These officers felt that evenings, weekends, and holidays were the times to make calls. If the officer wanted to make a home call at that time, the reimbursement was limited to compensatory time or it was not given at all.

The flat organizational structure also caused concerns about the system of promotions and changes in job titles. There was no promotion structure or reward system for officers who possessed expertise but did not want to be a supervisor. Many qualified officers chose not to become supervisors, if only because the supervisors never had the chance to leave the office.

> The recognition that one got was a significant part of the job. They don't pay you enough and the recognition that you get is a crucial part of the response that we have professionally. I don't expect accolades. I don't want to get my picture in the paper. We need the exposure and people don't care. The only time that people are interested in probation is when someone recidivates. No one realizes that there are some positive assessments and successes (Respondent 33).

These findings indicate that there are a number of important concerns and issues for which the officers feel change is necessary.

ANALYSIS

An examination of the problems outlined by these officers indicates that the department has a serious problem with increasing workloads and fiscal constraints while operating in a very dynamic environment.

Caseloads

The facts that budgets are down, caseloads are up, and the probation officers are unhappy have important implications for probation departments. Parsonage and Miller (1990) and Sieh (1990) have argued that the perception of danger was increasing among probation officers because they were not only supervising first offenders, but often had individuals with extensive criminal histories who were young, mentally unstable, substance abusers, and homeless (Respondents 8, 13, 23, 37). Though these clients might not complete any treatment programs, they refuse to be ignored, draw attention to themselves, and eventually end up putting further demands on the criminal justice system. Some of these people had participated in the intensive supervision program.

> A lot of ISP [Intensive Supervision Unit] clients are on probation for the sale of drugs and a lot of them are on for weapons, assaults, and robberies. The program was initially designed for the nonviolent offender...We now have people

in this program for manslaughter, rape, robbery, and weapons (Respondent 33).

The individual on probation is more violent and dangerous than in the past. I think that we are stepping into law enforcement without as much training as we should. We are doing things as they come along and we wonder if we did the right thing (Respondent 31).

The clients who begin serving probation in the ISP unit eventually graduate to regular adult supervision. One must assume that for many of these graduates, their problems have diminished but have not ceased. A high caseload means these clients will not get the attention they received while in the ISP unit, nor will they get follow-up on the referrals made for them.

With an average of 12 years in the department and several other years in other social agencies, these officers are experienced in some of the harsher aspects of life, particularly if they have worked in child protection services as many of them have. These officers are not naive social reformers, but social realists who understand that the job is changing. They have seen the changes that resulted from the social reform era of the 1960s, the abundance and demise of the Law Enforcement Assistance Administration (LEAA) in the 1970s, and the retrenchment of social service programs in the 1980s.

With the demise of many social programs, particularly those that employed their clients, the officer is required to encourage the client to find employment. This is particularly difficult when the client is unskilled and the pay is minimum wage. The officers realize the client can make more money selling drugs or may be so mentally disturbed that the officer can only hope the client will not end up in jail at the end of the day.

When the officers' work becomes overwhelming there is a tendency to downplay referrals and assume a control posture. The officers have not forsaken their training and desire to provide assistance to the client, but they realize that the most important function they perform is meeting the conditions of probation—a concrete indicator of the client's performance. These are minimum expectations with client casework only given lip service. The resulting tendency is to replace what began as a real occupational and social building process with "form reporting," often at monthly intervals (Jenkins, Heidemann & Caputo, 1985:103).

Many officers are happy to see a greater emphasis given to behavior control and are not motivated by the casework ideology. Many of them have law enforcement training and are qualified to carry guns and handcuffs. They are outspoken and unabashed in their interest in controlling behavior and are not afraid to argue that the client and society would be better served with the client in jail. This attitude is expressed publicly and in their offices where target silhouettes prominently hang on the wall or with the gun and handcuffs conspicuously hanging from their waist. The traditional social component of probation is unraveling and those officers who were trained on the proper casework approach for offenders' problems, are now able to express their long-repressed feelings about the desire to punish the criminal. These control-oriented officers now find, at least for the moment, their sense of frustration diminished while those still oriented to the casework model are experiencing more stress, frustration, and anomie.

The public welfare system emphasizes client accountability to reduce welfare fraud, and the police department emphasizes community relations under the rubric of "community policing." The probation department attempts to precariously balance these approaches by seeking to protect the community as well as to provide assistance to the client. At the heart of all three agencies is the problem of social control and how best to provide control while providing assistance.

Consequences of Decrementalism

The budgetary problems can be understood by considering the history of the nation's fiscal crisis, the dynamic nature of the environment, and the consequences of decrementalism—the breaking down rather than building up of institutional structures.

The fiscal history in this county indicates that the problems involving cutbacks have been in existence for the last 15 years. Like many other counties and cities, large sums of state and federal monies were channeled into jobs programs. Simultaneously, taxes were raised and government capital spending outpaced private capital expenditures in the inner city. Some cities experienced renewed growth brought on by tax incentive programs designed to bring private capital investment back into the community. Initially this process worked but lately the growth has lost its momentum. Large private real estate holdings have remained unoccupied and tax revenues have subsequently fallen. These communities continue to experience problems with the development of capitalism in their older urban centers.

To a certain extent these problems are a function of having been spoiled by the munificence of the Law Enforcement Assistance Administration. During the days of the LEAA the department had many more officers and a very active juvenile intake unit. Like many other cities, the response to budgetary cuts in this jurisdiction has been to maintain the prevailing levels of employment and budget totals in lieu of changing the program mix and priorities (Wolman & Davis, 1980:233). Officers now believe that most of the problems in the department are attributable to the shortage of funds and are not likely to ever change. This notion has resulted in a mind-set that certain things are not achievable or are too risky. The job is viewed as impossible under these conditions and consequently some officers view the job as a sinecure until retirement. Other officers are becoming frustrated with the conditions and would like to see substantive change initiated and completed.

Thus, the probation department has experienced decrementalism that not only affects officer morale, but may be jeopardizing the department's ability to provide basic probation services. There are various consequences to decrementalism which include: human resource erosion and the resulting decline in commitment, performance, and responsiveness; overcentralization and the resulting stifling of innovations and initiative; allocation shifts where power switches to the supervising officers away from unit supervisors and administrators; and lastly, decisional paralysis where policymakers are unable to make the difficult decisions and deny there is a crisis requiring substantive change (Levine, 1985:692).

Many of these consequences are evident in the department. While most of the interviewed officers claimed a commitment to their work, it is unclear how long they will sustain their effort in the face of continued job pressures. It is also likely that their definition of "good work" has changed, they have simply set their sights lower, and feel "good" when they can achieve modest gains. The department is certainly over-centralized, with only a deputy-director and director holding true administrative responsibility. Some other roles have taken on more responsibility, but bureaucratic authority is clearly in the hands of only a few people. The real power, however, is not held by the administrative staff but by the officers who work with clients.

Some officers would like to see greater accountability. Currently officers work independently and accountability is minimal as long as an officer provides timely reports. Finally, it appears as though the department has reached "decisional paralysis." Several statements indicated that difficult decisions were not being made and there was too little communication.

These problems tend to cluster together, threatening to produce a condition called "general service default," that occurs when the government is no longer capable of providing services that either augment or protect the quality of life in the community (Levine, 1985:692). The department appears to be at the point at which additional cuts will mean more than a proportional decline in services. Furthermore, the department is approaching the point at which even restored funding in the future might be ineffective in compensating for past losses.

If an agency is no longer seen as competent and valued by the workers, the potential for alienation exists. Through application of Seeman's (1959) sociopsychological concept of alienation, it is possible to argue the officers feel powerless to determine the occurrence of client successes. The officers realize, particularly with mandatory treatment cases, that aside from making the initial referral they are unable to influence the quality of treatment the clients receive. No data are collected on the clients' social adjustment and no evaluations are done in the department except for the special programs.

Furthermore, the work becomes meaningless when the officers are unable to understand the events that affect the future of the department particularly with the impending layoffs and budget cuts.

Normlessness occurs, accompanied by a sense of despair and apathy, when a standard of behavior for the officers' work is missing. Examples of this are found in the effort put into completing quarterly reports and inventories but ultimately nothing seems to come of them. The officers discern isolation from the outside world, which results in the development of a siege mentality, much like that already observed among police (See National Advisory Commission on Criminal Justice Standards and Goals, 1973). The officer feels that nobody understands his/her work, particularly because few members of the public seem to know the difference between probation and parole. Finally, self-estrangement sets in when an officer fulfills a role that is something less than what the officer would ideally like it to be. It is believed that these officers would like to provide a maximum level of assistance and control of the client.

> The purpose of describing these consequences of decremental adjustment to long-term fiscal stress is to underscore the point that short-sighted responses eventually produce departments that are not only smaller and cheaper but also weaker and less vital and, as a consequence, less able to cope with problems of crime and public order (Levine, 1985:692).

Recommendations

This section summarizes the officers' recommendations for responding to the department's problems. Most would like to see a more politically involved, aggressive leadership, better communication (particularly during crises), more mid-level managers willing to respond to problems, and a mentoring system. Some officers want to eliminate city boundaries or have caseloads rotated among a team of officers. They recommended an expansion of: intensive supervision, house arrest, equipment, staff, programs, and finally, community involvement.

Reforms that were not considered by these officers included the use of paraprofessionals to write presentence reports and volunteer probation officers to supervise the cases. When these strategies were proposed to the officers they were quickly dismissed. They gave the impression that the use of volunteers was another method for the administration to subvert their contract bargaining position, reduce their professional status in the community, and minimize their chances of getting out of the office at all, a highly valued job perquisite.

Other possible proposals not mentioned by these officers include streamlining the PSI, revising the classification system, banking probationary sentences, expanding diversion, making greater use of early termination, and furthering the development of specialized caseloads. In addition to neighborhood crime watch groups there might be neighborhood supervision of probationers. This will require a level of community organization most communities have not yet attained.

Substantive Change

Despite the officers' sincere beliefs in reforms, fundamental change seems unlikely. The current state of probation necessitates considering constant change in the environment. Nonequilibrium theory (Kiel, 1989) presents a view of public administration in which the processes of change in a modern organization produce fluctuations among many subsystems. This produces an array of qualitative changes throughout the entire criminal justice system. The seemingly unstable nature of open societies appears to provide the potential for novel forms of organization and complexity so indicative of modern democracies (Kiel, 1989:547).

Most importantly, nonequilibrium theory suggests that management should focus less on structural arrangements and more on organizational and administrative processes (Kiel, 1989:548). During cutbacks, instead of moving toward dramatic innovations that will permit the organization to anticipate and deal with future changes, there is a tendency to diminish both employee creativity and the willingness to accept change (Levine, 1979). Resource cutbacks may be seen to decline to a lower level of activity and complexity, in which destabilizing fluctuations are suppressed by stronger stabilizing forces (Kiel, 1989:549).

The response to any of these cutbacks can take a variety of forms. Departments are refocusing on statutory mandates where they can be enforced, on doing what the department does best, or where there is outside pressure to do the work, i.e. investigations. Some departments are expanding into areas where there is money, such as in programs for the developmentally disabled client or intensive supervision. Enterprising administrators are also emphasizing the punitive and law enforcement aspects of probation in an effort to re-establish judicial and public faith in probation (Baird, 1983). While there might be serious disagreements in a department about its goals, there is the general belief that if any department wants sufficient funding it merely needs to reorder its priorities and focus more attention on risk and control reduction (Cochran, 1989:17).

Some managers focus on building public constituencies and political support. Following the lead of most police agencies, the probation officers' association in the department studied has taken this initiative in an effort to establish a political base of support. The association has permitted officers to lobby for pay raises by emphasizing the law enforcement functions they perform and has also forced the administration to address some issues directly.

CONCLUSION

While this is a limited case study of one department, decrementalism, with its associated consequences, is likely to occur in many counties and states experiencing recurring budgetary problems. This condition should alert us to the potential hazards facing the community corrections movement. The movement's goals are ambiguous, and therefore achievements are difficult to measure (Clear, 1985:34). At the same time that public revenues are shrinking (or at least not growing), we are witnessing a shift in public opinion seeking harsher penalties for convicted offenders. In this setting, probation agencies have difficulties establishing a clear need for the function they perform and proving that they perform them well (Harlow & Nelson, 1982:1-2).

Probation departments have treated their problems as though they were the outcome of a money shortage, the influx of unwanted and multi-dysfunctional clients, or a lack of community support. Until recently, probation has not followed the lead of the police by emphasizing the risks of probation work and the control functions they perform. Moreover, seldom has a probation department gone public with its problems and sought public support. For years probation has been apologetic for the casework approach and the failures of the rehabilitation model. Moreover, probation is structured to follow the lead of community leaders and assume the mantle of protection provided by their offices. This means that the top administrator, for political reasons, can act as gatekeeper in releasing desired information about the department. The officers' and the judges' or executives' perceptions of the department may not coincide and may sometimes conflict.

Various reforms could lead to a more predictable organizational future. Organizational development as conceptualized by Bennis (1969) and as proposed for probation by Cochran (1982) would include planned organization-wide change incorporating the ideas of officers at all levels from all units within the organization. For any department experiencing the effects of decrementalism, establishing a broadly based task force set up within the department under the leadership of a member of the top administration would be a good start.

Drawing on the Likerts' (1976) work, Cochran (1982:117) argues that conflict that is dealt with on a win-lose basis will turn to destruction because victory brings feelings of elation to the winner, but defeat brings feelings of rejection, failure, and bitterness. Based on this premise, representatives from the court, the prosecutor's office, and the public defender's office (both juvenile and adult), should be included. This might counteract those who feel that public service workers suffer from indifference to their work and are only concerned with their salary, benefits, work schedule, working conditions, and job security. None of these goals are necessarily supportive of the desire to increase their overall agency productivity or personal performance (Fosler, 1980:287).

The objective of a task force should be to develop a strategic management plan. This requires a department to engage in both short-term and long-term planning and evaluation and to consider a wide array of possible options for providing probation services. The emphasis, however, is for options that are likely to provide services and still save money.

The task force has the responsibility of facilitating the establishment of various functions within the department. According to Levine (1985) these should include:

— forecasting and planning capacity

— decision-making authority

— a management philosophy to define the department's future

— rapid and accurate feedback

— budgetary flexibility

— performance incentives

— the ability to identify core services

— ability to target resources to high-priority programs and to cut low-priority programs

— ability to link service and expenditure decisions to economic development strategies

The problems of any probation department are neither temporary nor simply a reflection of its leadership. Solutions require a concerted effort on the part of the entire staff. As an incentive for the efforts, funding from grants can provide the necessary support to give some officers the needed time to make meaningful contributions to the project.

> The heads of most government agencies have learned over time that there is relatively little reward, aside from personal satisfaction, in doing things exceedingly well or showing imagination or initiative to improve programs.... In short, there is little incentive for improvement, but a great price to be paid for failure...Innovative managers are bound to make mistakes, suffer failures, and tread on toes, and consequently they are vulnerable to criticism and likely to accumulate political enemies. (Fosler, 1980:287)

REFERENCES

Adams, S. (1975). *Evaluation Research in Corrections.* Washington, DC: U.S. Government Printing Office.

Allen, H.E., C.W. Eskridge, E.J. Latessa & G.F. Vito (1985). *Probation and Parole in America.* New York, NY: The Free Press.

American Correctional Association (1977). *Manual of Standards for Adult Probation and Parole Field Services.* Rockville, MD: author.

Baird, C. (1983). *Report on Intensive Supervision Programs in Probation and Parole.* Washington, DC: National Institute of Corrections.

Bennis, W.G. (1969). *Organizational Development: Its Nature, Origins and Prospects.* Reading, MA: Addison-Wesley.

Clear, T. (1985). "Managerial Issues in Community Corrections." In L. Travis (ed.) *Probation, Parole, and Community Corrections,* pp. 33-46. Prospect Heights, IL: Waveland Press.

Cochran, D. (1982). "Issues in Organizational Development and Management of Probation in the 1980s." In G. Stephens (ed.) *The Future of Criminal Justice,* pp. 102-121. Cincinnati, OH: Anderson Publishing Co.

_____ (1989). "Correction's Catch 22—Can Probation Keep up its Reputation?" *Corrections Today,* 51(October):16-18.

Colley, L.L., R.G. Culbertson & E. Latessa (1986). "Probation Officers Job Analysis: Rural-Urban Differences." *Federal Probation,* 50(December):67-71.

Directors Report (1989). [Annual Reports 1984-1989: Probation Departments Case Summary Data]. Unpublished data.

Fosler, R.S. (1980). "Local Government Productivity: Political and Administrative Potential." In C.H. Levine & I. Rubin (eds.) *Fiscal Stress and Public Policy,* pp. 281-301. Beverly Hills, CA: Sage Publications.

Harlow, N. & E.K. Nelson (1982). *Management Strategies for Probation in an Era of Limits.* (Grant No. #CO-1). Washington, DC: National Institute of Corrections.

_____ (1990). "Probation's Response to Fiscal Crisis." In D.E. Duffee & E.F. McGarrell (eds.) *Community Corrections: A Community Field Approach,* pp. 165-183. Cincinnati, OH: Anderson Publishing Co.

Jenkins, R.L., P.H. Heidemann & J.A. Caputo (1985). *No Single Cause: Juvenile Delinquency and the Search for an Effective Treatment.* College Park, MD: American Correctional Association.

Kiel, L.D. (1989). "Nonequilibrium Theory and its Implications for Public Administration." *Public Administration Review,* 49(November/December):544-551.

Kline, S. (1989). *Bulletin: Probation and Parole 1988.* Washington, DC: Bureau of Justice Statistics.

Lauen, R.J. (1988). *Community-Managed Corrections.* College Park, MD: American Correctional Association.

Levine, C.H. (1979). "More on Cutback Management: Hard Questions for Hard Times." *Public Administration Review,* 39(March/April):316-325.

_____ (1984). "Retrenchment, Human Resource Erosion, and the Role of the Personnel Manager." *Public Personnel Management,* 13(Fall):249-263.

_____ (1985). "Police Management in the 1980s: From Decrementalism to Strategic Thinking." *Public Administration Review,* 45(November),691-699.

Likert, R. & J.G. Likert (1976). *New Ways of Managing Conflict.* New York, NY: McGraw-Hill.

McCarthy, B.R. & B.J. McCarthy (1991). *Community-Based Corrections,* Second Edition. Pacific Grove, CA: Brooks/Cole.

McCleary, R. (1978). *Dangerous Men: The Sociology of Parole.* Beverly Hills, CA: Sage Publications.

National Advisory Commission on Criminal Justice Standards and Goals (1973). *Community Crime Prevention.* Washington, DC: U.S. Government Printing Office.

O'Leary, V. (1987). "Probation: A System in Change." *Federal Probation,* 51(December):8-11.

Parsonage, W.H. & J.A. Miller (1990). *A Study of Probation and Parole Worker Safety in the Middle Atlantic Region.* (TA no. 98CO1GHF7). Washington, DC: National Institute of Corrections.

Petersilia, J., S. Turner, J. Kahan & J. Peterson (1985). *Granting Felons Probation: Public Risk and Alternatives.* (R-3186-NIJ) Santa Monica, CA: The RAND Corporation.

Seeman, M. (1959). "On the Meaning of Alienation." *American Sociological Review,* 24(December):783-791.

Sieh, E.W. (1990). "Probation Officers Perception of Danger: The Role of the Symbolic Assailant." Paper presented at the annual meeting of the American Society of Criminology, Baltimore, Maryland, November.

U.S. Department of Labor (1972). *Handbook for Analyzing Jobs.* Washington, DC: U.S. Government Printing Office.

Wolman, H. & B. Davis (1980). "Local Government Strategies to Cope with Fiscal Pressure." In C.H. Levine & I. Rubin (eds.) Fiscal Stress and Public Policy, pp. 231-248. Beverly Hills, CA: Sage Publications.

9

Control and the Use of Technology in Community Supervision

John T. Whitehead
East Tennessee State University

INTRODUCTION

Innovations are sweeping community corrections. Today's probation officer may be working in intensive supervision, house arrest, or electronic monitoring programs instead of traditional probation programs. The contemporary community corrections worker may be conducting curfew checks or collecting urine samples, whereas yesterday's officer was leading group counseling sessions or referring a troubled probationer to a community counseling agency. Today's officer possibly thinks of the job of community corrections as a job of surveillance whereas yesterday's officer often saw the job as one of service (Studt, 1973).

This chapter will examine contemporary changes in community corrections. It will describe such innovations as intensive supervision, house arrest, and electronic monitoring, attempt to gauge the extent of these practices, and place these developments in historical perspective. The chapter will then analyze some of the issues surrounding these practices, including the philosophy of the new programs, their effectiveness, their costs, their impact on personnel and on offenders, and the ethical implications of the innovative practices.

DESCRIPTIONS AND DIMENSIONS

Intensive supervision, house arrest, and electronic monitoring are best conceptualized as part of an array of intermediate sanctions or punishments lying between the extreme sanctions of prison and probation (Morris & Tonry, 1990).

Intensive supervision has been described as "one of the most popular and widely administered intermediate sanctions of the 1980s" (Lurigio, 1990:3). Operationally, intensive supervision involves reduced caseloads, greater contact between officers and offenders, curfews enforced by frequent home visits, a requirement that offenders be employed or perform community service, and drug testing (urinalysis). Recent statistics indicate that slightly more than 100,000 offenders are under intensive supervision (Byrne, 1990).

House arrest or home confinement can be conceptualized as one step up from intensive supervision in terms of the severity of the punishment (see, for example, Byrne, 1990). It can be described as a sentence of incarceration to one's residence rather than to a penal facility. Generally, the offender is under court order to remain at his or her residence except for a limited number of activities such as employment, community service obligations, and medical necessity. Approximately 10,000 were placed on house arrest in the late 1980s (Byrne, 1990).

In practice, distinctions between intensive supervision and house arrest become blurred. For example, an intensive supervision program in Alabama begun in the mid-1980s involved reduced caseloads, an employment or community service requirement, a curfew from 10:00 p.m. to 6:00 a.m., a supervision fee, and restitution (Smith, 1984). A Florida program labeled a house arrest program (Morris & Tonry, 1990) entails almost the exact same conditions.

Electric monitoring is best described as a practice of tracking the whereabouts of offenders by technological devices.[1] Rather than a sanction, it is a means of enforcing the curfew component of intensive supervision or the more stringent restrictions of house arrest. The latest report, the 1989 National Institute of Justice survey (Renzema & Skelton, 1990), indicates that the estimated daily monitored population in the United States has grown to 6,490 offenders for programs in 37 states, the District of Columbia, and Puerto Rico. About one-third of the offenders were under electronic monitoring for property offenses, 22 percent for drug offenses, another one-fifth for major traffic offenses, and approximately 12 percent for crimes against the person; the mean age of the offenders was 29.1 years and most (about 90%) were males.

For the purposes of this chapter, intensive supervision, house arrest, and electronic monitoring are considered together as related intermediate sanctions and strategies associated with intermediate sanctions. A complete list of intermediate sanctions would include fines, restitution, day fines, shock incarceration, and so on (see Morris & Tonry, 1990 for a thorough discussion of the entire range of intermediate sanctions). This chapter will focus on intensive supervision, house arrest, and electronic monitoring because they are a more severe set of sanctions than regular probation, yet not involving removal from one's residence.

HISTORICAL PERSPECTIVE

Two points are critical to place recent developments in community corrections in perspective. First, the recent developments are part of broader changes in corrections and criminal justice. Second, the innovations are *not* as innovative as they may appear to be.

As several chapters in this book report, corrections and criminal justice have been undergoing dramatic changes in the last 20 years. Very concretely, prison populations have risen dramatically (see Greenfeld, 1990). This alone has forced corrections officials to build new prisons and to devise other ways to cope with burgeoning numbers of prisoners, probationers, and parolees. More abstractly, the philosophy of corrections and criminal justice has changed from an emphasis on rehabilitation to an emphasis on retribution, deterrence, and incapacitation.

To simplify but still strive for accuracy, corrections has moved from a high concern for the offender to a concern with punishment and accountability: what Gordon (1990) has characterized as a get-tough policy. Along with this change in objectives, views of the offender have changed from a positivistic perspective to a neoclassical perspective (see, for example, Wilson, 1985); that is, the offender has been transformed from the pawn of sociological and economic forces to a free agent who is accountable and blameworthy. These historical changes have paved the way for the current emphasis on such tough interventions as intensive supervision, house arrest, and electronic monitoring; the new intervention strategies are the programmatic embodiment of those conceptual changes.

That intensive supervision, house arrest, and even electronic monitoring are not as innovative as they might appear is readily apparent to anyone familiar with the history of corrections, especially the history of corrections since the 1950s. These so-called innovations have historical precursors that show them to be recent refinements rather than radical reformations. Consider intensive supervision, for example. In the 1960s, California conducted a series of experiments with reduced adult supervision caseloads and with reduced juvenile caseloads in the belief that intensive supervision would be a more effective intervention than regular supervision. Unfortunately, that belief proved to be overly optimistic. At best, intensive supervision strategies showed mixed results in reducing recidivism (Carter & Wilkins, 1976).

The "new" intensive strategies resemble the old in that a key element is a reliance on reduced caseloads. Individual officers or teams of officers supervise perhaps 25 offenders. The contemporary strategies differ from older versions in that the philosophy is not rehabilitative but punitive-incapacitative with such contemporary developments as electronic monitoring that are used to keep track of offender whereabouts. It is intriguing that in actual practice the new and old forms of intensive supervision are not as different as they first appear. In-depth analysis of the California Community Treatment Project, for example, has shown that the program was punitive and incapacitative in its implementation. Although the program was inaugurated as a rehabilitative effort in which youths were supposed to be matched with appropriate parole officers, in actual practice 80 percent of the program youths were detained at least once, the average number of detentions was 2.8, and detained youths were kept in detention for an average of 20 days per detention (Lundman, 1984). Thus, a closer look at that intensive supervision experiment reveals that it was not implemented as intended and was punitive in practice. Clearly, today's so-called innovations are only innovative to the degree that one is unaware of history.

PHILOSOPHY OF SANCTIONS

A fundamental issue in the new intensive supervision movement is the philosophical question of what goals intensive supervision is trying to achieve. The simplistic answer to this question is that intensive supervision can satisfy all of the traditional goals of the criminal justice system: deterrence, retribution, incapacitation, rehabilitation, and others. In other words, arguments have been offered that intensive supervision is tough enough to be both deterrent and punitive, intrusive enough to be incapacitative, and dramatic enough to cause offender change (for a discussion of rationales, see Harland & Rosen, 1987). The problem with this answer is that such multiple goals create confusion and conflict. When the criminal justice system in general, or intensive supervision in particular, tries to be all things to all people, chaos results.

A more reasoned answer to the question is that intensive supervision is more limited in its aims. Specifically, Harland and Rosen (1987) contend that the major goal of intensive supervision is:

> To minimize risk during the supervision period, that probationers will reoffend or breach other conditions of their release, by restricting their opportunity and propensity to do so, via primarily the incapacitative and specific deterrent means of intensive regulation and monitoring of their

> whereabouts and conduct, and the corresponding increased
> threat of detection and strict enforcement of consequences
> in event of violation (1987:34).

In other words, Harland and Rosen argue that intensive supervision (and, by extension, house arrest) serves just two goals: incapacitation and specific deterrence. There is so much surveillance of the offender that there is little or no opportunity for the freedom of movement necessary to commit crime and the supervision generates enough fear of detection that the offender will refrain from crime.

Others argue that punishment can indeed be a goal of such programs as intensive supervision, house arrest, and electronic monitoring. Von Hirsch, for example, feels that these programs can be part of a sentencing structure that seeks proportionality and desert provided that the "degree of severity [of the community-based sanction] should reflect the degree of blameworthiness of the criminal conduct" (1990:163). He is concerned, however, that many offenders in such programs did not commit offenses serious enough to make the sanction a proportionate one. What often happens instead is that intensive supervision programs tend to be applied to offenders convicted of the least serious felonies because program organizers feel that such persons would be more likely to "cooperate" (von Hirsch, 1990:164).

Morris and Tonry (1990) also contend that intensive supervision, house arrest, and electronic monitoring can be part of a well-organized system of intermediate punishments lying between the extremes of prison and probation. A critical element of their perspective is their choice of the adjective "inter-mediate" rather than "alternative." Many have described such sanctions as alternatives to prison and thereby emphasized that the sanctions are by defini-tion intended to divert offenders from prison. Morris and Tonry (1990) con-tend that the new sanctions are not only for some offenders who would otherwise be incarcerated but are also appropriate for some offenders who would otherwise be placed on ordinary probation. In other words, their pri-mary focus is not diversion and cost savings but establishing a rational system of sanctions ranging from less to more severe. A consequence of their defini-tion is that studies showing questionable diversionary and cost savings impact (see below) do not radically undercut their call to implement the sanc-tions because the primary objective is a reasoned set of punishments rather than a quick fix to deal with spiraling prison populations and costs.

A partial resolution to the goal question is that intensive supervision pro-grams can take one of three primary goals: (1) the provision of crime control through incapacitation in a community setting, (2) punishment or just deserts, or (3) recidivism reduction by means of deterrence and rehabilitation (Byrne, 1990). Which goal is chosen will affect to a considerable degree how the pro-gram will operate.

An interesting related issue is that intended goals may be obscured while unintended goals take their place. Ball, Huff, and Lilly (1988) note, for example, that their original hope was that house arrest would be used to achieve reconciliation between the offender and the community. Consequently, they advocated the widespread use of volunteers to monitor house arrestees. They argued that because the offender would be involved with representatives of the local community rather than with government officials, it was hoped that the use of volunteers would contribute to the increased involvement of the public in the systems of criminal and juvenile justice (Ball et al., 1988:146). Experience, however, has shown that "those operating the criminal and juvenile justice systems may be more interested in maintaining tight, bureaucratic control over offenders than in opening supervision programs to the public" (Ball et al., 1988:146).

EVALUATION RESULTS

A second basic issue is the effectiveness of intensive supervision, house arrest, and electronic monitoring. Once the goals have been agreed upon, are the programs achieving those goals?

Despite the debate and confusion over progam goals mentioned above, when it comes to considering the effectiveness of the new programs, commentators agree that at least three concerns are crucial. One is the impact of the programs on recidivism: apart from any solution of the debate on program goals, are the programs having any effects on how many crimes offenders commit while they are under supervision and after the period of supervision? A second concern is cost-effectiveness: How much do the programs cost? Related to the cost-concern issue is the issue of diversion: If the programs are intended to divert offenders from prison, are they achieving that objective or are they simply widening the net and taking offenders from the ranks of regular probation?

Concerning first the question of recidivism, studies in Georgia and New Jersey have been optimistic. An evaluation of intensive supervision in Georgia found that only 40 percent of the intensives were rearrested during an 18-month follow-up, compared to 36 percent of the regular probationers and 58 percent of the incarceration sample (Erwin, 1987). An evaluation of the New Jersey intensive supervision program found that 12 percent of the intensives studied had an arrest that led to a conviction at the end of two years compared to a matched comparison group that served their ordinary prison term and then were paroled (Pearson & Harper, 1990). Thus, the assessment from New Jersey indicates that such programs are "clearly able to hold recidivism rates down to reasonable levels" (Pearson & Harper, 1990:79).

Probably the best-designed study to date has been the RAND Corporation study of three intensive supervision experiments in California, one of which included the use of electronic monitoring. Each of the counties involved in the study randomly assigned high-risk offenders to either intensive supervision or regular probation. After one year, Petersilia and Turner found that approximately 25 percent of the ISP offenders in each site had no new technical violations or new arrests, about 40 percent had technical violations only, and about one-third had new arrests. Furthermore, there were no significant differences in the severity of the offenses committed by experimental and control offenders who were arrested. Thus, the RAND results "suggest that ISP programs, as implemented in this study, are not effective for high-risk offenders *if effectiveness is judged solely by offender recidivism rates* (emphasis in original) (Petersilia & Turner, 1990:9).

Given the concern and demand for increased incapacitation and punitiveness, an ironical finding of the RAND study, however, is the authors' claim for the importance of a substantive treatment component in addition to mere surveillance. Petersilia and Turner found that "[A]t all three of the California study sites, offenders who received counseling, were employed, paid restitution, and did community service were shown to have less recidivism" (1990:10). This finding of the impact of treatment was also found in the Massachusetts intensive supervision program (Byrne, Lurigio & Baird, 1989).

The issue of the costs of the new programs has not been resolved. Superficial analyses suggest dramatic savings. Taking the number of offenders supervised in one of the new programs as *prima facie* evidence of the number of offenders diverted from prison, some analysts then simplistically compare the costs of keeping one offender in prison with the costs of supervising one offender in one of the new community supervision programs. The result is a claim for dramatic cost savings.

There are several problems, however, with such simplistic analysis. First, there is controversy as to whether such programs do actually divert would-be inmates from incarceration or instead capture would-be regular probationers into a more restrictive form of community supervision. Detailed analyses of intensive supervision programs in Florida, Georgia, and New Jersey, for example, have indicated that diversion occurred (Baird & Wagner, 1990; Erwin, 1987; Pearson & Harper, 1990). Critics, however, have questioned these claims (Byrne, 1990; Byrne et al., 1989; Tonry, 1990) and have asserted that many of the new programs have become more punitive options for offenders whom judges would normally *not* incarcerate. Judges continue to send similar or increased numbers of offenders to prison and begin to place persons they would normally place on regular probation into the new so-called "intensive" programs. In short, net-widening occurs.

Perhaps the best resolution of the controversy is a tentative conclusion that the programs divert some percentage of the offenders they supervise away from prison. For example, sophisticated analyses of the precise levels of diversionary impact in Florida and Georgia indicated that slightly more than half of the offenders in those programs were indeed diverted from incarceration (Baird & Wagner, 1990; Erwin, 1987).

Additionally, it is interesting to note that the one program that used a research design capable of a clear demonstration of whether diversion was taking place—the previously mentioned RAND Corporation study—did not even claim to be diverting offenders away from prison. California's intensive supervision programs, in other words, have utilized an experimental design with random assignment of offenders. The programs, however, are actually probation enhancement programs. Rather than attempt to divert offenders from prison, the California officials have "selected persons currently on probation whom they judged in need of more intensive supervision—participants were either high risk when granted probation or were showing signs of failing and potential revocation" (Petersilia & Turner, 1990:95). Ironically, this decision to divert from probation rather than from prison resulted in California's programs having accepted offenders at higher risk levels than Georgia's intensive program, which was supposed to be diverting people from prison (Petersilia & Turner, 1990).

A second difficulty with some of the claims of cost savings is that they often fail to include the costs of crimes committed by program participants during the supervision period. If an offender on intensive supervision or house arrest commits a crime during the supervision period, that offense involves costs to the victim(s) and processing costs for the criminal justice system. The recent RAND study of intensive supervision in three California counties included such costs in the evaluation and thus estimates of the actual costs of the new programs were considerably higher than cost estimates in previous studies that did not include those costs (Petersilia & Turner, 1990). Taking an extreme position, Tonry (1990) argues that the real comparison is between the number of crimes committed by offenders placed into such programs as intensive supervision, house arrest, and electronic monitoring *versus* the number of crimes that would have been committed if those same offenders would have been incarcerated. Because the latter figure is zero by definition, "all ISP [and like] programs that divert offenders from prison should increase crime victimization (Tonry, 1990:183).[2]

A third problem with simplistic cost analyses is that they fail to note that minimal decreases in prison populations are not enough to cause any prison closings. If a correctional system only places a small number of offenders into any new community program, the same number of prisons may still be needed. More importantly, many of the costs of operating a prison remain the same whether that prison has 500 inmates or 600 inmates. Heating, cooling, lighting, and maintenance costs and custody staffing may not vary with a difference of only 100 prisoners. Thus it may be erroneous to take a daily operating cost and calculate savings if no computation is made of the number of saved prison beds needed to generate cost savings across the board. As Tonry has observed:

> The reality is that one more prisoner costs the state only marginal costs—a bit of food, some disposable supplies, some record-keeping. Only when the numbers of people diverted from prison by a new program permit the closing of all or a major part of an institution or the cancellation of construction plans will there be substantial savings (1990:180).

In summary, to date, the evaluation research has been as expected: mixed. To put this conclusion more precisely but also more negatively, Byrne et al. contend that research to date has *not* provided the answers to these three critical questions:

1. How do we develop decision-making mechanisms that will result in true diversion rather than net-widening?
2. How do we provide the kind of community control that has both a short-term and long-term impact on offenders' behavior?
3. How do we develop cost-effective intermediate sanctions without jeopardizing public safety? (1989:39-40).

In Tonry's judgment, the research indicates that intensive supervision "fails to achieve its stated goals of diversion from prison, cost savings, and crime prevention" (Tonry, 1990:187). Previous experience with intensive supervision in particular and with correctional innovations in general suggests that future research will continue to show mixed results.

ETHICAL ISSUES

In a thought-provoking piece, von Hirsch (1990) notes several ethical concerns with new practices in community corrections. A basic concern is that any such innovations not insult or demean offenders but satisfy the standard of acceptable penal content:

> Acceptable penal content, then, is the idea that a sanction should be devised so that its intended penal deprivations are those that can be administered in a manner that is clearly consistent with the offender's dignity. If the penal deprivation includes a given imposition, X, then one must ask whether that can be undergone by offenders in a rea-

sonably self-possessed fashion. Unless one is confident that it can, it should not be a part of the sanction (von Hirsch, 1990:167).

Thus, von Hirsch is opposed to bumper stickers that advertise the drunk driver's offense because there "is no way a person can, with dignity, go about in public with a sign admitting himself or herself to be a moral pariah" (1990:168). Also, he approves of home visits:

only as a mechanism to help enforce another sanction that does meet our suggested standard of acceptable penal content...It is not plausible to assert that, without any other need for it, the punishment for a given type of crime should be that state agents will periodically snoop into one's home (von Hirsch, 1990:169).

A related concern is that both punitive and risk-control conditions of intensive supervision "are applied across-the-board without much attention to the individual circumstances of the case" (Clear & Hardyman, 1990:54). Every intensive offender, for example, may be subject to urinalysis checks for drug use even though many have never shown any indication of drug use. This can create a problem of discovering that an offender is adjusting positively on supervision except for recreational marijuana use.

The dilemma is how to react to the drug violation. A violation and incarceration would be an ironic twist to the stated intent of many programs to divert offenders from prison. A likely scenario is that "the probation officer is forced to play a type of game—warning the offender and noting the violation but trying to avoid action unless something else happens in the case" (Clear & Hardyman, 1990:54). Such game-playing is hardly new (see McCleary, 1978, for example) but cannot be avoided in face of the fiscal fact that the "resources simply do not exist to carry out all the threats made in the ISPs..." (Clear & Hardyman, 1990:54).

Another fundamental ethical concern is the contention that electronic monitoring is an insidious invasion of the privacy of the home that is enshrined in the Fourth Amendment. Corbett and Marx argue that electronic monitoring destroys the privacy of the home:

Figuratively, prisons have been dismantled, and each individual cell has been reassembled in private homes. Once homes start to serve as modular prisons and bedrooms as cells, what will become of our cherished notion of "home"? If privacy is obliterated *legally* in prison and if EM [electronic monitoring] provides the functional equivalent of prison at home, privacy rights for home confinees and family members are potentially jeopardized (1991:409).

Another problem with the "new" intensive supervision strategies is that they are not entirely new. As mentioned above, intensive supervision has been tried before, including a rather punitive-incapacitative version. The importance of the fact that intensive supervision has been tried before is that it is important not to slip into another round of the panacea phenomenon (Finckenauer, 1982). The mixed results found in the California Community Treatment Project and also in the California caseload studies suggest that the "new" intensive supervision efforts will also have mixed results. To expect that recent interventions are correctional cure-alls is to invite unnecessary disillusionment.

IMPACT ON WORKERS

A fourth consideration in the development of intensive programs is the impact such programs will have on the line personnel employed in these programs. Several scenarios are foreseeable. One is popular acceptance by workers. Given the greater role clarity in the recent intensive supervision programs compared to the role ambiguity and role conflict frequently found in traditional probation, positive worker attitudes are a distinct possibility.

Another possible scenario, however, is initial euphoria followed by more negative attitudes. Given the expectations of line officers to monitor offenders 24 hours a day, seven days a week, officers may temporarily experience the special aura of an exciting innovation only to sink into a depression occasioned by unrealistic expectations. Who wants to be on call 24 hours a day?

Due to the fiscal constraints on state and local government, it is very possible that officers in intensive supervision programs will be called on to perform such Herculean tasks without the resources for backups and relief. Physicians can join group practice arrangements to find some relief from never-ending demands, but the officers in these new programs will not have that luxury. Too many state and local governments are experiencing financial exigency to be optimistic about the resources that will be allocated to correctional programs.

Another possible reaction of line officers is that officers assigned regular probation caseloads may resent the special status and pay of intensive supervision officers. Regular caseload officers may also develop negative feelings about the reduced caseloads of intensive officers, especially if the regular caseload officers suspect that the intensive caseloads show little or no difference in risk levels compared to the regular probationers (Clear & Hardyman, 1990).

Evaluations of intensive supervision in Georgia, Illinois, and New Jersey have reported positive reactions of line personnel (Tonry, 1990). One partial inquiry into the effects of home confinement on a nonrepresentative sample of federal probation officers showed that the officers did not report widespread negative impacts even though overtime was routine (Beck, Kelin-Saffran &

Wooten, 1990). These findings suggest that negative effects on workers are not a necessary by-product of recent innovations. More research needs to be conducted, however, before firm conclusions are drawn, especially in light of the fact that corrections employment has proven to be conducive to stress and burnout (Whitehead, 1989; Williamson, 1990).

A more specific problem that intermediate punishments may pose for correctional workers is role conflict: "a tension between his control function and his casework function having to be both a policeman and a social worker" (Morris & Tonry, 1990:183). The enforcement of the conditions of intermediate punishments, such as urinalysis checks for drug use, necessarily places the officer in the role of an enforcer because there "is no way in which effective, regular, but unpredictable urine testing...can be made other than as a police-type function" (Morris & Tonry, 1990:185).

One way to resolve this is through team supervision of offenders placed on intermediate punishments. One team member emphasizes the enforcement of the conditions of the sanction and the other provides assistance. Another possible resolution is closer cooperation with local police (Morris & Tonry, 1990). Whatever approach is attempted, however, the basic conflict needs to be addressed.

OFFENDER CONCERNS

Another concern is the reaction of offenders to the programs. Although many assume that offenders would automatically prefer intensive supervision, house arrest, or electronic monitoring to prison, research in Oregon found that one-quarter of the offenders there chose prison over intensive supervision (Petersilia, 1990). Byrne interprets this finding to mean that "some offenders would rather *interrupt* their lifestyle (via incarceration) than deal with attempts to *change* it (via compliance with probation conditions)"(1990:23). Cynics or conservatives may wonder who really cares what offenders think, but probation officers know from experience that the attitude of the offender at the very least affects the quality of the supervision experience for officers.

From another perspective, there is concern that class bias may affect decisions regarding which offenders are selected for these programs. Some offenders may not have a private residence and thus be ineligible for house arrest. Some offenders may not able to afford supervision fees associated with either intensive supervision or house arrest, especially if those fees are high enough to offset the costs of expensive electronic monitoring equipment. Consequently, "there may well be a tendency to apply house arrest and electronic monitoring to the more privileged and to deny it to the indigent" (Morris & Tonry, 1990:217-218). In effect, this could lead to a dual system of sanctions: incarceration for the poor and alternatives for the wealthy.

PUBLIC ACCEPTANCE AND RELATED ISSUES

A key element of the new intensive supervision movement is the argument that the public will accept such programs in lieu of incarceration for select groups of offenders. That acceptance has yet to be demonstrated. A significant proportion of the public is prison-oriented and regards any lesser punishment as unacceptable. For example, a 1989 Gallup poll showed that 83 percent of Americans felt that their local courts were not harsh enough with criminals (Flanagan & Maguire, 1990). All the rational arguments and statistics that experts can muster will not convince some that even the new and "tougher" community supervision programs are "tough enough." Related to this problem is one of unrealistic public expectations. Even success rates of 90 percent are not good enough for some people who focus on the 10 percent who fail as sufficient evidence to discredit any alternative to incarceration.[3]

An important criticism of intensive supervision is that it has not done what it has claimed it would do: protect the public from dangerous, serious, high-risk criminals. The reason that intensive supervision fails to achieve this basic claim is simple: intensive supervision programs exclude dangerous, serious, and high-risk offenders from their caseloads. At least in Georgia and New Jersey, which represent two prototypes of model intensive supervision,

> a degree of community control that exceeds any previously experienced in this country...is applied to a target group of client volunteers, one-third or one-half of whom represent a minimal level of community risk—this while the ordinary probationer (who looks much the same [as the intensive probationer] in terms of risk) receives the usual degree of (often scant) attention (Clear & Hardyman, 1990:49).

An emerging issue concerning intensive supervision and house arrest is the absence of emphasis on rehabilitation. It is undeniable that many offenders in these programs have needs that are related to their criminal behavior. To focus only on punishment and incapacitation and to ignore such needs is like keeping a persistent problem student after school and not dealing with that pupil's learning difficulties. The modern school system includes school psychologists and special classes. The modern community supervision office cannot become the correctional counterpart of the old-fashioned one-room schoolhouse and the hickory switch.

The argument to retain some rehabilitative component in new programs of intensive supervision, house arrest, and electronic monitoring rests on several bases. Humanitarian concerns recognize that offenders are often deficient in such areas as education and employability and thus need assistance if claims of equal opportunity are to be more than patriotic platitudes. A pragmatic justification for including rehabilitative elements is that two recent evaluations of intensive supervision have suggested that interventions without such elements are not as effective as interventions with a treatment component (Byrne et al., 1989; Petersilia & Turner, 1990).

An issue that has been relatively disregarded is the question of what to do with offenders who violate their conditions of intensive supervision, house arrest, or electronic monitoring. The easy solution—to revoke their status and put them behind bars—represents "the same 'all or nothing' approach to probation violations...[in traditional] sentencing strategies" (Byrne, 1990:17). In other words, it is interesting to note that the need for intermediate sanctions is a justification for the use of intensive supervision, house arrest, and electronic monitoring but that same concept is ignored when it comes to violations. Thus it is refreshing to see that some intermediate sanctions proponents (Byrne, 1990; Pearson & Harper, 1990) are now calling for a wider range of responses to violations of intermediate sanctions conditions.

The most appropriate closure to this discussion of the controversial issues associated with the new intermediate sanctions is a call for legislators and policymakers to reconsider some basic issues. If intensive supervision, house arrest, and electronic monitoring are introduced into a correctional system without careful consideration, it is likely there will be little change and much confusion. As one observer has put it,

> Until that day [of serious consideration], judges who are frustrated by the lack of rigor of ordinary probation are likely to use newer intermediate punishments for the more villainous among the probation-bound rather than for the less villainous among the prison-bound for whom, in public declaration, they are designed (Tonry, 1990:189).

Consequently, Tonry calls for the introduction of legislative guidelines for sentencing in order to better structure the sentencing decisions of ordinary judges. The more basic issue is to examine the use of imprisonment in a particular jurisdiction, an issue that is often ignored in this country (Zimring & Hawkins, 1991).

CONCLUSION

Intensive supervision, house arrest, and electronic monitoring may be here to stay or may just represent the latest fads to have overtaken correctional policymakers. These programs currently appeal to officials faced with mushrooming prison populations and a country whose correctional philosophy embraces retribution, deterrence, and incapacitation as primary objectives.

At this point many questions about these innovative programs lack definitive answers. Their effectiveness and cost savings are still under scrutiny. Their unintended consequences are still being discovered.

It is clear that these progams are another chapter in the history of corrections. As such they have evolved from previous efforts and are not as revolutionary as some claim. Further, they will undoubtedly share the fate of all previous correctional practices: they will not be without problems.

If policymakers and the public can accept less-than-perfect programs, if both can have realistic expectations, then intensive supervision, house arrest, and electronic monitoring may make significant contributions to how American society responds to the correctional needs of this decade and the next. If policymakers and the public expect more than is reasonable, then these new programs will be as disappointing as previous efforts. Then future historians will categorize them as simply the latest in a series of panaceas following a familiar but disturbing pattern: "great early enthusiasm, widespread adoption, less-than-positive evaluations followed by disillusionment, and finally downscaling or elimination and receptiveness to the next panacea" (Corbett & Marx, 1991:409). Hopefully, future historians will find the former rather than the latter.

One final note: the fanfare surrounding intensive supervision, house arrest, and electronic monitoring tends to drown out the softer sounds of another recent trend in corrections. While some probation departments are stocking up on urinalysis kits and electronic monitoring equipment, others are pursuing victim-offender reconciliation, victim services, and restitution. For several years programs such as the Victim Offender Restitution Program and Genessee Justice (Picht, 1987) have been actually implementing sanctions that focus on justice and equity as well as estimated cost savings and the number of prison cells not utilized (for an overview, see Galaway, 1988). It is not surprising that in a dollars-driven, high-tech society even corrections officials will be fascinated with cost-benefit analysis and electronic wizardry. It is worth remembering that occasionally we rise above the bottom line and try to consider more noble goals.

NOTES

[1]   For a discussion of the technological aspects of the monitoring devices, see Morris and Tonry (1990). As with any electronic device, monitoring equipment can be subject to technical difficulties. As Morris and Tonry (1990) assert, however, it is reasonable to assume that such technical problems will be resolved.

[2]   Tonry (1990), of course, disregards any crimes that offenders may commit against other offenders or correctional personnel in the prison setting.

[3]   For a discussion of the argument that the public is less vindictive than assumed, see Umbreit (1989).

REFERENCES

Baird, S.C. & D. Wagner (1990). "Measuring Diversion: The Florida Community Control Program." *Crime and Delinquency,* 36(January):112-125.

Ball, R.A., C.R. Huff & J.R. Lilly (1988). *House Arrest and Correctional Policy: Doing Time at Home.* Newbury Park, CA: Sage Publications.

Ball, R.A. & J.R. Lilly (1986). "A Theoretical Examination of Home Incarceration." *Federal Probation,* 50(March):17-24.

Beck, J.L., J. Klein-Saffran & H.B. Wooten (1990). "Home Confinement and the Use of Electronic Monitoring with Federal Parolees." *Federal Probation,* 54(December):22-31.

Byrne, J.M. (1990). "The Future of Intensive Probation Supervision and the New Intermediate Sanctions." *Crime and Delinquency,* 36(January):6-41.

Byrne, J.M., A.J. Lurigio & C. Baird (1989). "The Effectiveness of the New Intensive Supervision Programs." *Research in Corrections,* 2(September):1-48.

Carter, R.M. & L.T. Wilkins (1976). "Caseloads: Some Conceptual Models." In R.M. Carter & L.T. Wilkins (eds.) *Probation, Parole, and Community Corrections,* pp. 391-401. New York, NY: John Wiley & Sons.

Clear, T.R. & P.L. Hardyman (1990). "The New Intensive Supervision Movement." *Crime and Delinquency,* 36(January):42-60.

Corbett, R. & G.T. Marx (1991). "No Soul in the New Machine: Technofallacies in the Electronic Monitoring Movement." *Justice Quarterly,* 8(September):399-414.

Erwin, B.S. (1987). *Final Report: Evaluation of Intensive Probation Supervision in Georgia.* Atlanta, GA: Georgia Department of Corrections.

Finckenauer, J.O. (1982). *The Panacea Phenomenon.* Englewood Cliffs, NJ: Prentice-Hall.

Flanagan, T.J. & K. Maguire (eds.) (1990). *Sourcebook of Criminal Justice Statistics 1989.* Washington, DC: U.S. Department of Justice.

Galaway, B. (1988). "Restitution as Innovation or Unfilled Promise?" *Federal Probation,* 52(September):3-14.

Gordon, D.R. (1990). *The Justice Juggernaut: Fighting Street Crime, Controlling Citizens.* New Brunswick, NJ: Rutgers University Press.

Greenfeld, L.A. (1990). "Prisoners in 1989." Washington, DC: U.S. Department of Justice.

Harland, A.T. & C.J. Rosen (1987). "Sentencing Theory and Intensive Supervision Probation." *Federal Probation,* 51(December):33-42.

Lundman, R.J. (1984). *Prevention and Control of Juvenile Delinquency.* New York, NY: Oxford University Press.

Lurigio, A.J. (1990). "Introduction." *Crime and Delinquency,* 36(January):3-5.

McCarthy, B.R. (1987). *Intermediate Punishments: Intensive Supervision, Home Confinement, and Electronic Surveillance.* Monsey, NY: Criminal Justice Press.

McCleary, R. (1978). *Dangerous Men: The Sociology of Parole.* Newbury Park, CA: Sage Publications.

Morris, N. & M. Tonry (1990). *Between Prison and Probation: Intermediate Punishments in a Rational Sentencing System.* New York, NY: Oxford University Press.

Pearson, F.S. & A.G. Harper (1990). "Contingent Intermediate Sanctions: New Jersey's Intensive Supervision Program." *Crime and Delinquency,* 36(January):75-86.

Petersilia, J. (1990). "Conditions that Permit Intensive Supervision Programs to Survive." *Crime and Delinquency,* 36(January):126-145.

Petersilia, J. & S. Turner (1990). "Intensive Supervision for High-Risk Probationers: Findings from Three California Experiments." Santa Monica, CA: RAND Corporation.

Picht, R. (1987). "Genesee Justice: County Makes Alternative Sentencing Work." *Los Angeles Times,* November 15, 1987, 4, 25.

Renzema, M. & D.T. Skelton (1990). "Use of Electronic Monitoring in the United States: 1989 Update." *NIJ Reports,* 9-13 (November/December).

Rosecrance, J. (1986). "Probation Supervision: Mission Impossible." *Federal Probation,* 50(March):25-31.

Schmidt, A.K. (1986). "Electronic Monitors." *Federal Probation,* 50(June):56-59.

Smith, F.V. (1984). "Alabama Prison Option: Supervised Intensive Restitution Program." *Federal Probation,* 48(March):32-35.

Studt, E. (1973). *Surveillance and Service in Parole.* Washington, DC: U.S. Department of Justice.

Tonry, M. (1990). "Stated and Latent Functions of ISP." *Crime and Delinquency,* 36(January):174-191.

Umbreit, M.S. (1989). "Crime Victims Seeking Fairness, Not Revenge: Toward Restorative Justice." *Federal Probation,* 53(September):52-57.

von Hirsch, A. (1990). "The Ethics of Community-Based Sanctions." *Crime and Delinquency,* 36(January):162-173.

Whitehead, J.T. (1989). *Burnout in Probation and Corrections.* New York, NY: Praeger.

Williamson, H.E. (1990). *The Corrections Profession.* Newbury Park, CA: Sage Publications.

Wilson, J.Q. (1985). *Thinking about Crime* (Revised Edition). New York, NY: Vintage Books.

Zimring, F.E. & G. Hawkins (1991). *The Scale of Imprisonment.* Chicago, IL: University of Chicago Press.

10

Community Residential Centers:
An Intermediate Sanction for the 1990s

Bernard J. McCarthy
University of Central Florida

INTRODUCTION

The intermediate sanctions movement swept through corrections in the 1980s. This movement was prompted by unprecedented prison crowding—the national prison population increased over 130 percent from 1980 to 1990 (Bureau of Justice Statistics, 1991a)—and a concern over the ineffectiveness of traditional probation/parole supervision in carrying out the purposes of punishment and in controlling crime (Petersilia, Turner, Kahan & Peterson, 1985). A broad array of programs was developed to handle offenders in community settings. These included house arrest, electronic monitoring, intensive probation and parole supervision, shock incarceration (boot camps) and the increased use of community service and restitution. Many of these sanctions were used in various combinations as communities experimented with alternative punishments.

A major effort was made by criminal justice policy analysts on the local, state, and federal levels of government to expand the range of correctional options available to judges and correctional agencies. The goals for these programs generally fell into two categories: first, to reduce the crowding of correctional institutions, and second, to improve the effectiveness of community correctional services.

Assessments regarding how well these programs accomplished either reductions in crowding or enhancements of community safety suggest that the innovations have fallen short of their objectives. The research to date, while limited, indicates that intermediate sanctions, particularly those defined as "front-end" strategies, have not had a major impact on prison crowding (United States General Accounting Office, 1990). Nor does the research indicate that these programs enhance public safety. Some studies report recidivism rates increase with the adoption of intensive supervision programs (Byrne, Lurgio & Baird, 1989). It is obvious that further work needs to be done in redefining existing programs and in program development, implementation, and coordination of correctional services.

COMMUNITY RESIDENTIAL CENTERS AS INTERMEDIATE PUNISHMENT

This chapter focuses on an important, yet underutilized, component of intermediate punishments commonly referred to as community residential centers or halfway houses, and examines how these programs can be used to reduce jail and prison crowding and enhance public safety.

Community residential center is a generic term that refers to a variety of programs such as: halfway houses, prerelease centers, transition centers, work-release centers, community treatment centers, community correctional facilities, and restitution centers. These facilities have the potential to make an impact on the crowding that occurs in jail and prison systems by providing a low-cost alternative setting for offenders serving their sentences and by providing an additional supervision resource for probation and parole agencies less restrictive than returning offenders to jail or prison.

Diversity is the essence of community residential centers. As J. Bryan Riley, executive director of the Massachusetts Halfway Houses, Inc., states: "Nobody could tell you what the average halfway house is like" (Hicks, 1987). Many of these programs are locally controlled and operated and serve local community needs. As a result, there is no single model of administration or operation. The programs may also serve as a link to other social service systems, particularly treatment systems outside of the criminal justice system (e.g., drug and alcohol programs).

Conceptually, community residential centers represent an integral link in the range of correctional services provided by local, state, and federal criminal justice systems. Unlike other forms of intermediate punishments, no uniform model exists regarding how these programs should be organized or run. The programs vary in degree of supervision and services provided but they may impose considerable restrictions on the liberty of the offenders residing in them.

As a correctional option, the community residential center provides a link between correctional supervision in the community and incarceration. These programs combine both community supervision and secure housing in a supervised setting (with supervision ranging from continuous to intermittent). The facilities may complement traditional probation and parole services, particularly for those clients who require more structure and discipline. They also bring together the public and private sectors. Many correctional agencies enter contractual arrangements with private vendors to provide community residential services. The services provided range from "three hots and a cot" (food and shelter) to comprehensive treatment centers.

In recent years the halfway house concept has been expanded to include a full range of services to the entire criminal justice system. They accommodate pretrial offenders unable to make bail, persons on probation who require close supervision, inmates assigned to work release, prereleasees and parolees and, more recently, as an intermediate sanction for offenders who violate the terms of their probation and parole. These facilities may also serve as a setting for drug and alcohol treatment. In line with developments in the field, the International Halfway House Association recently changed its name to the International Association for Residential and Community Alternatives as a reflection of the association's expanded scope of interests, activities, and functions.

Halfway houses have a long history in corrections. Since the earliest days of the first United States prison system (the Pennsylvania System of Prison Discipline), prison reformers have recognized the need for an intermediate setting between prison and the community, and have called for the development of transitional residences for inmates about to be released from prison (Powers, 1959). Halfway houses play a critical role in assisting inmates in negotiating the sometimes difficult adjustment from confinement in prisons or jails to life in the community.

Although these centers have been in existence since the early 1800s and are designed to address an extremely important issue in criminal justice, i.e., inmate recidivism, halfway houses or community correctional centers have remained on the periphery of corrections and have been underutilized by most correctional systems. The vast majority of offenders serving time in prison or assigned to community supervision status do not pass through these centers. Only a small percentage of prison inmates or prison releasees cycle through these programs.

TYPES OF CLIENTS

The type of client served by community residential centers varies from community to community depending on the type of agency operating the facility and the particular need the program addresses.

In their simplest form, these facilities serve a "halfway-in" or "halfway-out" function. In the first mode, the program involves clients who require more supervision than traditional probation offers or who have difficulty adjusting to the terms of probation. In the second, facilities serve as a prerelease mechanism for prison systems. These centers are normally operated by state departments of corrections or by private contractors who accept prison releasees (both prior to parole and after parole). In the parole group, these programs handle offenders who are leaving institutional facilities with special needs or who may pose a special risk to society (Beto, 1990).

Other centers are operated by private profit and nonprofit programs that handle substance abusers in a community setting and accept referrals from criminal justice agencies (e.g., the court or probation and parole agencies), as well as voluntary admissions. This area saw tremendous growth during the 1980s as private insurance companies provided for drug/alcohol treatment in their insurance coverage. Many for-profit hospitals have developed treatment programs to target this special group. Treatment programs typically involve a residential stay, followed by a graduated release involving day furloughs and brief, overnight visits, concluding with a period of day treatment.

Community residential centers service a wide variety of clients, from the ones deemed dangerous by society, i.e., felons released from prison, to probationers, and to citizens who are substance abusers who voluntarily enter treatment.

Prisoners are typically transferred to halfway houses as a transitional setting after serving a portion of their prison term. The facility provides a secure environment with close monitoring for the protection of society and usually furnishes services to the offender to aid in his/her successful return to the community.

Most state prison systems that operate community facilities have criteria, usually statutorily provided, that specify the types of offenders eligible to participate in these programs. Sex offenders and offenders deemed dangerous are often excluded from participation in these programs (Corrections Compendium, 1986). From a community protection point of view, these are the very offenders who would benefit the most from the secure setting and supervision provided by community residential programs. Offenders who represent a potential threat or danger to society or who have special problems and needs would be better served by placing them in a supervised setting while they become accustomed to life in the free world. One of the most important functions a residential center can provide is a semi-secure setting for correctional testing to determine if the offender is ready for release.

UNDERLYING PHILOSOPHY

The underlying theory behind community residential centers as well as other community sanctions is that offenders can be punished justly and effectively in a community setting. This notion assumes that the purposes of punishment can be accomplished; i.e., retribution or deserved punishment, deterrence, incapacitation, and rehabilitation (Clear & Cole, 1990). It also assumes that the punishment will be effective, in that the community will be protected and that the offender will not pose a danger to the community through higher rates of recidivism than if that offender had been sent to an institution. A second principle underlying the use of community residential centers is the concept of the least restrictive alternative. This principle suggests that only the custody required to serve the interests of justice be applied to the offender and the restrictions and deprivations of liberty one experiences be in proportion to the gravity of the offense committed and the danger one poses to others (see National Institute of Corrections, 1981). From a correctional administration point of view this principle calls for the efficient management of scarce correctional resources by matching prisoners with the appropriate correctional setting based on their needs and the risk they pose to themselves or society.

THE GOALS OF COMMUNITY CORRECTIONAL CENTERS

The overall goal of corrections is the protection of the public through the prevention of crime (American Correctional Association, 1966). Community residential centers address this general goal by providing: a semi-secure setting for offenders; continuous direct or indirect monitoring of offenders while they are involved in the program; and the provision of services (employment, counseling, etc.) that facilitate their adjustment to the prosocial community.

In addition to these general goals, community residential centers usually accomplish one or more of the following objectives:

1. To assist in the reintegration of offenders,

2. To reduce or ease overcrowding in jails or prisons,

3. To reduce correctional costs by providing a cost-effective intermediate sanction,

4. To provide an appropriate setting for the treatment of substance abuse problems.

The goals pursued by a particular program are a function of two key factors: (1) the need or function the program addresses in the community; and (2) the type of agency responsible for funding and operating the program. These factors will determine the role the facility will play in the local criminal justice system and the types of clients that will be served. Some programs pursue several of these objectives, others focus on one or two. As with most correctional programs, the goals are not mutually exclusive.

The Reintegration of Offenders

In the past, the primary justification for prerelease centers or halfway houses had been to assist in the reintegration of offenders (Allen, 1978). The

community residential facility or halfway house was conceived as an intermediate step between the prison and the community. It was assumed that the
offender would be in need of this transitional step for two reasons: first, the
separation from the community that results from incarceration, distances the
offender from his family, job and prosocial friends; and a gradual period of
readjustment would be required to ease a person back into community life.
Second, the institutional experience was viewed as essentially damaging and
debilitating and the offender would require a period of time in a setting where
he/she could decompress and reorient him/herself to living with noncriminals
and adjust to life in the community rather than a prison subculture.

The function of the facility would be to provide a supportive environment
for the offender while seeking employment and housing in the community,
while also providing varying levels of supervision to ensure the safety of citizens in the community.

High rates of recidivism by inmates released from prison point out the
need for a structured intermediate setting. A survey of inmates released from
prisons in 11 states found that 62 percent had been rearrested within three
years of release (Bureau of Justice Statistics, 1989c). Other research has
shown that of all offenders under community supervision, offenders released
from prison represent the greatest risk to the community (United States
General Accounting Office, 1990).

Impact on Crowding

A second objective is to reduce the crowding of correctional facilities. One
of the most critical problems confronting corrections in the 1990s is the crowding of correctional institutions. The prison population in the United States doubled in the decade of the 1980s. The Bureau of Justice Statistics recently noted
that prison systems required 1,100 new beds placed on line every week just to
keep pace with the growing prison population (Bureau of Justice Statistics,
1991a). Many prison systems have struggled to build additional capacity to
keep up with rapid increases in the inmate population.

Compounding the problem of crowding for prison systems has been the
active oversight of the federal courts. The courts have intervened in the operation of correctional systems when jails or prisons were perceived to be dan-
gerously overcrowded and in violation of the Eighth Amendment to the
United States Constitution (which prohibits cruel and unusual punishment). As
of January 1, 1990, 38 state agencies were under court order, 29 of which had
court-imposed population limits (Camp & Camp, 1990).

The crowding crisis has prompted criminal justice policy analysts to consider three sets of strategies to respond to the exigencies of crowding. The
first set of strategies commonly referred to as "front-end" strategies is
designed to reduce prison and jail populations by diverting prison-bound
offenders to alternative programs. A second set of strategies is designed to

expand the capacity of existing correctional institutions by adopting innova-tive techniques in construction and financing to expand existing capacity. A third approach involves developing "back door" strategies designed to reduce correctional populations by releasing offenders.

Community residential centers can be used with all three approaches. They could be used as an option for prison-bound offenders and as a correc-tional resource or housing option for overcapacity prisons, especially for offenders who do not require high-security settings. Finally, community resi-dential centers could be used as one component of a graduated release program.

Cost-Effective Intermediate Sanction

While crowding has created an unprecedented demand for correctional ser-vices, the cost of managing correctional populations has become a critical issue for governmental leaders. An increasing share of the justice tax dollar is being taken up by the costs of prison construction. A recent survey by Camp and Camp (1990) of state construction plans indicated that the planned construction by state correctional systems exceeded 5.7 million dollars in 1990. This same survey found that in 1990, the national average for building a single maximum-security bed was $75,341, a medium-security bed was $51,316 and a minimum-security bed was $29,170. The researchers found that more than 75 percent of the new beds planned were designated maximum or medium security.

Considerable savings in construction and operation costs can be realized when correctional systems can match the appropriate custody setting to the threat (and needs) of the offenders. To do so requires an adequate classifica-tion process that assigns appropriate custody settings based on an offender's needs and the risk he poses to society.

Research reported by the National Institute of Corrections (1981) indi-cates that prison systems routinely classify 40 to 50 percent of inmates to maximum custody. When objective classification instruments are used to determine the custody levels of inmates, only 8 to 15 percent of the inmate population is found in need of maximum-security custody.

In the 1980s, research called into question the effectiveness of traditional probation supervision and questioned whether community safety was actually endangered by probationers (Petersilia et al., 1985). A movement to improve the delivery of probation services and increase community protection swept across the country. This movement led to the adoption of sanctions that increased the super-vision levels of existing community sanctions without jail or prison confinement. Intensive probation supervision, electronic monitoring and house arrest were inno-vations that developed (see Chapter 9). In addition, shock incarceration and boot camps were also implemented by many jurisdictions (see Chapter 7).

The community residential centers, while intermediate sanctions, were apparently overlooked in the effort to find options to enhance traditional pro-bation and parole supervision. Moreover, with the stresses and strains of crowding on prisons, community residential centers could be used as a complement to probation or parole supervision, or as a part of a jail or prison sentence, or as a strategy for handling nonserious probation and parole violators.

Treatment Services

Community residential centers also provide a setting for the treatment of persons with substance abuse problems. These facilities provide a secure or semi-secure setting without the deprivations or harshness usually associated with the jail or prison environment. The coerciveness and punitiveness of correctional institutions are viewed by therapists as antithetical to the treatment concept. By providing treatment in a non-penal environment many of the negative aspects of confinement (e.g., prisonization) can be avoided.

SCOPE OF PROGRAMS

It is difficult to estimate the number of community residential centers in the United States because of their decentralized nature and the wide variety of clients the programs serve. An indication of the scope of these programs can be obtained by reviewing three sources of information.

First, the *1990 Membership Directory of the International Association of Residential and Community Alternatives* lists over 650 agencies and programs. This is a directory of programs and agencies that provide community-based services.

A second source of information comes from the American Correctional Association, which annually surveys programs operated by correctional systems throughout the United States. This annual directory reports that as of June 30, 1989, 21 states operated work-release programs, 20 states had programs defined as community facilities, and 23 states administered prerelease centers (American Correctional Association, 1990).

A third source of information regarding the number of programs comes from surveys of substance abuse programs. The number of substance abuse programs serving criminal justice clients is difficult to estimate because programs handle both criminal justice and non-criminal-justice clients, are both publicly and privately funded, and treat all types of substance abusers.

One survey of programs receiving government funding reported that in 1987, a total of 6,632 programs received state funds (residential and nonresidential) and over 450,000 drug clients were admitted (not including alcohol admissions) to these programs (Anglin & Hser, 1990). Another study focusing on residential programs estimated that there were over 500 therapeutic programs serving drug offenders in existence (De Leon, 1990).

According to the National Institute on Alcohol Abuse and Alcoholism, an additional 1.43 million people were treated for alcoholism in 1987, the majority in outpatient settings (United States Department of Health and Human Services, 1990). These types of programs overlap the criminal justice system and health-related systems. They provide services to clientele, some of whom are defined as offenders, others as patients. Many people who enter these programs do so voluntarily while others are required by criminal justice authorities (judges, probation officers, etc.). As a result, it is difficult to determine the size and number of programs that would fit the concept represented by community residential centers, but the numbers are huge. The information provided in this section, while not exact, provides some idea of the large number of clients that flow through community-based substance abuse programs across the nation.

COMMUNITY RESIDENTIAL CENTERS FOR INMATES

Prerelease Programs

Community residential centers that process prisoners about to be released to the community are referred to by several names that vary by jurisdiction. The names include community correctional facilities or centers, community treatment centers, prerelease centers, transition centers and work-release and restitution centers.

Prerelease centers focus on assisting inmates with their return to the community. These centers serve inmates about to be paroled, prisoners about to be released as a result of good-time (mandatory or conditional releasees) or offenders who already have a parole release date. These facilities serve as "decompression chambers" for prisoners returning to society.

In addition, in some systems, less serious offenders who are particularly vulnerable to the predators who dwell in high-security institutions are transferred to these facilities to serve their time as soon as they are admitted to a particular correctional system. Today, some states use these facilities as overflow valves for crowded correctional systems.

Prerelease centers are designed to provide inmates with a series of graduated release experiences that assist their return to the community. Typically, inmates are sent to these facilities 30 to 90 days prior to their release. Some facilities confine the inmate for the first two weeks while they are oriented to the program philosophy, participate in several how-to workshops, and generally adjust to the less secure environment.

These sessions are designed to teach prisoners how to look for work, how to complete job applications, and how to handle employment interviews. Group counseling sessions may also be conducted to address many concerns inmates have about returning to society.

In a typical program, the orientation phase is usually followed by a series of furloughs that are granted to find employment or housing, to see one's family or to secure needed treatment services. Once employment is obtained the resident is permitted (on work-release status) to leave the facility to go to work on a regular unsupervised basis.

Work-Release Programs

Work-release programs are designed to provide prison and jail inmates the opportunity to work at jobs in the community while serving their prison sentence. These programs can be implemented at any stage of confinement but in practice inmates are usually transferred to these facilities as they near their release dates.

Table 10.1

1989 Work-Release Population

STATE	PRISON POPULATION*	NUMBER ON WORK RELEASE	PERCENT OF TOTAL INMATE POPULATION
AL	13,559	1244	9
AZ	12,640	61	5
AR	5,759	266	5
CA	82,872	1256	1.5
DE	3,327	314	9
IL	22,576	793	3.5
IN	12,483	648	5
IA	3,654	195	5
KS	6,172	120	2
ME	1,505	114	7.5
MD	14,932	350	2
MA	6,757	492	7
MN	3,035	141	5
MS	8,224	29	.003
NE	2,277	306	13
NV	5,225	115	.02
NH	1,095	71	6
NJ	14,675	487	3
NY	48,644	2047	4
NC	17,536	1605	9
ND	513	3	.006
OH	28,076	235	.008
OK	9,444	895	9
PA	18,931	20	.001
RI	2,283	238	10
SC	13,737	775	5
SD	1,223	37	.03
TN	7,376	59	.008
VT	770	80	.08
WA	7,359	623	8
WV	1,414	203	14
WI	6,231	205	.03
WY	900	37	.04

* Note that not all of the states were included in this survey.

Source: American Correctional Association (1990). *Directory of Juvenile and Adult Correctional Departments, Institutions, Agencies & Paroling Authorities United States and Canada,* pp. xxii and xxiv. Laurel, Maryland.

There are a number of advantages associated with work-release programs. First, inmates are involved in productive labor in the community while serving their sentence; second, the state usually charges the inmate a fee for room and board and this helps offset the operating costs of the facility; and third, inmates become fiscally responsible (they pay taxes, accumulate savings, and pay off any court-ordered fines and restitution). In addition, once released, inmates have a job to support themselves and their family.

Despite the benefits associated with work-release programs, not all correctional systems have adopted the work-release concept. Table 10.1 indicates that very few inmates are participating in work-release programs. While seven states have 9 percent or more of their prison populations on work release, many other states have not yet developed the program beyond minimal participation. States with a high percentage of inmates on work-release status include: Alabama, Delaware, North Carolina, Nebraska, Oklahoma, Rhode Island, and West Virginia.

Many work-release facilities provide a full complement of services to inmates. These services range from substance abuse counseling, to job development and vocational education. For example, the Orange County Work Release Center in Orlando, Florida, provides prisoners with the opportunity to participate in a number of programs during nonworking hours. Programs range from High School Equivalency and Basic Education Classes for offenders with educational problems to Alcoholics Anonymous and Narcotics Anonymous programs for persons with substance abuse difficulties. A local technical school, Mid-Florida Technical Institute, provides free vocational education counseling and occupational classes for inmates during their nonworking hours. In addition, the work-release center also conducts random drug and alcohol testing as part of its programming.

Drug and Alcohol Treatment Programs

In the United States there is a growing network of community residential facilities that targets drug and alcohol offenders. These programs provide residential treatment services to offenders in a nonjail setting, which removes many of the contaminants associated with the prison and jail from interfering with the treatment process.

Because of their decentralized nature it is difficult to estimate the number and type of community residential programs providing treatment services to substance abusers in the United States. One recent study reported over 500 residential drug abuse programs in existence using the therapeutic community model of treatment (De Leon, 1990).

One of the major client groups served by community residential centers is persons with drug and alcohol problems (many of whom may not be officially designated as offenders because they are voluntary admissions). However, criminal justice clientele may enter programs from a number of decision-making points in the criminal justice system, including diversion from criminal court processing, as part of a criminal sentence imposed by a judge, or as a condition of probation or parole as specified by a probation or parole officer.

The typical model used by these facilities is the therapeutic community model fashioned loosely on the Synanon concept developed by a recovering alcoholic, Charles Dietrich (De Leon, 1990). Frequently these programs are contractually operated by nonprofit, private organizations. The programs generally require clients to remain in treatment for periods ranging from several months to a few years. Recovery, in fact, is viewed as a lifelong process.

The treatment provided in these settings involves drug abstinence, work, and the adoption of the 12 steps (of Alcoholics Anonymous). It also focuses on rebuilding the personality of the addict. Drug abuse is viewed as a symptom of a larger problem within the individual that must be treated to deal with the drug and alcohol use (De Leon, 1990). The treatment regimen is intense and all-encompassing. Encounter groups are used extensively: they focus on breaking down the client's resistances so that a rebuilding process may begin. The rebuilding phase involves a self-help process assisted by the efforts of the group, which has experienced similar problems. In many programs clients are required to work—as part of their treatment—maintaining the facility, and are initially assigned menial tasks. As they accept more responsibility for their behavior, they are assigned tasks with increased complexity, responsibility, and authority.

In the final stages of treatment, the client is gradually released to community life through daily passes that enable him/her to obtain employment and housing, and to reunite with supportive friends and family. The last step is the return to the community and independent living outside the program.

One example of such a program is Phoenix House, a major drug treatment program in New York City and a model for many other centers across the nation (Marriott, 1989). At Phoenix House, new residents are put to work on the service crew. They are responsible for various housekeeping chores, including cleaning bathrooms, sweeping and mopping floors, and kitchen duty. Through menial work, new members learn the philosophy of the house and undergo a humbling experience. The program is highly structured to provide a schedule that is routine, intensive, and supportive of the therapeutic objectives of the program.

Assessments of the effectiveness of this model of treatment appear to be positive for some clients who complete the total treatment program (Anglin & Hser, 1990). Research on program effectiveness indicates success rates that vary from 28 percent to 40 percent for persons who remain drug free (Anglin & Hser, 1990).

OTHER USES OF COMMUNITY
RESIDENTIAL CENTERS

Pretrial Release for Nondangerous Offenders

Some local justice systems have utilized community residential centers for the placement of selected (nondangerous) pretrial detainees who work in the community and are unable to secure a bond. These detainees are considered nondangerous, unlikely to flee, but without sufficient resources to obtain bond. Pretrial detainees are able to continue their employment in the community, maintain their family responsibilities (rent and family support) and resume their life in the community once sentenced, assuming they receive a probated term. Correctional administrators see some benefit in these programs because they allow them to select nondangerous offenders from overcrowded jails, thereby freeing beds for more serious offenders. In addition, local government usually collects fees from participants to offset the costs of confinement.

Residential Probation and Parole Supervision

Community treatment programs are also used in a number of different ways by sentencing judges and probation/parole agencies. They may be a residential condition of probation or parole for offenders in need of more structure, or as an increased penalty.

Some intensive probation programs are adding a residential component that restricts the person's movement at night to a specific supervised residential setting (Morris & Tonry, 1990). This option would be appropriate for persons who are unable to abide by curfews or the conditions of house arrest.

Handling Probation and Parole Revocations

Prison and jail crowding has forced correctional administrators to rethink the traditional policy of automatic recommitment to jail or prison for technical or legal violations of parole. The scarcity of bed space in correctional institutions has encouraged some correctional systems, such as Minnesota's Department of Correction, to develop a continuum of sanctions for probation violations. These options range from increasing restrictions and supervision, to intermittent confinement, to return to custody to serve out the remainder of the sentence, which is usually reserved for a severe violation (Herrick, 1989).

A survey by the *Corrections Compendium* reported that 21 percent of persons on parole in the United States in 1987 had their parole revoked (Herrick, 1989). In the past, a revocation based on either a technical or legal violation of parole usually resulted in a return to prison. Because of prison crowding and federal court-imposed limitations on populations, many states have developed intermediate steps to handle parole or probation violators. Table 10.2 provides an overview of how violators were processed.

Table 10.2
Non-Prison Alternatives for Parole Violators

Alternatives	Number of States
Change of Program Plan	40
Assignment to Treatment Centers	34
Work-Release or other Community Center	24
Electronic Monitoring	20
House Arrest	17
Intensive Supervision	7

Source: E. Herrick (1989). "Survey of Parole Violations," *Corrections Compendium*, March:8.

The prison crowding crisis has prompted correctional planners to analyze who goes to prison and why. Some research indicates that probation and parole violators make up a significant number of offenders who are admitted to prison each year. From a total of 460,798 prisoners admitted to prison in 1988, 122,156 or more than 25 percent were parolees or other conditional release violators who returned to prison and approximately 40 percent of these offenders received new sentences for additional crimes (Bureau of Justice Statistics, 1991b).

Restitution, Community Service, Day Reporting Centers and Other Forms of Intermediate Sanctions

The above sanctions can be used with a residential component while the offender is serving his/her sentence. For restitution and community service sentences, the individual may be housed in a minimum-security facility at relatively low cost while the sentence is served. Some offenders may need the structure provided by a community residential center to satisfy the punishment imposed by the court, while others may not be able to adequately support themselves while paying their debt to the victim or society.

Day reporting centers are a recent innovation that have been added to the range of sanctions available to a local correctional systems (Parent, 1990). Offenders under correctional supervision and in need of enhanced structure, discipline, and services are frequently referred to these centers. Program participants remain on community supervision but are required to be in contact with a reporting center up to several times per day or per week to account for their activities in the community. In addition, they may undergo drug and alcohol testing at the center or participate in some type of programming such as Alcoholics Anonymous, specialized group counseling, individualized counseling, or educational remediation programs. Participants may remain in the program from several weeks to a year.

Presently, community residential programs and day reporting systems are evolving in a manner that complements one another. A National Institute of Justice study by Parent (1990) found that 9 of 14 programs studied had close ties to community residential programs.

One county work-release program in Florida is presently experimenting with day reporting as the final phase of the release process. Inmates who are about to successfully complete their sentence at a work-release center can be phased into a day reporting status for the remaining portion of their sentence. As a result, badly needed bed space in the work-release center is made available to other qualified inmates housed in the severely overcrowded county jail. As day reporting gains acceptance as a method of supervision, community correctional centers will be increasingly used as a logical reporting site for participants.

ISSUES ASSOCIATED WITH COMMUNITY RESIDENTIAL CENTERS

A major obstacle to the growth of community residential centers is the reluctance of prison systems to expand their use. At the same time that prison and jail systems were experiencing unprecedented growth, prison systems routinely overclassified offenders (National Institute of Corrections, 1981). Many offenders do not require high levels of security to adequately protect the community and serve the purposes of punishment. Research suggests that many offenders could be placed in less secure settings without appreciably increasing the risk to the general public and at a considerably lower cost (Petersilia, 1987).

Despite the demands placed on capacity by crowding, many prison systems appear reluctant to build and operate a network of community facilities. A review of data indicates, paradoxically, that community residential centers are underutilized by many states (see Table 10.1). The *Annual Directory of the American Correctional Association* (American Correctional Association, 1990) reports that of a total inmate population of 645,609, 144,513 inmates were classified as minimum custody by state and federal prison systems. Inmates assigned this custody status are considered nondangerous and are usually eligible for community release. Yet only 14,837 inmates or approximately two percent of the total inmate population participated in work-release programs. An additional 5,000 inmates resided in facilities designated as community centers or homes.

It is apparent that only a small percentage of community-eligible inmates is participating in these programs. Prison systems are not utilizing community residential centers, even for a small part of their inmate population. Instead, they are relying on more traditional and costly means of managing offenders. This finding is noteworthy because of the tremendous cost involved in building and operating prisons.

The need to bring facilities on line much more quickly to accommodate rapid increases in population has encouraged some prison systems to consider alternative models for housing offenders. Unfortunately, it appears that prison systems are in the process of building medium- and maximum-security housing units and not minimum-custody facilities (Camp & Camp, 1990).

One explanation for the reluctance of correctional administrators to diversify the types of custodial settings they operate is their sensitivity to public reaction if an incident occurs involving an offender residing in one of these centers. The lesson of Willie Horton and the impact the case had on the presidential aspirations and political career of Governor Michael Dukakis of Massachusetts were not lost on correctional leaders and politicians in other states.

It is clear that only a very few offenders are placed on work-release status or other types of community correctional facilities. These centers remain an underutilized option available to state prison systems.

In addition to the incarcerated population, community residential centers are not being used to any great extent to assist inmates returning to the community as parolees. According to the American Correctional Association (1990), in 1989, 251,993 offenders were conditionally released from prison and another 73,250 were unconditionally released, yet only a very small percentage passed through halfway houses on their way back to the community. It is obvious even to the casual observer that most prisoners/parolees are not provided with the intermediate step of a transitional setting prior to release to the community.

PROSPECTS FOR THE FUTURE

Two key trends will emerge in the 1990s for community residential centers. The first is the continued growth in the number of community residential centers. Four major forces are shaping the use of these centers:

First, unprecedented crowding in state and local correctional facilities has forced many systems to rethink confinement policies. State and federal officials across the nation are evaluating whether the policy of collective incapacitation, which locks up all types of offenders, is reasonable and cost-effective. Justice systems across the United States at every level of government are presently considering alternatives to confinement. The search for solutions to the crowding crisis is difficult, particularly when balanced against public concern (and political rhetoric) regarding community safety. Community residential centers offer communities reasonable protection from offenders and, at the same time, assistance to clients returning to the community at a reasonable cost.

Second, there is a growing concern and awareness by the American people that the drug/alcohol problem in the United States will not be solved by simply locking up substance abusers. A recent national poll reported that 60 percent of the citizens surveyed favored putting drug users into treatment programs and only 28 percent favored punishing drug users (Media General/Associated Press Poll, 1990). Many citizens are realizing that simply incarcerating offenders will not appreciably affect a person's drug and alcohol use. In addition, treatment professionals are pointing out the need for treatment in a non-jail environment.

At the same time this awareness is growing, legislatures across the United States are mandating jail sentences for DWI (driving while intoxicated) offenders and drug users. Some correctional systems are responding to this increased flow of substance abusers by transferring these offenders to community residential centers. One administrator of a community corrections facility noted that his facility specialized in handling all types of substance abusers from "high-class" drunks serving mandatory jail sentences for repeat DWIs, to low-class crack addicts convicted for possession or attempting to possess cocaine.

Third, the growing inmate population has stretched the budgets of state and local governments. Incarceration is a costly government function and many state and local jurisdictions are starting to look upon jail and prison space as a valuable resource that needs to be used effectively and efficiently. In other words, individuals who do not pose a danger to the community should be placed in less secure environments. In addition, many jurisdictions are finding that in developing work-release facilities they can help offset the high cost of confinement by assessing user fees for prisoners participating in the programs. For example, the Department of Corrections in the state of Florida collects several million dollars a year from inmates participating in the state work-release program (Parent, 1990).

A fourth force driving the expansion of community residential centers is the movement to develop a range of intermediate sanctions. In 1985, the RAND Corporation released a report on felony probation (Petersilia, 1985) which revealed that in a study conducted in California, two-thirds of felons granted probation were rearrested and one out of two were convicted of new crimes. The inadequacies of traditional probation supervision became the subject of a national debate and sparked a reform movement to reshape probation supervision. This study crystallized the views of many that steps were needed to increase the safety of the community. These steps included expanding traditional probation and parole supervision practices to include house arrest, intensive probation supervision, and electronic monitoring. The utility of community residential centers as a correctional resource for enhanced community supervision is slowly being rediscovered by the corrections profession as prison and jail space becomes scarce.

A second major trend will be the further diversification of services provided by community residential centers. In some communities these centers are evolving into multiservice centers for the local criminal justice community. These facilities will handle a full range of offenders under one roof, ranging from individuals diverted from criminal justice processing but subject to informal probation, pretrial releasees, probationers in need of a secure setting, jail-sentenced offenders following work-release programs or day reporting schedules, minimum-security prisoners, prereleasees, and parolees.

As drug and alcohol testing continues to be emphasized as part of the supervision process, these centers may become testing centers for the local criminal justice community. Also, as the probation and parole population continues to increase, the need for an intermediate punishment for clients who violate the conditions of their community supervision will increase.

SUMMARY AND CONCLUSION

Community residential centers represent a promising, yet underutilized, resource in the search for effective and cost-efficient intermediate punishments. These programs can serve a wide variety of criminal justice agencies. The community residential center may be used as a pretrial detention option, as a condition of probation, as part of a sentence of confinement, as a transitional setting for offenders about to be released into the community from jail or prison, and as an intermediate sanction for violations of community supervision requirements.

These programs are developing across the country as local jurisdictions struggle to handle their correctional populations. One of their major advantages is the flexibility associated with the programs; they can be shaped to fit local needs and problems.

However, state prison systems have not developed these facilities to any great extent. Community residential centers show promise as a strategy for responding to prison crowding. These facilities offer a secure setting with supervision that provides a low-cost alternative to institutionalization while at the same time addressing community concerns over the safety issue.

The major weakness of this form of intermediate sanction is that policy development and implementation are not guided by research but by practice. Considerable innovation is taking place across the country but very little is guided by research. The trial and error process is both time-consuming and fraught with mistakes. Local, state, and federal program models, as well as the private sector, need to be evaluated and the findings disseminated so that exemplary program models can be replicated and ineffective program models can be improved or discarded.

REFERENCES

Allen, H. (1978). *Halfway Houses.* Washington, DC: U.S. Government Printing Office.

American Correctional Association (1966). *Manual of Correctional Standards.* College Park, MD: American Correctional Association.

———— (1990). *Directory of Juvenile & Adult Correctional Departments, Institutions, Agencies, and Paroling Authorities.* Laurel, MD: American Correctional Association.

Anglin, M. & Y. Hser (1990). "Treatments of Drug Abuse." In M. Tonry & J. Wilson (eds.) *Drugs and Crime.* Chicago, IL: University of Chicago Press.

Beto, D. (1990). "Linkage of Institution and Noninstitutional Treatment of Offenders in Texas." *International Association of Residential and Community Alternatives Journal.* III,4:20.

Bureau of Justice Statistics (1989a). *Parole in 1988.* Washington, DC: U.S. Department of Justice.

———— (1989b). *Prisoners in 1988.* Washington, DC: U.S. Department of Justice.

———— (1989c). *Recidivism of Prisoners Released in 1983.* Washington, DC: U.S. Department of Justice.

———— (1991a). *Prisoners in 1990.* Washington, DC: U.S. Department of Justice.

———— (1991b). "Sentenced Prisoners Admitted to State or Federal Jurisdictions by Type of Admission, 1989." *Correctional Populations in the United States, 1989.* Washington, DC: U.S. Department of Justice.

Byrne, J., A. Lurgio & C. Baird (1989). *The Effectiveness of the New Intensive Supervision Programs.* Washington, DC: Research in Corrections Series. National Institute of Corrections and the Robert J. Kutak Foundation.

Camp, G. & G. Camp (1990). *The Corrections Yearbook.* South Salem, NY: The Criminal Justice Institute.

Clear, T. & G. Cole (1990). *American Corrections.* Pacific Grove, CA: Brooks/Cole Publishing Company.

Corrections Compendium (1986). "Work Release Survey." (October):6.

De Leon, G. (1990). "Treatment Strategies." In J. Inciardi (ed.) *Handbook of Drug Control in the United States.* New York, NY: Greenwood Press.

Herrick, E. (1989). "Survey of Parole Violations." *Corrections Compendium,* March:8.

Hicks, N. (1987). "A New Relationship, Halfway Houses and Corrections." *Corrections Compendium*. XII,4:1.

Marriott, M. (1989). "Struggle and Hope from the Ashes of Drugs." *New York Times*, October 28:A1, 36.

Media General/Associated Press Poll (1990). "Attitudes Towards Proposals to Reduce Illegal Drug Use." In *Sourcebook of Criminal Justice Statistics 1989*. Washington, DC: Bureau of Justice Statistics.

Morris, N. & M. Tonry (1990). *Between Prison and Probation: Intermediate Punishments in a Rational Sentencing System*. New York, NY: Oxford University Press.

National Institute of Corrections (1981). *Prison Classification: A Model Systems Approach*. Washington, DC: U.S. Department of Justice.

Parent, D. (1989). *Day Reporting Centers for Criminal Offenders*. A Descriptive Analysis of Existing Programs. Washington, DC: National Institute of Justice. U.S. Department of Justice.

_____ (1990). *Recovering Costs Through Offender Fees*. Washington, DC: Office of Justice Programs. National Institute of Justice.

Petersilia, J. (1985). *Probation and Felony Offenders*. Research in Brief. Washington, DC: National Institute of Justice. U.S. Department of Justice.

_____ (1987). *The Influence of Criminal Justice Research*. Santa Monica, CA: RAND Corporation.

Petersilia, J., S. Turner, J. Kahan & J. Peterson (1985). *Granting Felons Probation: Public Risks and Alternatives*. Santa Monica, CA: RAND Corporation.

Powers, E. (1959). "Halfway Houses: A Historical Perspective." *American Journal of Corrections*, 21:35.

U.S. Department of Health and Human Services (1990). *Seventh Special Report to the U.S. Congress on Alcohol and Health*. Washington, DC: National Institute of Alcohol Abuse and Alcoholism.

U.S. General Accounting Office (1990). *Intermediate Sanctions: Their Impact on Prison Crowding, Costs and Recidivism are Still Unclear*. Washington, DC: U.S. General Accounting Office.

About the Authors

Peter J. Benekos is a Professor of Criminal Justice at Mercyhurst College and the Director of the Graduate Program in the Administration of Justice. He received his Ph.D. in sociology/criminology from the University of Akron. Benekos has published in the areas of community corrections, victimization, and the savings and loan scandals. His current research interests include corrections and public policy.

Robert Blair has been the Chairperson of the Department of Sociology at the College of Wooster in Wooster, Ohio, since 1988, and Professor of Sociology since 1971. He received his B.A. from Juniata College, and his M.A. and Ph.D. from Northwestern University. Blair teaches in the areas of criminal justice, deviance, qualitative and quantitative research methods.

Salvador Buentello is a gang specialist and a member of the State Classification Committee in the Institutional Division of the Texas Department of Criminal Justice, formerly the Texas Department of Corrections. For the past several years, Buentello has served as a leading consultant to the National Institute of Corrections on prison gang dynamics and management.

Marilyn Chandler Ford is the Research and Information Supervisor for the Volusia County, Florida Department of Corrections. She is responsible for developing and monitoring the Department's manual and computerized data bank and supervising the Booking Section. Ford has an M.A. and a Ph.D. from the School of Criminal Justice, State University of New York at Albany. She previously taught at Niagara University. Ford has published articles on jail overcrowding, juries, and youthful offenders.

Robert S. Fong is an Associate Professor in the Department of Criminal Justice at California State University—Bakersfield. Previously, he taught criminal justice for two years at the University of North Carolina at Charlotte and one year at East Carolina University. He received his Ph.D. in criminal justice from Sam Houston State University in Texas in 1987. From 1984 to 1988, Fong served as a special monitor for the Texas Department of Corrections in the historic prison case of *Ruiz v. Estelle*. His primary research interest is in the area of prison gangs.

Peter C. Kratcoski is the Chairperson of the Department of Criminal Justice Studies and Professor of Criminal Justice Studies and Sociology at Kent State University. He received his B.A. from King's College, his M.A. from the University of Notre Dame, and his Ph.D. from Pennsylvania State University. Kratcoski is author of *Criminal Justice in America: Process and Issues,* Second Edition (1984); *Juvenile Delinquency,* Third Edition (1990); *Correctional Counseling and Treatment,* Second Edition (1989); and numerous articles and book chapters. Kratcoski teaches in the areas of juvenile justice, corrections, and criminal justice administration.

Bernard J. McCarthy is a Professor of Criminal Justice at the University of Central Florida. He received his Ph.D. in Criminology from Florida State University. McCarthy is co-author of *Justice, Crime and Ethics* (Anderson, 1991). His research and writing have focused on the problems and issues of community corrections.

Alida V. Merlo is a Professor of Criminal Justice at Westfield State College in Westfield, Massachusetts. She received her Ph.D. from Fordham University. Most recently, she has published in the area of female offenders. Her current research interests include juvenile and adult corrections, and women and the law.

Francis T. Moore is the Corrections Administrator for Volusia County, Florida. He was previously on staff with the National Institute of Corrections in Denver, Colorado. He has a B.A. in Government from Fairfield University, Fairfield, Connecticut, and a J.D. from the University of Connecticut School of Law. Moore started his career in corrections as a jail correctional officer and has held every supervisory position up to and including director of a multi-institutional department. He has published in the area of jail overcrowding.

J. Michael Olivero is an Associate Professor in the Department of Law and Justice at Central Washington University. He received his Ph.D. from Southern Illinois University. Olivero is the author of *Honor, Violence, and Upward Mobility: Chicago Gangs 1970s to 1980s* (University of Texas Press, 1991) and is currently involved in assessing the AIDS problem in Mexican prisons.

Joycelyn M. Pollock-Byrne is an Associate Professor of Criminal Justice at the University of Houston—Downtown. She received her Ph.D. from the School of Criminal Justice, State University of New York at Albany and her J.D. from the University of Houston. She has done research in the areas of corrections, women in criminal justice, victimology, and ethics. Pollock-Byrne's published works include *Sex and Supervision: Guarding Male and Female Inmates* (Greenwood Press, 1986), *Ethics in Crime and Justice* (Brooks/Cole, 1989) and *Women, Prison and Crime* (Brooks/Cole, 1990), as well as articles about women in prison, teaching ethics, and victim services.

Edward W. Sieh holds a Ph.D. from Rutgers University. He is currently a Professor in the Criminal Justice Program at Niagara University. He has published several works in the area of employee theft, penal policy, and prison overcrowding. Currently, Sieh is involved in research projects relating to the probation system, the ideology of the Supreme Court, and the concept of justice as it is applied in the criminal justice system.

Ronald E. Vogel is a Professor of Criminal Justice and Chairperson of the Department of Criminal Justice at California State University—Long Beach. He received his Ed.D. from the University of Massachusetts at Amherst in 1978 and taught for 11 years in the Department of Criminal Justice at the University of North Carolina at Charlotte. Vogel's research interests are diverse and he has published on a variety of criminal justice issues.

John T. Whitehead is an Associate Professor in the Department of Criminal Justice and Criminology at East Tennessee State University. He received his Ph.D. from the School of Criminal Justice, State University of New York at Albany. He authored *Burnout in Probation and Corrections* (Praeger, 1989), and co-authored *Juvenile Justice: An Introduction* (Anderson, 1990). Whitehead's current research projects are an evaluation of the diversionary impact of intensive probation in Tennessee and an analysis of school victimization.